# CONTEMPORARY ISSUES IN ACCOUNTING AND FINANCE

# CONTEMPORARY ISSUES IN ACCOUNTING AND FINANCE

*Edited by*

A.R. MUJIBUR REHMAN

Akansha Publishing House
• Delhi • Guwahati • Visakhapatnam

**AKANSHA PUBLISHING HOUSE**
4649-B/21, Ansari Road
Daryaganj, New Delhi-110002
Phones: 23263193 / 9811582579 / 09435116718
Fax: 011-23263193
Email: ektabooks@yahoo.com
visit us: www.akanshapublishinghouse.com

*Contemporary Issues in Accounting and Finance*



First Published 2012

ISBN 978-81-8370-325-3



**PRINTED IN INDIA**

---

Published by Akansha Publishing House, New Delhi-110002 and printed at Harmain Offset Printers, Delhi.

# Contents

# Preface

Accounting occupies the centre-stage in the world of finance particularly in the areas of financial planning, reporting and control. Traditionally, accounting was expected to reflect only the true and fair view of the historical aspects of the day-to-day business transactions. But, of late, it has been globally realized that although accounting is basically historical in nature yet it provides the foundation that forms the basis of the facets like ascertaining the sustainability and feasibility of business and industrial ventures, fraud prevention and detection as well as ensure transparency in the conduct, recording, disclosure and control of business and industrial activities. Eventually these have led to the emergence of the issues of greater transparency, uniformity for the appropriate and adequate disclosure of corporate social responsibility. The development of the International Financial Reporting Standards (IFRS) is a clear evidence of the aforesaid submission.

This book is an edited volume and comprises scholarly articles and research papers contributed by eminent academicians of the country who have long experience of teaching and research in the respective areas of their interest. Besides them, couple of research scholars have also contributed papers based on the findings of their research works, and their papers are in the form of joint contributions with experienced faculty members of higher education institutions.

This book is aimed at focusing on the emerging issues in the areas of accounting and finance. In an attempt to fulfil this aim, the following are the main topics which have been dealt with in this book:

International Financial Reporting Standards (IFRS), Financial Reporting and Management Disclosure.

International Financial Management, Mutual Fund Industry in India- Accounting and Disclosure Practices thereof, Environmental Accounting in the context of Corporate Information Disclosure, Financial Reporting through Extensible Business Reporting Language (XBRL).

Short-run Managerial Decision Analysis, Operational Performance of Assam State Transport Corporation (ASTC), Budgetary Support for Protection against Climate Change.

Moreover some topics allied to finance and accounting yet relevant in the present context have also been included and these are:

Financial Inclusion, Internet Banking in India, Priority Sector Advances by Commercial Banks, Screen-Based trading, Security Trading: Pricing of IPOs.

The facts stated, conclusions arrived at, comments and views expressed in the papers are solely of the author. The Editor is not responsible for them, whatsoever.

This book is the output of the contribution made by the eminent scholars from all over the country.

I would like to offer my profound gratitude and thanks to all of them particularly to Dr. Shaikh Saleem (Aurangabad), Prof. G.P. Prasain (Imphal), Prof. Ranjan Kumar Bal (Bhubaneswar), Prof. Nikhil Bhusan Dey (Silchar), Prof. Sujit Sikidar (Guwahati), Prof. N. Panda (Shillong), Prof. Nayan Barua (Guwahati), Prof. A. Bhowal (Diphu), Prof. H.C. Gautam

(Guwahati). I am also grateful to Dr. A. Rajmoni Singh (Imphal), Dr. Kh. Dhiren Meetei (Imphal), Dr. Bhaskarjyoti Bora (Guwahati), Dr. Elangbam Nixon Singh (Aizawl), Dr. Joynal Ud-din Ahmed (Tura), Dr. Pinku Paul (Bhubaneswar) and Dr. Rajat Sharmacharjee (Silchar).

I am thankful to Sri M.P. Misra of Akansha Publishing House, New Delhi for shouldering the responsibility of converting the manuscripts to the present volume of the book within a shortest possible time.

Last but not the least my special thanks go to my wife Syeda Hasina, my son Mustafizur, daughter Zafreen and daughter-in-law Rukhsana for their constant support and encouragement and also for bearing with me as I was constantly involved with editing of this volume.

**A.R. MUJIBUR REHMAN**

# 1

# IFRS Opportunities and Challenges for India

**Shaikh Saleem**

International Financial Reporting Standards (IFRS) is a set of accounting standards, developed by the International Accounting Standards Boards (IASB) that is becoming the global standard for the financial statements. The International Accounting Standards Boards (IASB) is an independent accounting standards body based in London.

Today businesses are crossing their national boundaries, promoting the synchronization of accounting standards across the globe. The objective behind the IFRS is to create a common platform for the understanding of accounting internationally. By adopting IFRS a business can present its financial statements on the same basis as its foreign competitors, making comparisons easier.

While converting to IFRS is a complex process, these standards have important and positive implications for organizations and individuals that adopt them.

- For companies : Reduced cost of Capital and the ease of using one consistent reporting standard from subsidiaries in many different countries.

- For Investors : Better information for decision making, leading to broader investment opportunities.
- For National Regulatory bodies : Better information for market participants in a disclosure based system.

## STRUCTURE OF IFRS

### IFRS Comprises

1. International Financial Reporting Standards (IFRS) Standards issued after 2001.
2. International Accounting Standards (IAS) issued before 2001.
3. Interpretations originated from the International Financial Reporting Interpretations Committee (IFRIC) issued after 2001.
4. Standing Interpretations Committee ( SIC) issued before 2001

There is also a Framework for the Preparation and presentation of Financial Statements which describes some of the principles underlying IFRS.

### Content of IFRS Financial Statements

IFRS Financial Statements consist of IAS 1.8.

1. A Balance Sheet
2. Income Statement
3. Either a Statement of Changes in Equity (SOCE) or a Statement of Recognized Income or Expense ( SORIE)
4. A Cash Flow Statement
5. Notes, including a summary of the significant accounting policies.

Comparative information is provided for the previous reporting period (IAS 1.36). An entity preparing IFRS accounts for the first time must apply IFRS in full for the current and comparative period although there are transactional exemptions (IFRS 1.7).

### IFRS: THE GLOBAL SCENARIO

**Canada:** Required from 1 January 2011 for all listed entities and permitted for private sector entities, including not-for-profit organisations

**China:** Substantially converged national standards

**European Union:** All member states are required to use IFRS as adopted by the EU for listed companies since 2005

**Indonesia:** Convergence process is on

**Japan:** Permitted from 2010 for a number of international companies; decision about mandatory adoption by 2016 expected around 2012

**Republic of Korea**: Required from 2011

**Russia:** Required for banking institutions and some other securities issuers; permitted for other companies

**Saudi Arabia:** Not permitted for listed companies

**South Africa:** Required for listed entities since 2005

**Turkey:** Required for listed entities since 2008

**US:** Allowed for foreign issuers in the US since 2007; target date for substantial convergence with IFRS is 2011

*Source*: www.ifrs.org

## RELEVANCE OF CONVERSIONS OF IFRS TO INDIAN COMPANIES

Convergence of International Accounting Standards (IASs)with International Financial Reporting Standards (collectively referred to as IFRSs), issued by the International Accounting Standards Board (IASB) has gained momentum in recent years all over the world. The reason for this is obvious – as the capital markets become increasingly global in nature, more and more investors see the need for a common set of International Accounting Standards. About 113 countries presently require or permit use of IFRSs in preparation of financial statements in their countries. By 2011, the number is expected to reach 150.

Keeping in view the complex nature of IFRS, the Institute of Chartered Accountants of India (ICAI) in its concept paper has expressed the view that IFRSs should be adopted for the public interest entities such as listed entities, banks and insurance entities and large-sized entities from the accounting periods beginning on or after 1 April 2011. The countries which have adopted IFRSs have done so for similar types of entities.

## REGULATORY FRAMEWORK AND ENFORCEMENT OF ACCOUNTING STANDARDS

**The Institute of Chartered Accountants of India (ICAI)** is a statutory body established under the Chartered Accountants Act, 1949 (Act No. XXXVIII of 1949) for the regulation of the profession of Chartered Accountancy in India. During its more than fifty years of existence, the Institute has achieved recognition as a premier accounting body in the country for its contribution in the fields of education, professional development, maintenance of high accounting, auditing and ethical standards. The ICAI now is the second largest accounting body in the whole world.

### Accounting Standards Issued by ICAI

To date, the Institute of Chartered Accountants of India has issued 31 Accounting Standards. These are numbered AS-

1 to AS-7 and AS-9 to AS-31; AS-8 is no longer in force having been merged with AS-26. The compliance of Accounting standards issued by ICAI have become a statutory requirement with the notification of Companies (Accounting Standards) Rules, 2006 by the Government of India. ICAI has set an internal deadline of aligning its Accounting Standards with IFRS by April 2011.

### *Legal Recognition of Accounting Standards issued by ICAI under the Companies Act (1956)*

The Companies Act (1956) provides the basic requirements relating to financial reporting of all companies incorporated in India. The Act requires the preparation, presentation, publication, and disclosure of financial statements, as well as an audit of all companies by a member-in-practice certified by the Institute of Chartered Accountants of India (ICAI). Under the Act, the Central Government has the power, by notification in the Official Gazette, to constitute the National Advisory Committee on Accounting Standards (NACAS), to advise the Central Government on the formulation and laying down of accounting standards for adoption by companies or class of companies. For this purpose, the Act requires that NACAS has to consider accounting standards issued by the ICAI when recommending accounting standards to the Government. While, as stated earlier, the ICAI bases its accounting standards on the corresponding IASs/IFRSs, NACAS also specifically considers the deviations – and reasons, if any – from the corresponding IAS/IFRS while reviewing ICAI accounting standards. In case the NACAS is not satisfied about any deviation, it requests ICAI to amend the standard to comply with IFRS. ICAI generally deviates from the corresponding IAS/IFRS because of the following factors:

- Legal and regulatory environment prevailing in the country;

- Alternatives permitted in IFRSs would lead to incomparable financial information;
- Economic environment within the country;
- Level of preparedness of industry.

***Legal recognition of accounting standards by other regulators Reserve Bank of India***

The Reserve Bank of India (RBI) was established to regulate the issue of banknotes and keeping reserves to secure monetary stability in India, as well as to generally operate the currency and credit system of the country to its advantage. **The Banking Regulation Act (1949)** empowers the RBI to regulate financial reporting of the financial sector, including banks and financial institutions. One of the Schedules to the Banking Regulation Act prescribes formats for general purpose financial statements (e.g. balance sheet, and profit and loss accounts) and other disclosure requirements. Banks are also required to comply with requirements of the Companies Act (1956), provided they are consistent with the Banking Regulation Act. The RBI has issued circulars requiring banks to comply with the accounting standards issued by ICAI.

**Securities and Exchange Board of India**

The Securities and Exchange Board of India (SEBI) Act protects investors and regulates the securities market. Listed companies in India are required to comply with the requirements prescribed by the SEBI in its Act of 1992 and the Securities Contracts (Regulation) Act of 1956, which provides for the regulation of securities transactions. To protect investor interests, SEBI has issued a listing agreement which specifies disclosures applicable to listed companies in addition to other applicable auditing and accounting requirements. In particular, it requires compliance with the accounting standards issued by ICAI.

## The Insurance Regulatory and Development Authority (IRDA)

The Insurance Regulatory and Development Authority (IRDA) regulates the financial reporting practices of insurance companies under the Insurance Regulatory and Development Authority Act (1999). This Authority has been constituted to regulate, promote and ensure orderly growth of the insurance business and reinsurance business. Insurance companies and their auditors are required to comply with the requirements of the IRDA regulations of 2002 titled "*Preparation of Financial Statements and Auditor's Report of the Insurance Companies*", in preparing and presenting their financial statements and the format and content of the audit report. IRDA regulations require compliance with the accounting standards issued by ICAI.

## Opportunities in Adopting IFRS

### *One Financial Reporting Platform*

Convergence to IFRS, by all group entities, will enable company managements to view all components of the group on one financial reporting platform. This will eliminate the need for multiple reports and significant adjustment for preparing consolidated financial statements or filing financial statements in different stock exchanges.

**Reduce Cost of Capital:** Migration to IFRS will lower the cost of raising funds, as it will eliminate the need for preparing a dual set of financial statements. It will also reduce accounts' fees, reduce risk premiums and will enable access to all major capital markets as IFRS is globally acceptable.

**Investor Friendly:** Investors want the information that is more relevant, reliable, timely and comparable across the jurisdictions. Financial statements prepared using a common set of accounting standards help investors better understand investment opportunities as opposed to financial statements prepared using a different set of national accounting standards. For better understanding of financial statements, global investors have to incur more cost in terms of the time and efforts to convert the financial statements so that they can confidently compare opportunities. Convergence with IFRS contributes to investors' understanding and confidence in high quality financial statements.

**Access to International Capital Markets:** Many Indian entities are expanding or making significant acquisitions in the global arena, for which large amount of capital is required. The majority of stock exchanges require financial information prepared under IFRS. Migration to IFRS will enable Indian entities to have access to international capital markets, removing the risk premium that is added to those reporting under Indian GAAP.

**Fair Value Accounting**: In Indian GAAP, business combinations with few exceptions, are recorded at carrying values rather than fair values of net assets acquired. Purchase consideration paid for intangible assets not recorded in the acquirer's books is usually not reflected separately in the financial statements; instead the amount gets added to goodwill. Hence, the true value of the business .combination is not reflected in the financial statements. IFRS will overcome this flaw, as it mandates accounting for net assets taken over in a business combination at fair value. It also requires recognition of intangible assets, even if they have not been recorded in the acquiree's financial statements.

**Facilitate International Business:** As the markets expand globally the need for convergence increases. The convergence benefits the economy by increasing growth of its international business. It facilitates maintenance of orderly and efficient capital markets and also helps to increase the capital formation and thereby economic growth. It encourages international investing and thereby leads to more foreign capital flows to the country.

**Facilitates Foreign Fund Raising:** The industry is able to raise capital from foreign markets at lower cost if it can create confidence in the minds of foreign investors that their financial statements comply with globally accepted accounting standards. With the diversity in accounting standards from country to country, enterprises which operate in different countries face a multitude of accounting requirements prevailing in the countries. Convergence of accounting standards simplifies the process of preparing the individual and group financial statements and thereby reduces the costs of preparing the financial statements using different sets of accounting standards.

**Opportunities to accounting professionals:** Convergence with IFRS also benefits the accounting professionals in a way that they are able to sell their services as experts in different parts of the world. The thrust of the movement towards convergence has come mainly from accountants in public practice. It offers them more opportunities in any part of the world if same accounting practices prevail throughout the world. They are able to quote IFRS to clients to give them backing for recommending certain ways of reporting.

**Growth Prospects to New Sector:** Benefits from the adoption of IFRS will not be restricted to Indian corporates. In fact, it will open up a host of opportunities in the services sector. With a wide pool of accounting professionals, India can emerge as an accounting services hub for the global community. As IFRS is fair value focused, it will provide significant opportunities to professionals including, accountants, valuations experts and actuaries, which in-turn, will boost the growth prospects for the BPO/KPO segment in India.

**Benchmarking with Global Peers :** Adoption of IFRS will enable companies to gain a broader and deeper understanding of the entity's relative standing by looking beyond country and regional milestones based on global business environment, rather than merely local ones.

## Challenges Involved in Adoption of IFRSs

### *Convergence with IFRSs in India*

A financial reporting system supported by strong governance, high quality standards and a sound regulatory framework is key to economic development. Indeed, high quality standards of financial reporting, auditing and ethics form the foundations of the trust that investors place in financial information and therefore play an integral role in contributing to a country's economic growth and financial stability. As the forces of globalization prompt more and more countries to open their doors to foreign investment and as businesses expand across borders, both the public and private sectors are increasingly recognizing the benefits of having a commonly understood financial reporting framework, supported by strong globally accepted standards. The benefits of a global financial reporting framework are numerous and include:

1 Greater comparability of financial information for investors;

2 Greater willingness on the part of investors to invest across borders;

3 Lower cost of capital;

4 More efficient allocation of resources; and

5 Higher economic growth.

However, before these benefits can be fully realized, there must be greater convergence to a single set of globally accepted high quality standards.

International convergence is a goal that is embraced in the mission of the International Federation of Accountants (IFAC) and shared by IFAC members, international standard-setters and many national standard-setters.

ICAI endeavours to bridge the gap between Indian accounting standards and International Financial Reporting Standards by issuing new accounting standards and ensuring that existing Indian accounting standards reflect any changes in international thinking on various accounting issues. In this regard, it should be noted that ICAI is making a conscious effort to bring the Indian accounting standards into line with International Financial Reporting Standards by revising existing accounting standards. ICAI has so far issued 29 Indian accounting standards corresponding to IFRSs. In view of the above, Indian accounting standards (ASs) are largely in step with the IFRSs.

## Challenges for small and medium-sized entities and accounting firms

In emerging economies like India, a significant part of the economic activities is carried on by small- and medium-sized entities (SMEs). Such entities face problems in implementing the accounting standards because of:

- Scarcity of resources and expertise with the SMEs; and
- the Cost of compliance is not commensurate with the expected benefits.

## India seeks to push date for IFRS switch by two years

Chairman of an influential parliamentary committee has urged the prime minister to delay the rollout of global accounting norms by at least two years, saying India need to enter into a dialogue with other countries to modify the proposed norms to suit local practices.

"India should engage in a dialogue with USA, Japan and China to get IASB (international accounting standards board – the global standard setter) to modify IFRS after taking into account the ground realities applicable to India and Indian companies," said Murli Manohar Joshi, chairman of the public accounts committee, in a letter to Prime Minister Manmohan Singh.

"We should focus our attention on ... the areas where Indian accounting standards differ with IFRS, so that by 2013 or by 2015, the stabilised IFRS can take into account the concerns of Indian accountants and Indian companies," he said in the letter. Economies such as US and Japan which have already deferred IFRS implementation by 2015, Mr. Joshi said.

The Ministry of Corporate Affairs, which is the administrative ministry coordinating the convergence scheme, said the process is in schedule.

"We've not seen the contents of the letter. As of now we can only reaffirm our position that the convergence process is on schedule and all the regulatory formalities will be met with," said a senior official with the ministry of corporate affairs.

Convergence to IFRS is part of India's commitment at the G20, a global forum of the world's largest economies. Convergence typically means that Indian companies will not be required to follow IFRS principles in totality, but they need to follow standards that are aligned to global norms. Many of the converged standards have suggested changes in norms relating to real estate and foreign exchange.

The government has charted out a three-phase IFRS convergence process for Indian companies with the first phase beginning in April 2011. In the first lot, all companies listed on the BSE and NSE and those with net worth higher than. 1,000 crore will be covered.

The convergence requires preparedness not just at the level of companies that follow it, but also from the government in respect of regulatory policies. Some of the regulations that are yet to be aligned for the convergence include taxation laws, existing Company law provisions.

Approximately 120 nations have accepted IFRS for domestic listed companies. Of these, about 90 countries have made it mandatory for their companies to follow IFRS.

Currently, India does not require its companies to follow the IFRS. However, as per its commitment to the G20, India will converge its domestic accounting standards with IFRS in a phased manner from April 1, 2011.

## Issues to be Addressed

The Indian GAAP has conceptual differences with IFRS and our legal and regulatory frameworks need to be amended to adopt IFRS as written by the International Accounting Standards Board (IASB), the standard setting body of IFRS. IASB requires that compliance to IFRS be explicit and in an unreserved manner. The bridge between Indian GAAP and IFRS needs legal sanctions through Parliament for the adoption of IFRS in India.

## Concept of a group

The Companies Act (The Act) treats Indian companies as separate legal entities, while IFRS promotes a group concept, where individual legal entities lose their individual relevance to the overall economic entity, the group, except for legal or tax compliance. The Act does not specifically deal with consolidated accounts or their auditors' reports. Hence the form of accounts adopted by a group can be different from the format specified by the Act for individual companies.

Our tax laws assess individual entities as separate units for tax and do not assess the group as a single taxable entity. Hence the role of consolidated accounts has no relevance for tax purposes. In many countries like the US, the group could be the primary unit for tax assessment in one legal jurisdiction and the consolidated accounts then become relevant.

## Fixed Assets

There is a significant distinction between the Act and IFRS for fixed assets — the description of assets itself. The Act defines a class of assets whereas IFRS promotes a concept of components of fixed assets based on their usefulness. This means that various significant components embedded in an asset having different useful lives will be depreciated separately. It would be appropriate to depreciate the engines and airframe of an aircraft using different lives. Another key difference with the Indian GAAP and the Act is on the definition of cost. Under IFRS, the fair estimate of the retirement obligation of an asset is discounted to a fair value and recognised as a liability. The corresponding costs are capitalised with the fixed assets. In India, future costs are not allowed to be discounted and capitalised and they are recognised as a liability when they become an obligation.

The Companies Act prohibits depreciation on revaluation of fixed assets to be reflected in the profit and loss account as such depreciation is netted off against the reserve specifically created on revaluation in the balance sheet. IFRS is based on fair value concepts and where a company revalues its fixed assets to reflect its current value, the depreciation of the revalued assets is routed through the income statement and affects the earnings.

## Capital and Reserves

If we look at the capital side of the balance sheet, the Companies Act requires capital instruments to be separately disclosed as equity and preference shares and there are separate provisions that govern the issue of these instruments and their relative legal rights. Similarly, convertible debentures or bonds, whether they are in Indian or foreign currency, have specific rules relating to their issue and disclosure in the accounts. There are also foreign exchange regulations which would also come into play relating to these bonds. IFRS treats debentures, bonds or preference shares that are convertible into equity shares as compound instruments, that need to be segregated into a debt and an equity portion based on their relative fair values. Similarly, a redeemable preference share for cash will normally be a debt. Such re-classification of preference shares to debt or equity or creating equity instruments from bonds or debentures will need sanction of the Companies Act, which lays down rules on how such instruments are to be issued and shown in the accounts. Mere segregation by using IFRS principles will not comply with the Act, nor will it retain the legal rights and obligations that are associated with these instruments. This leaves a gap between our current laws and IFRS.

Reserves in a balance sheet arc a result of past profits following Indian GAAP and are available to shareholders either as dividend or distributed on dissolution. Upon transition to IFRS, an entity will have an increase or deduction of reserve just by the application of the new GAAP. A shareholder could have more distributable reserves or conversely if the reserves get wiped out, it could leave him poorer due to such a change.

How changes in GAAP affect the wealth or earnings of the shareholders will be the cornerstone of decisions.

## IFRS and Initial Public Offerings (IPO)

Some other areas of attention would be the rules relating to initial public offerings (IPO). Under the current laws, five years of audited financial accounts under Indian GAAP form the base financial information for an IPO. When we transition to IFRS in 2011, we are not sure whether all the five years of accounts for a company need to be under IFRS or the law will allow a part thereof, say, three years. The efforts a company needs to make if they are to re-cast their accounts to IFRS for the past five years will be significant. How the Act and SEBI will define this requirement will be important for companies looking for an IPO in the next few years.

## Correction of Past Errors

Correction of errors under IFRS can be made in the years they pertain to, even if they are audited and adopted by the shareholders. Currently, past errors in India are shown as adjustment relating to previous years in the current year as no changes can be made to the accounts as adopted by shareholders. Furthermore, no specific disclosure relating to the error is required to be made. If we go the route of IFRS, the restatement of material errors is a feature that Indian companies and their auditors will need to be aware of. Whether or not this triggers a number of lawsuits in the future against the company and their auditors, only time will tell.

These are some of the indicative areas where an amendment to the law needs to be made if we are to converge with IFRS. We have a choice of having specific differences in India between the accounting principles followed here and those under pure IFRS. These divergences are euphemistically referred to as 'IFRS Lite' and are not considered by the SEC and IASB as explicit compliance of IFRS. IFRS promotes the principle that the same economic transaction happening in New York, New Delhi or São Paulo will have the same accounting result. The question is, how different India wants to be in this regard.

## Road Map for IFRS convergence in India

The ICAI has already announced a road map for full convergence of Indian Accounting Standards by April 1, 2011. The move towards IFRS has also been endorsed simultaneously by the Ministry of Company Affairs (MCA), government of India. The ICAI and other fora like Indian Banks Association (IBA) have been holding various workshops/ meetings and promoting awareness about the daunting task ahead for the Indian entities in this respect.

In another important initiative, the Ministry of Companies Affairs (MCA) government of India has recently set up a high powered core group under the chairmanship of the Secretary MCA to study the impact of IFRS and to understand the preparedness of Indian entities in implementing IFRS.

Recently the ICAI has brought a list of over 400 companies that should converge their accounting practices with IFRS by April 2011. The first list comprises 439 companies. It includes BSE sensex companies NSE- Nifty companies that have raised debt over $50 million abroad, financial sector companies, public accountable companies (with total borrowings of over 1000 crore). Indian subsidiaries of foreign companies that have implemented IFRS at the parent company and companies outside these categories with capital of over $50 million abroad.

IFRS convergence will entail a change in accounting process depending on company's complexity, it will need a change in its IT and ERP systems, management information system and the companies will have to employ values for various valuations.

IFRS compliance is huge opportunity for consultants, IT companies and Tax experts. Companies will have to train their accountants and finance personnel on IFRS. After IFRS convergence bench marking Indian companies will be more accurate with their global peers.

## CONCLUSION

Irrespective of various challenges, adoption of IFRSs in India has significantly changed the contents of corporate financial statements as a result of:

- More refined measurements of performance and state of affairs, and
- Enhanced disclosures leading to greater transparency.

With the rapid liberalization process experienced in India over the past decade, there is now a huge presence of multinational enterprises in the country. Furthermore, Indian companies are also investing in foreign markets. This has generated an interest in Indian GAAPs by all concerned. In this context, the role of Indian accounting standards, which are becoming closer to IFRSs, have assumed a great significance from the point of view of global financial reporting.

Indian companies using the Indian accounting standards are experiencing fewer difficulties accessing international financial markets, as Indian accounting standards are becoming closer to the IFRSs. Indian standards are expected to converge even further in the future, especially after the challenges mentioned in study are addressed over the next few years.

## REFERENCES

1. http://www.indiaprwire.com/pressrelease/financial-services/2008032
2. http://www.thehindubusinessline.com/2007/01/04/stories/2007010400100900.htm
3. http://www.ou-mba.ac.in/i/6.pdf
4. www.iasplus.com/asia/2008ifrsindiangaap.pdf

5. http://www.business-standard.com/india/news/kaushik-dutta-mindgaap-indiaifrs/344217
6. http://en.wikipedia.org/wiki/Institute_of_Chartered_Accountants_of_India
7. http://en.wikipedia.org/wiki/International_Financial_Reporting_Standards
8. Source: www.ifrs.org
9. www.economictimes.com

# 2

# International Financial Management - An Overview

**G.P. Prasain & Kh. Dhiren Meetei**

**ABSTRACT:** International business means any business activity or transactions that transcend the national border. It is, however, doubtful whether some of the business transactions which cross national border can be regarded as real international business. International business has three methods. They are:

(i) international trade,

(ii) contractual methods and

(iii) foreign investment.

International trade is growing faster than the world output, indicating a growing proportion of the national output is traded internationally or that the international market is more dynamic than the national markets. International trade is primarily multinational in character, but bilateral trade closely exist in many cases. Bilateral trade, often known as counter-trade is a sort of bartering of goods in various ways. Sometimes we see industrial counter-trade or the buy-back agreement that involves the sale of industrial equipment or turn-key plants in exchange for the products manufactured by the industrial plant so delivered.

*Foreign investment is another method of international business. Broadly there are two types of foreign investment, namely foreign direct investment (FDI) and portfolio investment. FDI refers to investment in a foreign country where the investor retains control over the investment. It typically takes the forum of starting a subsidiary, acquiring a stake in an existing firm or starting a joint venture in the foreign country.*

## Introduction

Beginning in the 1980s, there has been an explosion in international investments, through mutual funds and other intermediaries by the individual and through direct investments by institutions. On the other side, capital raising is increasingly is occurring across national boundaries. The financial manager must search for the "best price" in a global marketplace, sometimes while making use of currency and other hedges. To accommodate the underlying demands of investors and capital raisers, financial institutions and instruments have changed dramatically. Financial deregulation, first in the United States and then in Europe and in Asia, has prompted increased integration of world financial markets. As a result of the rapidly changing scene, the financial manager today must have a global perspective. International business has been propelled by large cross-border flows of finance. While the private financial flows are invariably commercial in nature, financial flows related to Official Development Assistance have also implications for business. Official Development Assistance refers to grants and soft loans from official sources, with the objective of promoting economic development and social welfare. Investments resulting from Official Development Assistance also provide opportunities for private business, besides the general economic improvements such investments may promote. The economic liberalization that swept across the world, has very significantly changed the environment for international private financial flows. At the same time, the surging international capital flows, in its turn are substantially impacting the business environment, have also implications for business.

Today along with the growth in trade, cross-border capital flow and, in particular, direct investments have also grown enormously. The world has witnessed the emergence of massive multinational corporations with production facilities spread across the world. Liberalization, integrations and innovation have created a giant international financial market, which is extremely dynamic and complex. The market presents the finance manager with a bewildering menu of funding techniques, investment vehicles, risk management products and speculative opportunities. Financial engineering is no more a fancy jargon but a reality. For those who are willing to master its complexities, the market provides endless opportunities for creative financial management; for the unwary, it is a minefield.

## Objectives of the study

The present paper presents a birds-eye view of international financial management. The main objectives of the paper are:

(i) to discuss the international business and its methods

(ii) to elaborate the multinational corporation and its impacts on international financial functions

(iii) to explain the nature and scope of international financial management

(iv) to make a comparison between domestic financial management and international financial management

(v) to draw the concluding remarks of the paper.

## International business & its methods

International business means any business activity or transactions that transcend the national border. It is, however, doubtful whether some of the business transactions which cross national border can be regarded as real international business. International business has three methods. They are:

(i) international trade,

(ii) contractual methods and

(iii) foreign investment.

International trade is growing faster than the world output, indicating a growing proportion of the national output is traded internationally or that the international market is more dynamic than the national markets. International trade is primarily multinational in character, but bilateral trade closely exist in many cases. Bilateral trade, often known as counter-trade is a sort of bartering of goods in various ways. Sometimes we see industrial counter-trade or the buy-back agreement that involves the sale of industrial equipment or turn-key plants in exchange for the products manufactured by the industrial plant so delivered.

## Foreign Investment

Foreign investment is another method of international business. Broadly there are two types of foreign investment, namely foreign direct investment (FDI) and portfolio investment. FDI refers to investment in a foreign country where the investor retains control over the investment. It typically takes the form of starting a subsidiary, acquiring a stake in an existing firm or starting a joint venture in the foreign country. On the other hand, if the investor has only a sort of interest in investing the capital in buying equities, bonds, or other securities abroad, it is referred to as portfolio investment. With reference to foreign investment in India, foreign investment may be classified as shown in Fig. 2.1.

As per RBI Bulletin January 2011 dt. 12.1.2011 table No. 44- Foreign Investment inflows under the heading of financial year-wise FDI equity inflows from April 2000 to November 2010 in India can be shown under Table 2.1(A):

There are three forms of foreign direct investment. They are:

(i) **Greenfield investment**: It can be made through opening of branch in a host-country or through making investment in the equity capital of the host -country firm.

(ii) **Merger and Acquisitions**: Mergers and Acquisitions are either outright purchase with a running foreign company abroad or an amalgamation with a running foreign company. While in the former, the acquiring company maintains its existence and the target company loses its existence. In the latter case, both lose their existence in favour of a new company.

(iii) **Brownfield investment**: It is a combination of greenfield investment and Mergers and Acquisitions. It exists when a company first goes for an international Merger and Acquisition and then makes huge investment for replacing plant and machinery in the target company.

International business takes different forms, like exporting, licensing, contract manufacturing, foreign assembly, foreign production, joint venturing, etc. The extent of internationalization could vary under each of these methods. Exporting, the most traditional mode of entering the foreign market, is quite a common one even now. Licensing and franchising, which involve minimal commitment of resources and effort on the part of the international marketer are very easy ways of entering

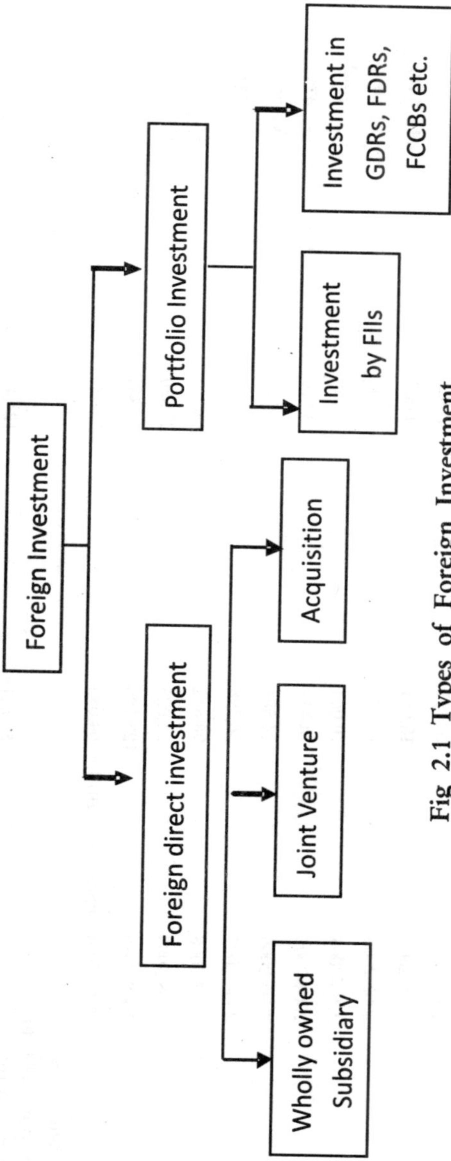


Fig 2.1 Types of Foreign Investment

**Table 2.1(A)**
**Year wise FDI Equity Inflows**
**(As per DIPP's FDI data base-equity components only)**

| Sl. No. | Financial Year (April-March) | Amount of FDI Inflows (including advance) | | %age growth over previous year (in terms of US $) |
|---|---|---|---|---|
| Financial Year 2000-2001 | | In Crores | In US$ million | |
| 1. | 2000-2001 | 10,733 | 2,463 | - |
| 2. | 2001-2002 | 18,654 | 4,065 | (+) 65% |
| 3. | 2002-2003 | 12,871 | 2,705 | (-) 50% |
| 4. | 2003-2004 | 10,064 | 2,188 | (-) 19% |
| 5. | 2004-2005 | 14,653 | 3,219 | (+) 47% |
| 6. | 2005-2006 | 24,584 | 5,540 | (+) 72% |
| 7. | 2006-2007 | 56,390 | 12,492 | (+) 125% |
| 8. | 2007-2008 | 98,642 | 24,575 | (+) 97% |
| 9. | 2008-2009 | 123,025 | 27,330 | (+) 11% |
| 10. | 1009-2010 | 123,120 | 25,834 | (-) 05% |
| 11. | 2010-2011 (upto Nov. 2010)+ | 64,083 | 14,025 | - |
| Cumulative Total (From April 2000 to November 2010) | | 556,819 | 124,436 | - |

**Source:** *RB's Bulletin* January 2011 dt. 12.01.2011 (Table No. 44 (B) Foreign Investment Inflows)

the foreign markets. Under contract manufacturing, a company doing international marketing contracts with firms in foreign countries to manufacture or assemble the products while retaining the responsibility of marketing the product. This is a common practice in international business. The establishment of an assembly operation represents a cross between exporting and overseas manufacturing.

Joint venture is a very common strategy of entering the foreign market. In the widest sense, any form of association which implies collaboration for more than a transitory period is a joint venture. Strategic alliance has been becoming more and more popular in international business. This strategy seeks to enhance the long-term competitive advantage of the firm by forming alliance with its competitors, existing or potential in critical areas, instead of competing with each other.

## Multinational Corporations and their impacts on International financial functions

According to an ILO report, "the essential nature of the multinational enterprises lies in the fact that its managerial headquarters are located in one country (referred to for convenience as the "home country") while the enterprise carries out operations in a number of other countries as well ("host countries").[1] Obviously, what is meant is "a corporation that controls production facilities in more than one country, such facilities having been acquired through the process of foreign direct investment. Firms that participate in international business, however large they may be, solely by exporting or by licensing technology are not multinational enterprise".[2]

Financial executives in multinational corporations face many factors that have no domestic counterparts. These factors include exchange and inflation risks; international differences in tax rates; multiple money markets, often with limited access;

currency controls and political risks, such as sudden and creeping expropriation.

When examining the unique characteristics of multinational financial management, it is understandable that companies normally emphasize the additional political and economic risks faced when going abroad. However, a broader perspective is necessary if firms are to take advantage of being multinational. The ability to move people, money and material on a global basis enables the multinational corporation to be more than the sum of its parts. By having operations in different countries, the MNC can assess segmented capital markets to lower its overall cost of capital, shift profits to lower its taxes and take advantage of international diversification of markets and production sites to reduce the extent of risk of its earnings. Multinationals have taken the old adage of "don't put all your eggs in one basket" to its logical conclusion.[3]

The costs of ensuring that managers maximize shareholders' wealth is known as agency costs. The magnitude of agency costs can vary with the management style of the MNC. A centralized management style can reduce agency costs because it allows managers of the parent to control foreign subsidiaries and therefore reduces the power of subsidiary managers. However, the parent's managers may make poor decisions for the subsidiary if they are not as informed as subsidiary managers about financial characteristics of the subsidiary. Decentralized management style is more likely to result in higher agency costs because subsidiary managers may make decisions that do not focus on maximizing the value of the entire MNC. Yet, this style gives more control to those managers who are closer to the subsidiary's operations and environment. To the extent that subsidiary managers recognize the goal of maximizing the value of the overall MNC and are compensated in accordance with that goal, the decentralized management style may be more effective.[4]

The main thrust of a global MNC is the global thinking-the state of mind-spread of its activities and assets in different countries. It is distinguished by agility of penetration into new market segments, seeking out new markets integrating marketing in one place with manufacture in another place; Research and Development in yet another place and embracing financing opportunities on a global basis. The global manager manages change, anticipates the forthcoming changes and plans for them. The quality of decision making is initial for prospect of survival and growth is MNC. The basic goal of his operations in a global scale is how to maximize the wealth of the shareholders of his company. Some centres may be bad or poor profit earners but the overall operations of all centres are taken into account in accounting for profitability.

## Definition of International Financial Management

International financial management (IFM) is concerned with the management of international business (IB)-related financial functions, commonly known as the international financial functions.[5]

International finance is designed to better develop those skills that equip to understand and appreciate the international financial issues that companies face when they operate in separate countries. It covers various international financial management issues, which are essential for those who are engaged and active in international business management. It discusses various issues related to international capital markets, foreign exchange rate determination and global financial management. It provides an integrated perspective on the topics of foreign currency and exchange rates, international financial linkages, international financial markets and investment, financing and risk management in a global context. It requires the interactions between exchange rates and cross-border trade and capital flows, inflation, interest rates, economic growth and government policy. The principal focus of the subject are financial instruments used in international financial markets such as currency options, forwards, futures and swaps as well as bonds, equities and other innovative securities.

## Nature and scope of International Financial Management

International business has been propelled by large cross-borders flows of finance. The increasing globalization of trade and investment has led to the emergence and dominance of multinationals which control about two-thirds of the world trade and investment. Corporate investments across borders grew 4 times faster than global output and 3 times faster than international trade between 1983 and 1990s.[6]

The subject of foreign exchange is, in the words of H.E. Evitt, "that section of economic science which deals with the means and methods by which rights to wealth in one country's currency are converted into rights to wealth in terms of another country's currency."[7] Foreign exchange is the system or process of converting one national currency into another, and of transferring money from one country to another (Dr. Paul Einzing).[8] The discussion of the foreign exchange market and of the various activities therein forms the subject-matter of international financial management.

The IMF (International Monetary Fund) is primarily a short-term financial institution -a lender and a borrower - and a central bank of central banks and secondarily, aims at promoting a code of conduct among members for orderly exchange arrangements and international monetary management. The main function of the IMF is to promote exchange stability and encourage multilateral trade and payments. It is also a financing institution and has schemes for provision of short-term finance for meeting the balance of payments purposes. It provides international liquidity in tune with the requirements of world trade and fosters the growth of world trade and freer system of payments. Gold was originally the unit of account in which the various currencies were denominated. So, the functioning of IMF and the determination of exchange rate form an integral part of the international financial management.

Foreign exchange exposure is a measure of the potential that a firm's profitability, cash flow and market value will change because of a change in exchange rates. A major responsibility of financial managers in multinational enterprises is to manage these currency exposures. There are four different types of foreign exchange exposure namely, transaction, operating, accounting and tax exposure. Operating exposure measures the change in the present value of a firm resulting from a change in its future operating cash flows due to an unexpected change in exchange rates. The change in present value depends on the effect of an exchange rate change on the firm's future sales volume, prices and costs. International financial management covers all the areas of foreign exchange exposure.

A firm needs to achieve a certain global cost and availability of capital in order to compete successfully in both its domestic and foreign markets. Global integration of capital markets has given many firms access to new and cheaper sources of funds beyond those available in their home markets. Designing a capital sourcing strategy requires that management agree upon a long-run financial objective and then choose among the various alternative paths to get there. MNC must consider how to maintain access to global capital markets, reduce risk through international diversification, minimize foreign exchange risk due to raising foreign currency-denominated debt and meet the expectations of international portfolio investors. International financial managers must manage interest rate risk. Interest rate risk affects both the liability and asset side of a firm's balance sheet. There are three important interest rate risk management instruments; namely, forward rate agreements, interest rate futures and interest rate swaps. So, global capital market to minimize its costs of capital and maximize its access to capital forms a part of international financial management.

Foreign investment decisions analyze how a firm transitions from the international trade stage to become a full-blown multinational firm. Foreign direct investment- theory and strategy-analyses the decisions whether, where and how to undertake foreign direct investment (FDI). The theory of comparative advantage is the basis for international trade. However, market imperfections create a rationale for the existence of multinational enterprises. Political risk assessment and management shows how to adjust for political risk in foreign investments. It explains how to define measure and manage foreign investment risks. Multinational tax management describes the global tax environment. It analyzes how tax treaties between countries attempt to provide a level playing field for competing MNC. Furthermore, different types of taxes, such as the value added tax, complicate the MNC's goal of minimizing its worldwide tax burden. Multinational capital budgeting introduces the foreign complexities that must consider when undertaking a capital budgeting analysis of foreign project. Cross-border mergers, acquisitions and valuation introduce the increasingly important field of cross-border mergers and acquisitions, which is a viable alternative to a Greenfield direct foreign investment. Since the MNC needs to attract and retain international portfolio investors in order to gain its global cost and availability of capital, risk reduction through international diversification is important to both parties. So the FDI involving long term investment decision, often know as international capital budgeting forms a part of international financial management.

International financial market embraces variety of source-beginning from the international development banks, such as the World Bank, International Finance Corporation and regional development banks, such as Asian Development Bank etc. to the Eurocurrency market and international securities market. The international financial functions are related to the raising of funds from different windows of the international financial market and also to the related activities, such as financial swap and interest-rate risk management. The study of IFM covers all these activities.

At the end of the financial year, the international firm tries to consolidate the financial statement of all the units so as to assess the global profit and global financial status. International firms often resort to transfer pricing in order to siphon pre-tax profit from a high-tax country to a low-tax country and thereby to maximize the global profit despite close watch by the government authorities. IFM thus deals with international accounting and international tax strategy and all the related activities.

The government of different countries records all types of flow of funds on the debit and credit sides so as to know the net flow of funds into the economy or out of the economy. The statement recording the transactions is known as balance of payments in which the performance of the entire external sector is reflected. The major items of India's Balance of payment for the 2007 to 2010 are as under Table 2.1(B).

IFM covers essentially the study of the balance of payment, external indebtedness and its management.

## International Financial Management: Different from the Domestic Financial Management.[9]

Table 2.1(c) details some of the main differences between international and domestic financial management. These component differences include institutions, foreign exchange

**Table 2.1(B)**
**Major Items of India's Balance of Payments (US $ million)**

| Particulars | (2007-08) (PR) | (2008-09) (P) | Apr-Dec. (2008-09)(PR) | Apr-Dec (2009-10)(R) |
|---|---|---|---|---|
| Exports | 166,163 | 175,184 | 150,520 | 124,473 |
| Imports | 257,789 | 294,587 | 248,967 | 213988 |
| Trade Balance | -91626 | -119,403 | -98446 | -89515 |
| Invisible, net | 74592 | 89,587 | 70931 | 59185 |
| Current A/c Balance | -17034 | -29817 | -27516 | -30330 |
| Capital A/c* | 109,198 | 9737 | 7136 | 41630 |
| Change in Reserve # | -92164 | 20080 | 20380 | -11330 |

(+ indicate increase; -indicate decrease)
(*including error & omissions; # on BOP basis excluding valuation; P: Preliminary, PR: Partially revised, R: revised)
Source: Reserve Bank of India Report.

**Table 2.1(C)**
**What is Different About International Financial Management?**

| Concept | International | Domestic |
|---|---|---|
| Culture, history and institutions | Each foreign country is unique and not always understood by MNC Management | Each country has a known environment; base case |
| Corporate Governance | Foreign countries' regulations and institutional practice are all uniquely different | Regulations and institutions are well known |
| Foreign Exchange risk | MNCs face exchange risks due to their subsidiaries, as well as import/export and foreign competitors | Foreign exchange risks from import/export and foreign competition, but not from subsidiaries |
| Political risk | MNCs face political risks because of their foreign subsidiaries and high profile | Negligible political risks |
| Modification of domestic finance theories | MNCs must modify finance theories like capital budgeting and cost of capital because of foreign complexities | Base case |
| Modification of domestic financial instruments | MNCs utilize modified financial instruments such as options, future, swaps and letters of credit | Base case |

and political risks and the required modifications of financial theory and financial instruments.

International financial Management requires an understanding of cultural, historical and institutional differences such as those affecting corporate governance. Although both domestic firms and MNCs are exposed to foreign exchange risks, MNCs alone face certain unique risks that are not normally a threat to domestic operations such as political risks.

MNCs also face other risks that can be classified as extensions of domestic finance theory. For example, the normal domestic approach to the cost of capital, sourcing debt and equity, capital budgeting, working capital management, taxation and credit analysis needs to be modified to accommodate foreign complexities. Moreover, a number of financial instruments that are used in domestic financial management have been modified for use in international financial management. Examples are foreign currency derivative, interest rate and currency swaps and letter of credit.

## Why study International Finance?

A study of international finance will help the finance manager in the following ways:[10]

(1) He will be able to know how international events will affect the firm and the economy as a whole and what steps could be taken as correctives - to take advantage of positive events and guard against adverse ones.

(2) He may be able to know anticipate events which could enable the firm to benefit-change in exchange rates, interest rates, inflation rates, growth and various countries, national income overall and per capita. He may be able, in many cases, to anticipate political events as well.

Further, increased volatility in exchange rates as a result of flexible exchange rate system prevalent in many countries has made the knowledge of international finance imperative. Knowledge of international financial management is helpful not only to those who work in multinationals but also to those who export and import. It is also helpful to those companies which are operating in domestic markets but compete with firms producing abroad and selling in their markets because they may be affected by international developments like changes in exchange rates.

The second half of the twentieth century has also experienced a vast magnitude of lending international and regional developments. The movement of funds mostly to the developing world and the reverse movement of funds in forms of interest and amortization payments needed proper management. Besides, there were big changes in the character of the international financial market with the emergence of Euro banks and offshore banking centre and of various instruments, such as Euro bonds, Euro notes and Euro commercial papers. The nature of the movement of funds became so complex that proper management became a necessity and the study of international financial management became highly relevant. In fact, international financial management suggests the most suitable technique to be applied at a particular moment and in a particular case in order to hedge the risk.

## CONCLUSION

International financial management deals with the financial decisions taken in the area of international business. The growth in international business is, first of all, evident in the form of highly inflated size of international trade. It would thus be seen that the importance of international financial management can be traced to the sectoral and national interdependence which leads to international economic, commercial and financial relations as between countries. International trade, aid and financial flows account for the bulk of such transactions as between nations. The basic economic principles of efficiency, productivity and least cost optimization process necessitate the use of inputs both domestic and foreign and flow of goods and services across national borders, provided there are no barriers to such flows. The result is the exchange of goods and services involving payments and receipts as between countries and exchange of one currency for another and borrowing and lending of money or near money assets across borders. The transactions and trading in foreign currencies, foreign assets or liabilities and foreign claims constitute the international financial system and are the subject matters of International Financial Management.

## REFERENCES

1. ILO, *Multinational Enterprises and Social Policy*, ILO, Geneva 1973, p.3.
2. Leonard Gomes, *International Economic Problems*, Macmillan Press, London, 1978,p.119.
3. Alan C. Shapiro, *Multinational Financial Management*, Prentice-Hall of India Pvt. Ltd. New Delhi, 1996, p.17.
4. Jeff Madura, *International Financial Management*, Thomson Asia Pvt. Ltd. Singapore, 2001, p.5.
5. V. Sharan, *International Financial Management*, Prentice-Hall of India Pvt. Ltd. New Delhi, 2008, p.3.
6. The Economist, *Multinationals: A Survey*, March 27, 1993, p.5.
7. Cited in V.V. Keshkamat, *Foreign Exchange and Exchange Control*, Vivek Publications, Bombay, 1976, p.3.
8. Cited in V.V. Keshkamat, *ibid.*, p.3
9. Eiteman, Stonehill, Moffett and Pandey, Multinational Business Finance, Dorling Kindersley (India) Pvt. Ltd. 2007,p.3.
10. R.L. Varshney & S. Bhashyam, *International Financial Management: An Indian perspective*, Sultan Chand & Sons, New Delhi, 2001, p.8.

# 3

# Growth of Mutual Fund Industry in India

**Ranjan Kumar Bal & Pinku Paul**

The mutual fund industry in India has evolved little over four decades but the real impetus has come after the changes in the mutual fund regulations in early 80s. Private and foreign mutual funds are operating in the Indian market and constitute a substantial portion of the mutual fund industry. Today the industry consists of Unit Trust of India, mutual funds sponsored by public sector banks and insurance corporations, private and foreign mutual funds. The age long journey of the Mutual fund Industry of India comprises five distinct phases with growing asset under its management. Still now the journey is rolling up and achieving new heights.

## Evolution of Mutual Funds in India

The formation of Unit Trust of India marked the evolution of the Indian mutual fund industry in the year 1963. The primary objective at that time was to attract the small investors and it was made possible through the collective efforts of the Government of India and the Reserve Bank of India. The history of mutual fund industry in India can be better understood divided into following phases:

## Phase I. Establishment and Growth of Unit Trust of India - 1964-87

Unit Trust of India enjoyed complete monopoly when it was established in the year 1963 by an act of Parliament. UTI was set up by the Reserve Bank of India and it continued to operate under the regulatory control of the RBI until the two were de-linked in 1978 and the entire control was transferred in the hands of Industrial Development Bank of India (IDBI). UTI launched its first scheme in 1964, named as Unit Scheme 1964 (US-64), which attracted the largest number of investors in any single investment scheme over the years.

UTI launched more innovative schemes in 1970s and 80s to suit the needs of different investors. It launched ULIP in 1971, six more schemes between 1981-84, Children's Gift Growth Fund and India Fund (India's first offshore fund) in 1986, Master share (India's first equity diversified scheme) in 1987 and Monthly Income Schemes (offering assured returns) during 1990s. By the end of 1987, UTI's assets under management grew ten times to Rs 6700 crores.

## Phase II. Entry of Public Sector Funds - 1987-1993

The Indian mutual fund industry witnessed a number of public sector players entering the market in the year 1987. In November 1987, SBI Mutual Fund from the State Bank of India became the first non-UTI mutual fund in India. SBI Mutual Fund was later followed by Can bank Mutual Fund, LIC Mutual Fund, Indian Bank Mutual Fund, Bank of India Mutual Fund, GIC Mutual Fund and PNB Mutual Fund. By 1993, the assets under management of the industry increased seven times to Rs. 47,004 crores. However, UTI remained to be the leader with about 80% market share.

**Table 3.1**
**Amount Mobilized and Asset under Management**

| 1992-93 | Amount Mobilized | Assets Under Management | Mobilization as % of Gross Domestic Savings |
|---|---|---|---|
| UTI | 11,057 | 38,247 | 5.2% |
| Public Sector | 1,964 | 8,757 | 0.9% |
| Total | 13,021 | 47,004 | 6.1% |

**Source**: www.appuonline.com/mf/knowledge/industry.html.

## Phase III. Emergence of Private Sector Funds - 1993-96

The permission given to private sector funds including foreign fund management companies (most of them entering through joint ventures with Indian promoters) to enter the mutual fund industry in 1993 provided a wide range of choice to investors and more competition in the industry. Private funds introduced innovative products, investment techniques and investor-servicing technology. By 1994-95, about 11 private sector funds had launched their schemes.

## Phase IV. Growth and SEBI Regulation - 1996-2003

The mutual fund industry witnessed robust growth and stricter regulation from the Securities and Exchange Board of India (SEBI) after the year 1996. The mobilization of funds and the number of players operating in the industry reached new heights as investors started showing more interest in mutual funds.

Investors' interests were safeguarded by SEBI and the Government offered tax benefits to the investors in order to encourage them. SEBI (Mutual Funds) Regulations, 1996 was introduced by SEBI that set uniform standards for all mutual funds in India. The Union Budget in 1999 exempted all dividend incomes in the hands of investors from income tax. Various Investor Awareness Programmes were launched during this phase, both by SEBI and Association of Mutual Funds in India (AMFI), with an objective to educate investors and make them informed about the mutual fund industry. In 1999, there was a significant growth in assets under management which amounted to Rs 68,472 crores and the gross mobilization of funds from investors are presented in Table 3.2.

## Phase V. Growth and Consolidation - 2003 Onwards

In February 2003, the UTI Act was repealed and UTI was stripped of its Special legal status as a trust formed by an Act of Parliament. The primary objective behind this was to bring all mutual fund players on the same level. UTI was re-organized into two parts:

1. The Specified Undertaking,
2. The UTI Mutual Fund

The Specified Undertaking of the Unit Trust of India with assets under management of Rs.29,835 crores as at the end of January 2003, representing broadly, the assets of US 64 scheme, assured return and certain other schemes is functioning under an administrator and under the rules framed by Government of India and does not come under the purview of the Mutual Fund Regulations.

The UTI Mutual Fund Ltd, was sponsored by SBI, PNB, BOB and LIC. It is registered with SEBI and functions under the Mutual Fund Regulations. With the bifurcation of the erstwhile UTI, which had in March 2000 more than Rs.76,000 crores of assets under management, and with the setting up of a UTI Mutual Fund, conforming to the SEBI Mutual Fund Regulations.

**Table 3.2**
**Gross Funds Mobilization**

| GROSS FUND MOBILISATION (RS. CRORES) | | | | | |
|---|---|---|---|---|---|
| From | To | UTI | Public Sector | Private Sector | Total |
| 01-April-98 | 31-March-99 | 11,679 | 1,732 | 7,966 | 21,377 |
| 01-April-99 | 31-March-00 | 13,536 | 4,039 | 42,173 | 59,748 |
| 01-April-00 | 31-March-01 | 12,413 | 6,192 | 74,352 | 92,957 |
| 01-April-01 | 31-March-02 | 4,643 | 13,613 | 1,46,267 | 1,64,523 |
| 01-April-02 | 31-Jan-03 | 5,505 | 22,923 | 2,20,551 | 2,48,979 |
| 01-Feb.-03 | 31-March-03 | * | 7,259* | 58,435 | 65,694 |
| 01-April-03 | 31-March-04 | - | 68,558 | 5,21,632 | 5,90,190 |
| 01-April-04 | 31-March-05 | - | 1,03,246 | 7,36,416 | 8,39,662 |
| 01-April-05 | 31-March-06 | - | 1,83,446 | 9,14,712 | 10,98,158 |

**Source:** www.appuonline.com/mf/knowledge/industry.html

Presently Unit Trust of India operates under the name of UTI Mutual Fund and its past schemes (like US-64, Assured Return Schemes) are being gradually wound up. However, UTI Mutual Fund is still the largest player in the industry.

The industry has also witnessed several mergers and acquisitions examples of which are acquisition of schemes of Alliance Mutual Fund by Birla Sun Life, Sun F&C Mutual Fund and PNB Mutual Fund by Principal Mutual Fund. Simultaneously, more international mutual fund players have entered India like Fidelity, Franklin Templeton Mutual Fund etc. There are 35 funds houses as at the end of March 2009. This is a continuing phase of growth of the industry through consolidation and entry of new international and private sector players. Recently a new Mutual Fund house has launched Shinsei Asset Management (India) Pvt. Ltd. ("Shinsei AMC") sponsored by Shinsei Bank, Limited ("Shinsei Bank" or "Bank") making the Mutual Fund Industry a 36 member Industry.

## WORKING OF MUTUAL FUND

A Mutual Fund is a trust that pools the savings of a number of investors who share a common financial goal. The money thus collected is then invested in capital market instruments such as shares, debentures and other securities. The income earned through these investments and the capital appreciations realized are shared by its unit holders in proportion to the number of units owned by them. Thus a mutual fund is the most suitable investment for the common man as it offers an opportunity to invest in a diversified, professionally managed basket of securities at a relatively low cost. The figure 3.2 below describes broadly the flow of funds in a mutual fund:

There are many entities involved and the diagram below illustrates the working of mutual fund (Fig. 3.3):

## GROWTH IN ASSETS UNDER MANAGEMENT

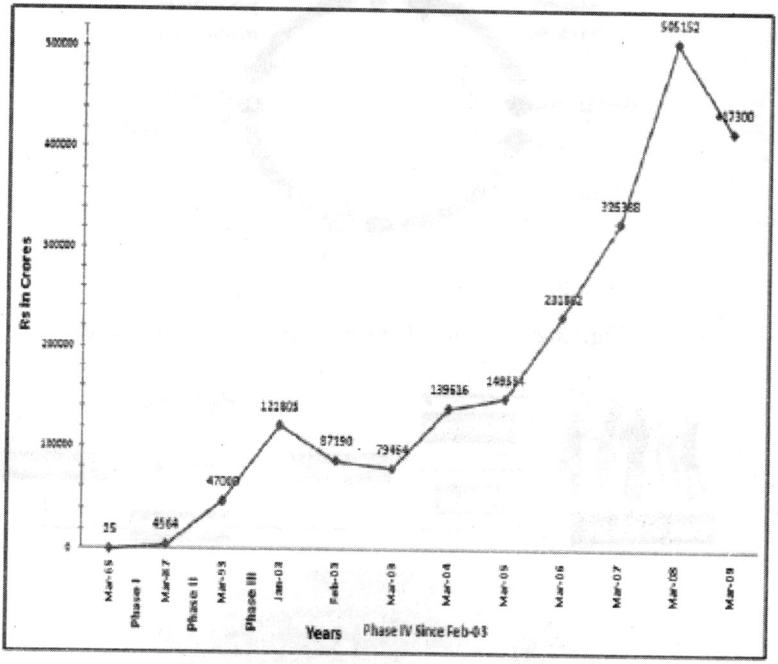


**Fig. 3.1. Growth of Asset under Management**

**Note:** Erstwhile UTI was bifurcated into UTI Mutual Fund and the Specified Undertaking of the Unit Trust of India effective from February 2003. The Assets under management of the Specified Undertaking of the Unit Trust of India has therefore been excluded from the total assets of the industry as a whole from February 2003 onwards.

**Source:** www.amfiindia.com

A mutual fund is usually either a corporation or a business trust. Asset Management Company (AMC), approved by Securities Exchange Board of India (SEBI), manages the funds by making investments in various types of securities. Custodian, registered with SEBI, holds the securities of various schemes of the fund in its custody. According to SEBI Regulations, two thirds of the directors of Trustee Company or board of trustees

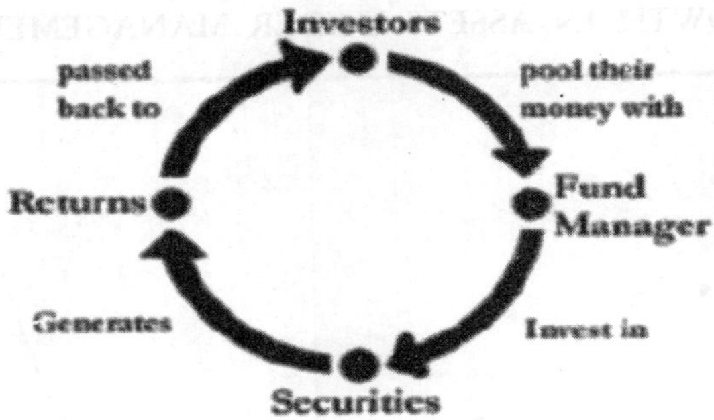


Source: www.amfiindia.com

**Fig. 3.2. Flow of Funds in a Mutual Fund**

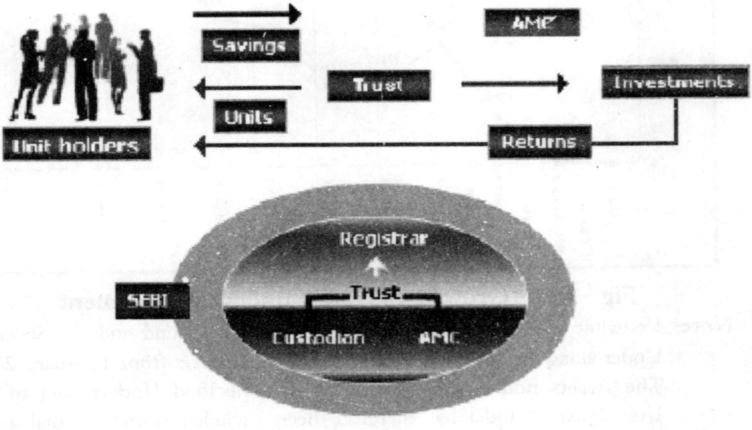


**Source**: www.mutualfundindia.com

**Fig. 3.3. Working of Mutual Fund**

must be independent. The Association of Mutual Funds in India (AMFI) reassures the investors in units of mutual funds that the mutual funds function within the strict regulatory framework. Its objective is to increase public awareness of the mutual fund industry. AMFI also is engaged in upgrading professional standards and in promoting best industry practices in diverse areas such as valuation, disclosure, transparency etc.

## Types of Returns associated with Mutual Funds

There are three ways, where the total returns provided by mutual funds can be enjoyed by investors:

Income is earned from dividends on stocks and interest on bonds. A fund pays out nearly all income it receives over the year to fund owners in the form of a distribution.

If the fund sells securities that have increased in price, the fund has a capital gain. Most funds also pass on these gains to investors in a distribution.

If fund holdings increase in price but are not sold by the fund manager, the fund's shares increase in price. You can then sell your mutual fund shares for a profit. Funds will also usually give you a choice either to receive a cheque for distributions or to reinvest the earnings and get more shares.

The risk return trade-off indicates that if investor is willing to take higher risk then correspondingly he can expect higher returns and *vice versa* if he pertains to lower risk instruments, which would be satisfied by lower returns. For example, if investors opt for bank FD, which provide moderate return with minimal risk. But as he moves ahead to invest in capital protected funds and the profit-bonds that give out more return, which is slightly higher as compared to the bank deposits, but the risk involved also increases in the same proportion. Thus investors choose mutual funds as their primary means of investing, as Mutual funds provide professional management, diversification, convenience and liquidity. That doesn't mean mutual fund investments as risk free. This is because the money that is pooled in are not invested only in debts funds which are less riskier but are also invested in the stock markets which involves a higher risk but can expect higher returns. Hedge fund involves a very high risk since it is mostly traded in the derivatives market, which is considered very volatile.

**Risk Hierarchy of Mutual Funds**

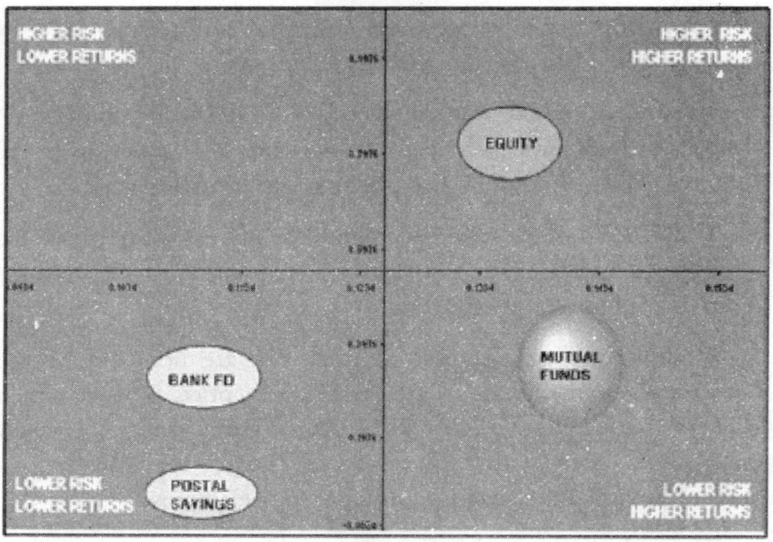


**Source**: www.appuonline.com/mf/knowledge/industry.html

**Fig. 3.4. Risk Return Matrix**

## Risk Hierarchy of Different Mutual Funds Schemes

Different mutual fund schemes are exposed to different levels of risk and investors should know the level of risks associated with these schemes before investing. The graphical representation hereunder provides a clearer picture of the relationship between mutual funds and levels of risk associated with these funds:

## Pros and Cons of investing in Mutual Funds

For investments in mutual fund, one must keep in mind about the pros and cons of investments in mutual fund.

## Advantages of Investing Mutual Funds

- *Professional Management* - The basic advantage of funds is that, they are professional managed, by well-qualified

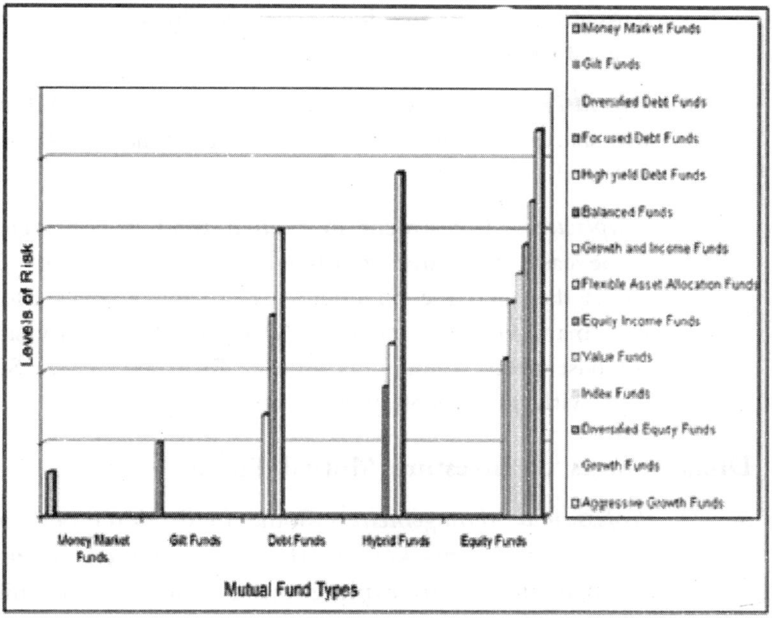


Source: www.appuonline.com/mf/knowledge/industry.html

**Fig. 3.5. Risk Hierarchy of Different Mutual Funds Schemes**

professional. Investors purchase funds because they do not have the time or the expertise to manage their own portfolio. A mutual fund is considered to be relatively less expensive way to make and monitor their investments.

- *Diversification* - Purchasing units in a mutual fund instead of buying individual stocks or bonds, the investor's risk is spread out and minimized up to certain extent. The idea behind diversification is to invest in a large number of assets so that a loss in any particular investment is minimized by gains in others.
- *Economies of Scale* - Mutual fund buy and sell large amounts of securities at a time, thus help in reducing

transaction costs, and help to bring down the average cost of the unit for their investors.

- *Liquidity* - Just like an individual stock, mutual fund also allows investors to liquidate their holdings as and when they want.
- *Simplicity* - Investment in mutual fund is considered to be easy, compared to other available instruments in the market, and the minimum investment is small. Most asset management companies (AMC) also have automatic purchase plans whereby as little as Rs. 2000, where SIP start with just Rs.50 per month basis.

## Disadvantages of Investing Mutual Funds

- *Professional Management* - Some funds don't perform in neither the market, as their management is not dynamic enough to explore the available opportunity in the market, thus many investors debate over whether or not the so-called professionals are any better than mutual fund or investor him self, for picking up stocks.
- *Costs* – The biggest source of AMC income is generally from the entry & exit load, which they charge from investors, at the time of purchase. The mutual fund industries are thus charging extra cost under layers of jargon.
- *Dilution* - Because funds have smallholdings across different companies, high returns from a few investments often don't make much difference on the overall return. Dilution is also the result of a successful fund getting too big. When money pours into funds that have had strong success, the manager often has trouble finding a good investment for all the new money.
- *Taxes* - When making decisions about your money, fund managers don't consider your personal tax

situation. For example, when a fund manager sells a security, a capital-gain tax is triggered, which affects how profitable the individual is from the sale. It might have been more advantageous for the individual to defer the capital gains liability.

## Mutual Fund Houses in India

**Table 3.3**
**Total Asset under Management for all Mutual Fund houses**

| Sl. No. | Name of the Asset Management Company | Average Assets Under Management As on March 2009 (Rs. in Crores) |
|---|---|---|
| 1 | 2 | 3 |
| **A** | **BANK SPONSORED** | |
| **(i)** | **Joint Ventures - Predominantly Indian** | |
| 1 | Canara Robeco Asset Management Co. Ltd. | 4,744 |
| 2 | SBI Funds Management Pvt. Ltd. | 26,383 |
| | Total A (i) | 31,127 |
| (ii) | Joint Ventures - Predominantly Foreign | |
| 1 | Baroda Pioneer Asset Management Company Limited | 1,132 |
| | Total A (ii) | 1,132 |
| (iii) | OTHERS | |
| 1 | UTI Asset Management Company Ltd | 48,754 |
| | Total A (ii) | 48,754 |
| | Total A (i + ii + iii) | 81,013 |

*(contd.)*

| 1 | 2 | 3 |
|---|---|---|
| B | INSTITUTIONS | |
| 1 | LIC Mutual Fund Asset Management Co. Ltd. | 23,092 |
| | Total B | 23,092 |
| C | PRIVATE SECTOR | |
| (i) | INDIAN | |
| 1 | Benchmark Asset Management Co. Pvt. Ltd. | 1,069 |
| 2 | DBS Cholamandalam Asset Management Ltd. | 1,023 |
| 3 | Deutsche Asset Management (India) Private Ltd. | 9,355 |
| 4 | Edelweiss Asset Management Limited | 22 |
| 5 | Escorts Asset Management Ltd. | 182 |
| 6 | IDFC Asset Management Company Private Limited | 14,362 |
| 7 | J.M. Financial Asset Management Pvt. Ltd. | 4,788 |
| 8 | Kotak Mahindra Asset Management Co. Ltd. | 18,204 |
| 9 | Quantum Asset Management Co. Pvt. Ltd. | 57 |
| 10 | Reliance Capital Asset Management Ltd. | 80,963 |
| 11 | Religare Asset Management Company Private Limited | 6,023 |
| 12 | Sahara Asset Management Co. Pvt. Ltd. | 146 |
| 13 | Tata Asset Management Ltd. | 17,030 |
| 14 | Taurus Asset Management Co. Ltd. | 208 |
| | Total C (i) | 153,432 |
| (ii) | FOREIGN | |
| 1 | AIG Global Asset Management Company (India) Private Ltd. | 3219 |
| 2 | FIL Fund Management Private Ltd. | 6,173 |
| 3 | Fortis Investment Management (India) Private Ltd. | 5,811 |
| 4 | Franklin Templeton Asset Management (India) Private Ltd. | 19,205 |
| 5 | Mirae Asset Global Investment Management (I) Private Ltd. | 162 |
| | Total C (ii) | 32,728 |

| 1 | 2 | 3 |
|---|---|---|
| (iii) | JOINT VENTURES - PEDOMINANTLY INDIAN | |
| 1 | Birla Sun Life Asset Management Co. Ltd. | 47,096 |
| 2 | DSP Merrill Lynch Fund Managers Ltd. | 14,412 |
| 3 | HDFC Asset Management Co. Ltd. | 57,956 |
| 4 | ICICI Prudential Asset Management Co. Ltd. | 51,432 |
| 5 | Sundaram BNP Paribas Asset Management Co. Ltd. | 9,267 |
| | Total C (iii) | 180,163 |
| (iv) | JOINT VENTURES - PREDOMINANTLY FOREI | |
| 1 | Bharti AXA Investment Managers Private Limited. | 196 |
| 2 | HSBC Asset Management (India) Private Ltd. | 9,575 |
| 3 | ING Investment Management (India) Private Ltd. | 2,529 |
| 4 | JPMorgan Asset Managemenxt (India) Private Ltd. | 2,454 |
| 5 | Morgan Stanley Investment Management Pvt. Ltd. | 1,346 |
| 6 | Principal PNB Asset Management Co. Pvt. Ltd. | 6,757 |
| | Total C (iv) | 22,857 |
| | Total C (i + ii + iii + iv) | 389,180 |

**Source**: www.mutualfundsindia.com.

As per the data released by Association of Mutual Funds in India (AMFI), as on 31st March 2009, 35 members are presently operating in the Indian mutual fund industry. The average assets under management (AAUM) of the 35-member mutual fund industry was Rs. 4, 17,300 crores as against Rs. 5, 05,152 crores as at the end of the previous year. 551 new schemes were launched during the year as against 612 in the previous year. The amount mobilized was Rs. 1, 03,177 crores as against Rs. 1, 60,773 crores in the previous year. Total Funds mobilized during the year stood at Rs. 54, 26,353 crores as against Rs. 44, 64,376 crores in the last year representing an increase of 22%. Redemptions at Rs. 54, 54,650 crores were 27% higher than the redemptions of Rs. 43, 10,575 crores in the previous year. On a net basis, there was an outflow of Rs. 28,297 crores as compared to an inflow of Rs.153, 801 crores in the last year.

## CONCLUSION

The Fiscal year 2008-09 was a challenging year that the Fund Industry passed through (Kurian, 2009). Industry till May 2008 was growing at the annual growth rate of about 50% per annum. Since then, there was a marked deceleration in the growth of Assets under Management till September 2008. Thereafter, reflecting the financial 'Tsunami' which erupted elsewhere but impacted our economy also to some extent, the AUM started declining over the year and though it recovered somewhat in the last quarter, the month end AUM for March 2009 was over 17% lower than the previous year. The fiscal year 2008-09 was a challenging year. The Fund Industry passed through the Financial Tsunami. However, the situation has been changing, and changing for the better. The industry witnessed a robust growth in the Fiscal 2009-10 with AAUM Rs. 6,13,979 Crores as on 31st March 2010, representing an increase of 47%.

## REFERENCES

Appuonline: IT enabled financial services. (2008). "Mutual Fund Industry in India", as at http://www.appuonline.com/mf/ knowledge / industry.html.

Brown, B.J., Goetzman, W. (1997). "Mutual fund styles", Journal of Financial Economics, Vol. 43, pp.373-99.

Chakrabarti, Anjan and Rungta Harsh. (2000). "Mutual Funds Industry in India: An in-depth look into the problems of credibility, Risk and Brand", The ICFAI Journal of Applied Finance, Vol.6, No.2, April, pp.27-45.

Kulshreshta, C.M. (1994). Mastering Mutual Funds, Vision Books, New Delhi.

Kurian, A. P. (2009), 'Newsletter of The Association of Mutual Funds Industry in India', Vol. VIII Issue IV, January - March as at http:// www.amfiindia.com/ spages/ aqu-vol8. pdf-issueIV.pdf

McWhinney, Jim. (2006). "Evolution of MF A Brief History Of The Mutual Fund", as at http://www.investopedia.com /articles/ mutual fund /05/ MFhistory.asp.

Sadhak, H. (1997). "Mutual Funds in India – Marketing Strategies and Investment Practices", Response Books, Sage Publication ltd., New Delhi.

Sarkar, A.K. (1991). "Mutual Funds in India: Emerging Trends", Management Accountant, Vol.26, No.3, pp.171-194.

Srinivsasn, Ajay. (1999). "Mutual Funds: The New Era", Chartered Secretary, Sept., A 262.

The Hindu Online edition of India's National Newspaper, Saturday, May 06, (2006). "Bright future for mutual funds industry: study", as at http:/ www.hindu.com/2006/05/06/stories/2006050606071700.htm

Tripathy, Nalini Prava, (1996). "Mutual Fund in India: A Financial Service in Capital Market", Finance India, Vol. X, No. 1, March, pp. 85–91.

Vidya Shankar, S. (1990). "Mutual Funds – Emerging Trends in India", Chartered Secretary, Vol.20, No.8, pp.639-640.

## WEBOGRAPHY

http://www.amfiindia.com/showhtml.aspx?page=mfconcept

http://www.amfiindia.com/showhtml.aspx?page=mfindustry

http://www.amfiindia.com/spages/aqu-vol9-issueIII.pdf

http://www.mutualfundindia.com

http://www.mutualfundsindia.com/news

# 4

# Accounting and Disclosure Practices of Mutual Funds in India

**Rajat Sharmacharjee & Nikhil Bhusan Dey**

**Abstract**: A mutual fund is an institutional device through which investors pool funds of savers to invest in a diversified portfolio of securities, thus, spreading and reducing risk. It aims at minimizing risk while ensuring steady return. Since mutual funds act as financial intermediary collecting funds from small investors and investing them in securities ,their interest should be protected. Proper accounts and accounting reports should be prepared and submitted to the fund holders at regular intervals to enable them to know about their investments and financial results. Under SEBI (MF) Regulations and other allied Acts of the country ,mutual funds are required to maintain proper books of accounts, records and documents. This paper attempts to highlight the reporting and disclosure practices of mutual funds in India. The study is based on secondary sources. Books, research articles, newspapers, internet etc. are reviewed and consulted for the purpose of the study.

**Keywords**: *Net Asset Value (NAV) .GAAP, SEBI, AMC*

## Introduction

Mutual fund is an investment vehicle through which investors pool their funds under the direction of an investment manager. The funds are invested in a wide variety of securities in such a way as to minimize risk while ensuring steady return. The mutual fund industry is a fast growing sector of the Indian capital market. Mutual funds entered the Indian capital market with the establishment of UTI in 1964. Public Sector Banks and Financial Institutions began to establish mutual funds in 1987. The Private Sector and Foreign Institutions were allowed to set up mutual funds in 1993. The Indian mutual fund industry has grown tremendously in the last decade and it is a very important and dynamic sector in Indian capital market.

Mutual funds have become a major vehicle for mobilization of savings, specially, from the small and household sectors of Indian economy. These savings are invested in the capital market through appropriate and prudent portfolio methods to optimize earnings to enable the fund holders to have better benefits in the shape of dividends and capital appreciation.

As mutual funds use public money, proper accounts and accounting reports should be prepared and submitted to fund holders at regular intervals to enable them to know about their investments and financial results. These annual accounts should be prepared in the manner prescribed by the Securities and Exchange Board of India (SEBI) and other allied Acts of the country. The annual accounts should be audited by qualified auditors and audit reports should be annexed with the annual accounts and reports along with proper annexures relating to the performance. Trustees' report about the manner and performance of each mutual fund schemes should be given exclusively for each scheme. The present paper is divided into four sections, viz, Section I provides an overview of accounting principles that guide various aspects of mutual funds; Section

II deals with accounting and disclosure practices of mutual funds in India; section III deals with valuation policies of mutual funds in India and section IV relates to concluding remarks.

## SECTION I

### Accounting Principles

Accounting is a language of business. As a language, accounting communicates the results of business activities to various interest groups including the owners and holders who have stake in business. Accounting is the process of recording, classifying, summarizing, analyzing and interpreting the financial transactions and communicating the results thereof to the person interested in such information. The accounting cycle depends on accounting principles popularly known as Generally Accepted Accounting Principles (GAAP). Accounting principles may be defined as those rules of action or conduct which are adopted by the accountants universally while recording accounting transactions. The following chart shows the different elements of GAAP.

All these principles are more or less adapted to the frame of a business as well as mutual funds. Accounting principles and standards set for regulating measurement and disclosure of information should ideally stem out of an accepted conceptual framework. The various aspects of the conceptual framework that would underlie the analysis of accounting information provided by mutual funds are stated hereunder.

In mutual funds, funds are managed by trusts by pooling funds from investors. The costs of additional disclosure and provision of additional information is completely passed on to the investor. The plea for additional disclosures should be evaluated with the overriding constraint of keeping benefits greater than the costs involved. Again, mutual funds are distinctly different from traditional business and hence the traditional

**Generally Accepted Accounting Principles (GAAP)**

| Assumptions | Principles | Modifying principles | Accounting Standards |
|---|---|---|---|
| 1. Accounting Entity | 1. Dual Aspect | 1. Materiality | At present 33 accounting |
| 2. Accrual | 2. Revenue Recognition | 2. Conservatism | standards are available |
| 3. Going Concern | 3. Cost | 3. Cost Benefit | (AS – 1 to AS – 33) |
| 4. Money Measurement | 4. Matching | 4. Timeliness | |
| 5. Accounting period | 5. Full Disclosure | 5. Consistency | |
| | 6. Objectivity | 6. Substance over legal form. | |
| | | 7. Industry Practice. | |

balance sheet, income statement, reporting forms and accounting methods are different. The net assets of the fund, changes to the net assets over an accounting period etc. should be reported. Another important aspect is that in the Indian context, the users of information would be mainly the individuals. The important characteristics of such users would be the inability to get information from other sources, limited ability to process information and the subjective nature of decision making process. Simple and easily understandable reporting methods are important in this connection. Also the concept of relevance and reliability manifests significantly in the accounting practices of mutual funds. The principle of conservatism as applied to mutual funds is creating certain anomalies in revenue recognition and provisioning for depreciation and doubtful incomes. The accrual principle is applied to arrive at true and fair income measurement. Thus for accounting and reporting purposes of mutual funds' transactions, accounting policies, standards and principles are adopted following Accounting Standard (AS)-1 issued by the Institute of Chartered Accountants of India (ICAI). Moreover, SEBI guidelines and provisions of the Companies Act are also followed.

## SECTION II

### Accounting and Disclosure Practices of Mutual Funds

Mutual funds like other business organizations prepare their annual accounts to disclose their performance. The financial statement and annual report should be prepared following the provision of the SEBI, the Companies Act, 1956, Income Tax Act, 1961 and Indian Trusts Act. Under SEBI (MF) Regulations, mutual funds are required to maintain proper books of accounts, records and documents. It, under Regulation 47, requires that the books of accounts should be such as to explain its transaction and to disclose it at any point of time the financial position of the mutual funds. The records and statements should give a true and fair view of the state of affairs of the fund.

Accounting policy of a mutual fund involves the selection of certain specific methods of measuring and reporting of financial information from amongst alternatives that may be available. Uniform accounting procedures would help for inter-firm comparison. Although diversity in accounting treatment cannot be eliminated, it should be minimised. The prescription and enforcement of accounting and reporting norms for mutual funds are made in order to serve the requirements and purposes of both fund holders SEBI and government authorities, with the purpose: the disposition of the assets and their performance have to be known to the unit holders and the financial statement should enable evaluation of income earned on the amounts and financial position. In the annual reports, mutual funds have to disclose the accounting policies that have been adopted by them. Material alterations to reported income, due to changes in accounting policy should also have to be quantified, reported and disclosed.

In India, mutual funds are required to prepare Revenue Account and Balance Sheet in an accounting year. The accounting year is consisting of 12 months commencing from 1st April of current year ending at 31$^{st}$ March next. Revenue Account is prepared by mutual funds following the guidelines of SEBI and Accounting Standards issued by the ICAI, Indian Trusts Act, the Indian Companies Act, Income Tax Act and the Trust Agreement and Charter on each mutual fund scheme.

In regard to 'Accounting Requirements', the Ministry of Finance, Government of India has issued the following guidelines on February 14, 1992.

(i) Mutual funds should be required to segregate their earnings as current income, short term capital gains and long term capital gains.

(ii) Accounting for all the schemes should be required to be done for the same year ending.

(iii) For all quoted instruments, mutual funds must calculate weekly NAV at the last available closing market prices. For unquoted investment, the valuation may be done once weekly either at cost or by any other method authorized by SEBI.

(iv) The SEBI will have the right to call for any information regarding the operations of the mutual funds and any of its schemes.

(v) SEBI will require from every mutual fund at least the following periodic reports, in addition to any other it may see fit:

a. Copies of the duly audited statements of accounts including the Balance Sheet and the Profit and Loss account for the fund and for each scheme, once a year.

b. Six monthly un-audited accounts as above.

c. A statement of movement in net assets for each of the fund, every quarter.

d. A portfolio statement, including changes from the previous periods, for each scheme, every quarter,

(vi) SEBI shall also lay down the accounting policies to be complied with by all mutual funds and the format and contents of the financial statements and other reports.

(vii) SEBI can after due investigation impose penalties on mutual funds for violating the guidelines as may be necessary.

## Revenue Account

It is a statement of expenses, incomes and surplus of mutual funds as specified in SEBI (MF) Regulations.

## Expenses

Regulation 50 requires all the expenses of a mutual fund to be clearly identified and appropriated to individual schemes. As per the Regulation, an Asset Management Company (AMC) can charge the mutual fund with the following expenses:

i. Initial issue expense.

ii. Recurring administrative expenses.

iii. Investment management and advisory fee.

Initial issue expenses are very crucial for the successful launching of a scheme. The significance of these expenses is that to the extent of these expenses, the investible fund or the corpus raised automatically stands reduced. Thus, to safeguard interest of small investors, SEBI has imposed a limit on these expenses. Initial issue expense in respect of any one scheme shall not exceed six per cent of the fund raised under that scheme. These expenses include brokerage, commission and incentives, marketing and advertisement expenses, lead manager fee, processing and record keeping, printing and distribution, legal fee etc. These expenses are typically capitalized and written off over the tenure of the scheme. All mutual funds uniformly capitalize the expenses as 'Deferred Revenue Expenditure' in the Balance Sheet. But the manner of amortization is not uniform with all the mutual funds. Depending the earning capacity of the particular scheme, some funds retain the flexibility to increase the extent of amortization in a particular year, as decided by the trustees. If the income is more in a particular year, the amount of amortization would be more. When the income of a particular scheme is low, the amortization amount would be less. Thus, the amount of amortization would be flexible over the tenure of the scheme. Unamortized initial expenses will be shown in the Balance Sheet. Commission is paid only once in regard to 'close-ended scheme' while it is recurring in case of an 'open-ended scheme.' If commission is paid only once in the tenure of the scheme, it is amortized over the period of tenure, if it is fixed. If the scheme is open ended and commission is paid regularly, the amount of current year will be charged to Revenue Account.

Recurring or ongoing administrative expenses include marketing and selling expenses, custodian fee, transfer fee, legal fee, audit fee, interest expenses, directors fees, brokerage and transaction costs arising on account of sale or purchase of securities from money market or capital market, accounting fee payable to agencies. Each AMC may charge the mutual fund with investment management and advisory fee. This fee is the compensation paid to AMC for handing the investment of the fund. It is the fee from which AMC is to meet expenses like office rent, salaries and stationery etc. Such fee should be disclosed in the offer document. As an incentive besides management fee, a bonus may be payable if the fund out performs some specified market index or a stipulated growth rate. As per Schedule VI of SEBI (MF) Regulations, total expenses charged to the fund, except initial issue expenses shall not exceed three per cent of the net weekly average net assets.

Other expense items of Revenue Account include depreciation on investment, provision for bad and doubtful debts / incomes, loss on sale / redemption of investments, loss on inter scheme transfer / sale of investments, deferred revenue expenses written off. SEBI requires under Regulation 52 that before declaring any dividend in respect of any scheme, every mutual fund shall provide for depreciation on investments. In case of mutual funds, depreciation is the difference between the aggregate market value of investment and the carrying cost or aggregate cost of the investment and it is charged as direct expenses and debited to Revenue Account. However, a question arises how to compute the aggregate market value of investment.

There in no settled law or specific accounting standard in India to take care of biasness of the mutual funds. Mutual funds in India value quoted investments at year end market rates. But there are different alternatives available for the rates on the last date e.g. closing rate, opening rate or mid-market rate. As per international accounting practice, investment should be valued at mid-market rate. However, in India, SEBI desires that depreciation on investment should be to the satisfaction of its auditors and method of depreciation is to be disclosed in the notes to the accounts.

Prior to 1989-90, UTI charged depreciation on investments on line by line basis. Such method as per UTI was very conservative since it required making provisions for every instance where market price has fallen below purchase price. Since 1990-91, UTI changed its method of depreciation following international practice, to the global method.

SEBI also authorizes mutual funds to provide for bad and doubtful debts or doubtful incomes and doubtful deposits and current assets. All such provisions again should be to the satisfaction of the auditor of the scheme.

## Incomes

All the incomes of mutual funds are to be accounted for in its Revenue Account. As per SEBI (MF) Regulation 49, every mutual fund shall in its accounts make a disclosure by segregating its earnings into short term capital gains, long term capital gains and other incomes. But the Revenue Account format suggest disclosures as to incomes from dividends, interests, profits on sale/redemption of investments, profits on inter scheme transfer. Accounting policy in respect of recognition of revenue and income from investments should be disclosed. In absence of any specific directions from SEBI, norms laid down as to recognition of incomes specified in AS-13, issued by ICAI under paras 12,13,21 and 22 may be adhered to even by mutual funds.

## Dividend

Dividend is a very important element of income to mutual fund. Both cash basis and accrual basis of accounting are used for recognizing dividend as income of mutual fund. . Under cash basis, actual cash receipts and actual cash payments are recorded which gives rise to actual position on dividend. In accrual basis, income is recognized and all possible adjustments like dividend accrued, dividend received in advance etc, are considered.

## Interest Income

Interest income includes : (i) Interest on fixed income securities, interest on short term securities, interest on long term securities, and (ii) Interest on money market instruments, commercial bank deposits. All mutual funds in India treat interest income on accrual basis.

## Profit on Sale of Investments

Mutual funds earn profits from: (i) sale of investments to third parties, (ii) profit on redemption of investments; and iii) profit on transfer of investments to another scheme in their own fund. Profits from these sources are required to be separately disclosed.

## Other Incomes

Mutual funds also earn income from other activities such as front end fees, service charges, commitment charges on firm allotments and private placements, interest on advance subscriptions underwriting commissions and stand by charges. In regard to accounting treatment of incomes in 'other income category' there are certain bases of allocation of such income to revenue. Such incomes are allocated by spreading the revenue over the life of the asset, or the tenure of the scheme, whichever is less. Another method of allocation and appropriation of such income is over the period of three years, recognizing 50 percent of the income in the first year, 30 percent in the second year and 20 percent in the third year. Another item appearing in Revenue Account on income side is 'profit on inter-scheme transfer/sale of investment'. Schedule VI of the Regulation requires that such transfers should be done at the prevailing market price for quoted investments on spot basis. In UTI, the relevant practice is as under:

i) Quoted investments at the market rate prevailing on the date of transaction.

ii) Unquoted debentures and bonds at a value determined on the basis of the current rate of yield

iii) Other investments at book value.

## Appropriation of Surplus

Matching expenses and incomes obviously give the surplus generated or loss incurred during an accounting period. Indian, mutual funds appropriate its surplus as per the SEBI Regulations or as per the wishes of the Board of Trustees. Regulation 51 states: 'Every mutual fund shall, as soon as may be, after the closing of the annual accounts, distribute by way of dividend to the holders of the units in accordance with these regulations, an amount, which shall not be less than ninety (90) percent of the profit earned during the year in respect of that scheme." This condition is not applicable for cumulative investment scheme or a growth oriented scheme in respect of which full disclosure of the nature of the scheme has been made to investors at the time of the offer. For such cases, as per the wishes of Board of Trustees, surplus may be distributed or may be transferred to reserves. The Revenue Account given in Schedule VII of the SEBI Regulations does not provide for presenting appropriation of income. It is only in the footnotes it specifies that the appropriation of the surplus by way of transfer to reserves and dividend distributed shall be disclosed in the Abridged Revenue Account.

## Balance Sheet

As per SEBI Regulations, mutual funds are required to prepare Balance Sheet at the end of the year. Such prepared Balance Sheet along with Revenue Account is to be submitted to SEBI within a period of six months from the date of closure of the relevant financial year.

Assets side of the Balance Sheet includes investment, deposits, fixed assets, other current assets, deferred revenue expenditure.

The liabilities side discloses the corpus of the scheme under the head unit capital, reserves and surplus, loans, current liabilities and provisions. For open ended policies, unit capital may go on changing on account of either sale or purchase of the units. But in the case of close ended schemes, there is possibility of only reduction in unit capital since these schemes can only buy back units. The paid up value of units so redeemed is cancelled against unit capital receiving advices from Registrars and difference between the acquisition cost and paid up value can be dealt with in general reserves or Revenue Account as decided by the Board of Trustees.

Regarding reserves and surpluses, there is no bar as to which reserves it can create. However, if any reserve other than the specified reserves are to be maintained, its nature is to be disclosed adequately. All transfers from / to reserves shall be separately disclosed for each type of reserve.

Although, no mutual fund is permitted to allow to borrow funds to finance its investments (Regulation 41 and Schedule VI), yet in Balance Sheet a separate head is prescribed for loans,.

Details of all loans are to be separately shown along with details of securities, if any.

## Format of Revenue Account and Balance Sheet

It is interesting to note that the formats of Revenue Account and Balance Sheet of mutual funds are just a replica of the format evolved by UTI over a period. The basic feature of formats prescribed by SEBI is that mutual funds have to spell out their accounting policies relating to investment and other important matters such as recognition of revenue and income, depreciation policy for investments, valuation of investments etc. UTI, the oldest mutual fund in India, has also been enclosing statement of Significant Accounting Policies forming part of the accounts for the year. The following Annexures (1A and 1B) shows the formats of Revenue Account and Balance Sheet followed by mutual funds as per SEBI (MF) Regulation, 1993.

### 1. A: Revenue Account

| | Current year Amount | Previous year Amount |
|---|---|---|
| INCOME | | |
| Dividend | | |
| Interest | | |
| Profit on Sale of Investments/Redemption | | |
| Profit on inter-scheme transfer/Sale | | |
| Other Inome | | |
| a. Total Income | | |
| EXPENSES | | |
| Trusteeship fees | | |
| Rent | | |
| Office and administrative expenses | | |

*(contd.)*

| | |
|---|---|
| Provision for depreciation | |
| Provision for doubtful debts | |
| Deferred revenue expenses | |
| Other expenses | |
| b. Total Expenses | |
| Surplus of the year (a) – (b) | |
| Appropriations. | |

## 1. B: Balance Sheet

| | Schedule Reference | Current year Amount | Previous year Amount |
|---|---|---|---|
| Sources of Funds | 1 | | |
| Unit Holder's Funds | | | |
| (i) Unit Capital | | | |
| (ii) Reserves and Surplus Loans | | | |
| Current Liabilities and provisions | 2 | | |
| Total | | | |
| Application of Funds | | | |
| Investment | 3 | | |
| Deposits | 4 | | |
| Other Current Assets | 5 | | |
| Fixed Assets | | | |
| Deferred Revenue Expenditure | 6 | | |
| Total | | | |

## SECTION III

### Valuation Policies of Mutual Funds

Mutual funds maintain and manage portfolio of investments judiciously to optimise income and profits. At the end of every year, valuation is to be made on investments to show the true and fair values. Depending on the accounting conventions, assets of an entity are valued at historical cost or market value. While business enterprises tend to value assets at historical cost, investment companies rely on market value. Mutual funds in India adopt the following practice for valuation of investments:

a. Investments are stated at cost or written down cost.

b. The aggregate cost of investments is compared with the aggregate market value to determine appreciation or depreciation in the value of investments for arriving at the market value of investments.

c. Quoted investments are taken at year end market rates.

d. Unquoted equity shares are taken at cost.

e. Money market obligations are taken at book value.

f. Government securities are taken at book value.

g. Quoted share warrants are taken at the year end market rates. Unquoted share warrants are taken at the year end market rates of the relative shares discounted for dividend element, if any, as reduced by the cost of acquisition payable in cases where it is higher than the market value, the value of warrants is nil.

h. Convertible debentures and bonds where composite market quotations are not available, the market value of the convertible portion is taken at the year end market rates applicable to relevant equity shares, discounted for dividend element, if any. The non-convertible debenture is taken at market down cost calculated at the current rate of yield.

## Net Asset Value (NAV)

Mutual funds most relevant disclosure for investors is NAV. It is the mirror depicting the worth of investment made per unit. It is an indicator of the capital appreciation of the funds under the scheme as on the date of the NAV. It is calculated by dividing the aggregate value of the net assets of the scheme by the number of outstanding units under the scheme.

$$NAV = \frac{(M+O) - L}{U}$$

where,

M = Market value of securities / investment made

O = other assets

L = Total liabilities

U = Number of units outstanding

SEBI (MF) Regulation, 1993 requires NAV calculation and publication at least in two daily newspapers at intervals not exceeding:

a. One month in respect of open-ended scheme; and

b. Three months in respect of close-ended schemes.

## Audit of Mutual Fund Accounts

Under Section 226 (1) of the Companies Act, 1956, every mutual fund is required to get its accounts audited by a qualified auditor in order to assure authenticity of books of accounts. Audit report shall be a part of Annual Report of the mutual fund. The auditor, as usual, gives a certificate with respect to receipt of all information and as to the fact that the Balance Sheet and Revenue Account give a true and fair view of the schemes.

## SECTION IV

### Concluding Remarks

Mutual funds in India have been following the general standards of accounting and reporting applicable to other businesses. Though the mutual funds altogether a separate category of organization, they adopt the general business accounting basis to exhibit their accounts and annual reports to its unit holders. They follow the GAAP and Accounting Standards set out by the ICAI. They prepare and present financial statements, viz, Revenue Account, Balance Sheet, Trustees' Report and Audit Report, disclosing all relevant facts.

However, accounting for mutual funds is an area where SEBI is still to go a long way to ensure systematic, quantitative and qualitative information not only for itself but for investors and public at large. Mutual funds are to make public their correspondence with companies they have invested in. Some mutual funds in India like SBI Mutual Fund, Can Bank Mutual Fund, Morgan Stanley Mutual Fund etc. are regularly sharing some of their information with their investors through periodic newsletters. But still in the field of disclosures of objectives, operations and transparency of all dealings, Indian mutual funds have a long way to go.

The observation of Dr. Dave highlights that Indian provisions stand very small in contrast to their counterpart in USA. "The SEC obligations on record keeping in USA are very interesting and relevant investment companies are called upon to maintain complete business details for a period of six years, especially journals containing an itemized daily record of all purchases or sales of securities. Equally note worthy is the SEC insistence that every investment advisor, depositor and principal underwriter for a registered investment company must maintain all appropriate documents covering his transactions with an investment company. We in India are quite far from such onerous but well intentioned statutory obligations. And yet, a true globalization to be preceded by a realization by the entire mutual fund industry infact, the entire securities industry, that truthful disclosures, fair conduct and transparency in dealings are basic responsibilities of the entire financial service sector and basic rights of investors."

Absence of accounting norms has made the accounting information of different funds incomparable. Different valuation methods, treatment of income and expenses, depreciation etc. can change completely the story of a mutual fund accounting performance. However, on these issues SEBI constituted a broad based Committee in May 1994, to examine accounting standards and policies for mutual funds. The Committee consists of Pratip Kar, the Executive Director of SEBI, B.G. Daga, General Manager of UTI, Dr. L.C. Gupta, Chief of the Society for Capital Market Research and Development, Y.H. Malegam, Senior Partner of Billimoria and Co., well known Chartered Accountants, P.G. Kakodkar, Managing Direcor of SBI Mutual Fund and Sudhir Virendra, Managing Director of Taurus Mutual Fund. However, the move has been prompted by the need to bring about standardization in accounting practices in the industry thereby increasing credibility and comparability of accounting information.

## BIBLIOGRAPHY

Bansal, K.L. and Agarwal, J.D., (1996), *Mutual Funds-Management and Working*, Deep and Deep Publications, New Delhi.

Rao, P.M, (1997), *Current Issues in Accounting Standards*, Kanishka Publishers, New Delhi.

Rao, P.M., (1999), *Corporate Social Accounting and Reporting*, Deep & Deep Publications, New Delhi.

Sankaran. S., (2008), *Indian Mutual Funds Handbook*, Vision Books, New Delhi.

Singh, H.K. and Singh. M, (2001), *Mutual Funds and Indian Capital Market*, Kanishka Publishers, New Delhi.

Singh. D (2003), *Mutual Funds in India*, Rajat Publications, New Delhi.

Tripathy N.P., (2007), *Mutual Funds in India - Emerging Issues*, Excel Books, New Delhi.

Websites of UTI, SEBI and various Mutual Funds.

# 5

# Financial Reporting Through Extensible Business Reporting Language (XBRL) - A New Paradigm

**Sujit Sikidar & Suparna Ghosh**

**Abstract**: The present paper makes an attempt to explore the meaning and nature of XBRL. It emphasizes on examining the mechanism of use of XBRL and the requirements for application of XBRL for financial reporting. It highlights the areas of application of XBRL in accounting and financial information.

## Introduction

The corporate entity uses accounting as language of business. The language is used for communication between the company *vis-à-vis* the outside world. The mandate of communication of a corporate entity for disclosing its financial information and sharing the same with the various interested user groups of the said information has been stipulated both as a statutory requirement as well as other professional stipulations. It is equally true more in respect of the listed entities, because a wide range of investors and other stakeholders look at this information for their investment decisions as well as for other managerial decisions.

When investment decisions are made basing on the financial information reported through corporate reporting mechanism it entails pecuniary interest on the part of user of information.

This gives rise to the responsibility of the management to ensure that the information so shared in the corporate reports is having a bearing on their responsibility. It manifests management responsibility towards the third party in respect of information sharing with pecuniary implication addressed to a wide spectrum of stakeholders.

The need for sharing of information by the management of the corporate entities specially for those listed in any stock exchange anywhere in the world is not confined to the supplier of information The demand for true and fair information is increasing day by day The shareholders and other stakeholders, therefore, appoint an auditor to safeguard their interest so far as it relates to information. The onus of certifying and attesting the information through the mechanism of audit and assurance has been cast on the auditors. As a result, the agency theory propounded by Watt and Zimmerman comes to play a role in information sharing. Obviously attempts have been made at different times to improve the quality of information in order to make it understandable, meaningful, usable, uniform, reliable, free from personal bias, fairly representative of factual and authenticate information of a listed corporate entity.

The traditional concepts of historical cost, going concern value, constant dollar accounting, and accrual system have paved the way for fair value accounting, mark to market value, negotiated value coming into force at the beginning of first decade of 21$^{st}$ century.

As a process of improvising paper based manually handled information, attempts have been made to transform them into online IT supported information system. This system is popularly known as extensible business reporting language (XBRL). Medium of communicating the corporate information has been shifted with sophisticated quickly disseminable information software such as XBRL. The basic instinct of accounting as language of reporting the state of affairs of a business entity remains valid. Rapidity of the flow of information form one network to another network has been enhanced through XBRL. Having considered the aforesaid issues the present researchers have ventured into a task of penning down their research findings embodied in the present form of the article.

## Objectives

The present article has been prepared with the following objectives-

1. To explore the nature and meaning of XBRL
2. To analyze the mechanism of the use of XBRL and its requirements for application of business reporting.
3. To focus on the application of XBRL in financial reporting.

## Methodology

The present work is a descriptive type of research based on contemporary work in financial information system. The work is based on secondary data collected form published books, research articles published in professional journals and other websites.

## Meaning of XBRL

Extensible business reporting language (XBRL) is an accounting and financial linkage for the use in the internet.

It is a structured but adaptable computer language developed to solve a problem. XBRL shows several relationships such as associating the cash position and cash flow of an entity in related financial statements. Its task is associating numbers with variables and matching a name to a picture. However, in using language in an internet there is a constraint. For e.g.: In pre XBRL computer language, such as hyper text mark up language (HTML), such information cannot be processed directly by the recipients' application software. HTML is a unit but it cannot process the other relevant information. Hence, the reported data must be rekeyed in form acceptable to given customized software. XBRL is an intelligent internet language that can be used in business entities by both the parties namely provider of information and user of information from the financial statements. XBRL bridges the communication gap between the preparers and the user of financial statements on the internet. In fact XBRL is based on the extensible mark up language (XML), by which both the contents and relationships can be easily established between the users and preparers of financial information.

XBRL has become the standard way of recording, storing and transmitting business, financial information from the computer information providers to the information users. It is capable of use throughout the world wherever XBRL is available for a wide variety of business purposes. It will act as a cost saving device, enhances efficiency in information storing, processing and retrieving in business and government related organizations.

XBRL runs open discussion groups where non-members can ask for specific help. Members willing to use XBRL can gain support from a range of internal groups software tools which are meant for specific tasks and are listed on the tools page on the website of XBRL. XBRL has discussion groups in which members of the public can participate.

XBRL international, a non-profit organization which is engaged in developing XBRL stated that it is a language for the electronic communication of business and financial data which is revolutionizing business reporting around the world. It provides major benefits in the preparation, analyses and communication of business information. It offers cost efficient improved accuracy and quicker dissemination of business information through software. XBRL is not only confined to intra-organization communication line but engulfs in the information needs of all the third parties and other stakeholders (Shashi Kanta Choubey, XBRL, The Management Accountant, October, 2010, page-812).

## Nature of XBRL

XBRL is an open standard free of license fees. Instead of treating financial information as a block of text as in a standard internet page for a printed document, XBRL provides an identifying tag for each individual item of data. This is computer readable. A company's net profit, net worth, current asset, current liability as its unique tag. (www.xbrt.org). A computer can treat XBRL data intelligently, it can store, retrieve, process, analyze, select and exchange it with other commuters connected between provider of information and its user.

It possesses the same qualities of an information technology related information such as quicker handling of information, reducing the changes of errors, permitting automatic checking of information and quicker use for managerial purpose. XBRL is powerful and flexible version of extended mark up language (XML). Mark- up language contains not only the codes that enable computers to interpret data but also descriptive information to help humans to understand the function of each element in a document. Mark up languages have indicators called tags. XML based languages create either documents or files used by variety of organizations, developers, industries (Ellen Perlman, Eileen Mullin, *Programming the web using XML*, Tata Mcgraw Hill Publishing Company Ltd. New Delhi, 2004).

## Mechanism of use of XBRL

XBRL solves the problem by tagging individual items of data in a way that another computer can understand and work with it. Tagging is a metaphorical term for assigning coded identifiers to data. We have realized that a fully tagged datum would be described in an efficient way which is capable of retaining its identity and can be read correctly by a user's application software. As we have mentioned here that for using XBRL in easy-to-use format there is an intervention of XML. XML is a general purpose mark-up (tagging) standard for creating languages to standardize the data exchange between different computing platforms and applications. (Hilmielifoglu, Joel Siegel, 2004). XML can be used to define new document formats by combining and reusing other formats in order to exchange information in an environment that do not share common platforms. As a pre-condition to the use of XML it is necessary to add structure and context to unstructured information which can be transmitted to the other computers of other users.

The most fundamental steps involved in XBRL are tagging data and applying a style sheet to the tagged data with a view to convert XBRL files into a document; that document is ultimately readable and appears to be paper report like a printed financial statement. From our research investigation from the www.kpmg.com dated 17$^{th}$ August. 2010 it is revealed that tagged process is governed by the XBRL, specifications. It also explains how to create taxonomics and instant documents. Taxonomics are tagging dictionaries and instant documents are the files sent by a reporting entity to a recipient to deliver XBRL data. The working mechanism of XBRL has been demonstrated in the diagram (Fig. 5.1)

## Requirements for application of XBRL for business reporting

XBRL is an open standard maintained by a not for profit organization called XBRL International created in 1999 with funding from American Institute of Certified Public Accountants (AICPA), USA with more than 450 companies supporting the use of XBRL language.

However, a few selected important parameters are relevant for designing XBRL and formatting it as business language, Financial information and accounting data are formatted in XBRL language in respect of generally accepted accounting principles (GAAP). They can use XBRL language free of charge. XBRL ensures access to financial information and furnishes more accurate and reliable extraction of information. It is for this reason Securities Exchange Commission of the USA choose the term interacting data to refer to XBRL reports.

- US banking regulators have required quarterly call reports to be filled in XBRL since October, 2005.
- The Securities Exchange Commission of USA introduced a financial reporting programme in XBRL format and in September, 2006 it announced efforts to prepare electronically reporting system to receive XBRL filings.
- The standard setter for audits of Securities Exchange Commission registrants the public company oversight board (PCOB) has issued guidelines for complying with XBRL language.
- China, Spain, the Netherlands and the UK have mandated their companies to use XBRL.
- The Tokyo Stock Exchange has accepted XBRL information since early 2003: the Canadian Stock

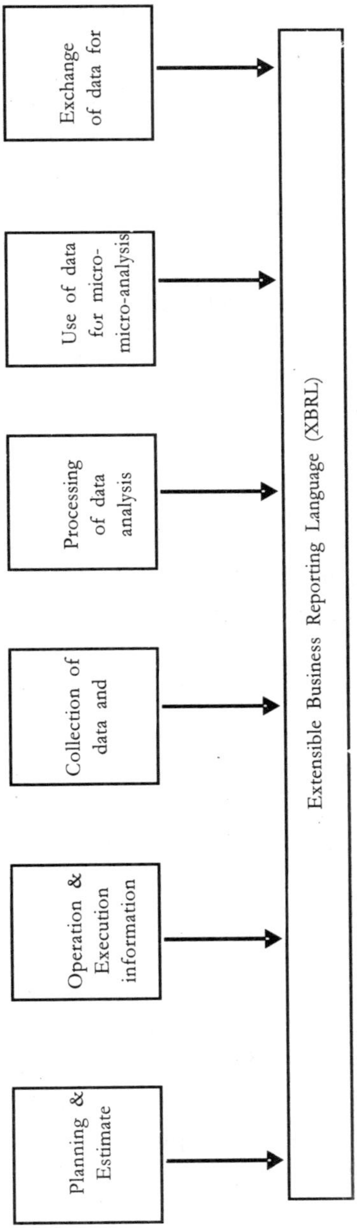


**Reference**: Shashi Kanta Choubey, XBRL, The Management Accountant, October, 2010.

**Fig. 5.1. The Working Mechanism of XBRL**

Exchange Commission has accepted XBRL data since May, 2007.

XBRL tags financial information with a precise contextual description. It is used for reporting of data as per generally accepted accounting principles. Investors can have access to XBRL information from the web page for their informed investment decision purposes.

## Use of XBRL information in financial reporting

With reference to our objective No. 3 stated above we now proceed to discuss about the use of XBRL in financial reporting as indicated below

### Tax advice:

The information relating to provisions of income tax, service tax, GST and VAT can be stored in XBRL software. It can accommodate the aforesaid information for a large number of clients which can be used for filing the electronic return to various tax authorities, government regulating agencies.

### Auditing Services:

The audit and assurance services can be efficiently discharged by the use of XBRL software. The financial information extracted from the books of clients can be stored in XBRL software. The auditor in course of his attestation function can access the clients information.

### Use for International Clients:

While discharging the consultancy job for international client in respect of global takeover and merger, valuation of properties in case of merger, ascertainment of profit at the pre-acquisition and post-acquisition stage, sharing of the profit among the two corporate entities, determination of swap equity ratios for exchange among the two companies in merger and acquisition can be done by assigning a unique tag within the XBRL.

## Providing benefits to third parties:

Statements can be mapped into XBRL using XBRL software tools designed for the purpose. Data from accounting databases can be extracted in XBRL format. It is not necessary for all information providers to use XBRL even the third party products can achieve the transformation.

XBRL is wider than mere MIS because it derives the use of not only the internal agencies but also the external users. IASB has taken an initiative for imparting training to professional accountants and is also trying through XBRL to integrate it with IFRS. XBRL is useful for preparation of financial statements, internal reports, external report and electronic filing of information for the purpose of rendering add on service to the clients spread across the globe Most of the accounting professional bodies around the world have acquired the membership of XBRL and they are trying to utilize XBRL for preparation of financial statements, internal reports, external reports, export-import reports and other international business needed for business information. The professional accounting bodies aim to provide quality financial information to the investing public. The chartered accountant professional members can position themselves to the development of XBRL and can render value added services and provide valued knowledge for their clients. Once the professional chartered accountants get exposure to XBRL they can guide their client organizations to enter into a new digital world, solve business issues and capitalize on opportunities.

The International Accounting Standard Board is currently developing a taxonomy which reflects international financial reporting standards (IFRS). National XBRL jurisdictions will extend this taxonomy to reflect their particular local implementation of IFRS. Taxonomics will thus be available to enable those reporting under IFRS in different countries to use XBRL enhancing efficiency and comparability, as adoption of IFRS expands around the world.

## Findings and Conclusion

The securities market regulator has imposed a condition called auditors' certificate on compliance of conditions of corporate governance. Our research findings try to bring into focus the crafty language used by the auditor in certifying the compliance of corporate governance in respect of a company under our study:

The auditor has examined the compliance of conditions of corporate governance by the concerned company for the year ended 31st March, 2010, as stipulated in clause 49 of the listing agreement of the said company with stock exchanges.

The compliance of conditions of corporate governance is the responsibility of the management. Auditor's examination was limited to procedures and implementation thereof, adopted by the company for ensuring the compliance of the conditions of corporate governance.

It is neither an audit nor an expression of opinion on the financial statements of the company. It further stated " in our opinion and to the best of our information and according to the explanations given to us and the representations made by the directors and the management certify that the company has complied with the conditions of corporate governance as stipulated in clause 49 of the above mentioned listing agreement. We further state that such compliance is neither an assurance as to the future viability of the company nor the efficiency for effectiveness with which the management has conducted the affairs of the company".

We, therefore, conclude that disclosure of authentic information is an area of benchmark between management and auditor vis-à-vis the outside third parties. Every agency involving reporting does not like to venture into crossing the territorial benchmark of their professional commitment. The third parties have to apply their rational judgment to use that information. We feel the XBRL would bridge the users' information expectation gap and make it publicly available to the various interested user groups and other stakeholders. We know that information is power and pecuniary benefits can be derived out of information. XBRL poses a question as to how far we open to transparency. (www.xbrl.org;www.iasb.org).

## REFERENCES


Hilmielifoglu, Joel Siegel, Extensible Business Reporting Language (XBRL). The Management Accountant, Institute of Cost and Works Accountant (Kolkata). No.8, August, 2004, pp: 670 & 671.

Ellen Perlman, Eileen Mullin, Programming the web using XML, Tata Mcgraw Hill Publishing Company Ltd., New Delhi, 2004, Page no. 2

Shashi Kanta Choubey, XBRL, The Management Accountant, October, 2010, page 812.

www.xbrt.org

www.onesource.com

www.kpmg.com

www.xbrl.org

www. iasb.org

# 6

# How Indian Managers Perceive Corporate Social Responsibility and Reporting? - A Survey

**N. Panda & A.N. Shankar**

**Abstract:** Drawing on propositions from social identity theory and signalling theory, it is observed that firms' corporate social performance (CSP) is associated with managers' intensity of involvement in CSP. Legitimisation of corporate social responsibility (CSR) has posed challenges to both working managers and trainees. Businesses have to adopt practices that ensure ethical, legal, commercial and public expectations. CSR must be inter woven in the routine business, by engaging all stakeholders, strategies to support individual managers to make socially responsible decisions conforming ethical behaviour and law. Management training institutions, academicians and corporate bodies are concerned about the changing scenario of contemporary business strategies; it is their role to sensitise trainees regarding CSR. An increasing concern over three decades about CSR has brought about the present study with an objective to investigate into how the Indian managers perceive CSR with regard to its objective, function, accountability, transactional Implications, and outcomes.

**Keywords**: Corporate Social Responsibility, Transactional Implications, Managers' Perception, Corporate Social Performance

Managers are moral actors. Within every domain of CSR, they are obliged to exercise such discretion as is available to them, towards socially responsible outcomes. In Carroll's (1979) CSR classification, a firm's discretionary responsibilities are those areas of voluntary social involvement not specifically prohibited to or demanded of companies because of their economic, legal, and ethical responsibilities. Further research work (Aupperle, Carroll, and Hatfield, 1985) has emphasized that discretionary responsibilities are the least weighted of all a firm's social responsibilities. The domain of discretionary responsibility typically has been operationalised as corporate philanthropy, or occasionally as corporate involvement in public-private partnerships or collaborative social problem-solving ventures. Clearly, as reflected in the low conceptual weight given to it in Carroll's (1979) scheme, discretionary responsibilities defined in this manner are subject to a "last in, first out" LIFO method of placement on a firm's action inventory. To date, the business and society field has not built a concept of discretion, or discretionary social responsibility that is related to the standard concept of managerial discretion. However, the focus since the mid-1980s on business ethics, decision making, value conflicts, and so on, clearly points to the need that a principle of socially responsible human action should be articulated. A company's social responsibilities are not met by some abstract organisational actor; they are met by individual human actors who constantly make decisions and choices (Wood, 1990). Ackerman (1975: 32-33) wrote about corporate social responsibility as 'the management of discretion', referring not to philanthropy or community involvement programs, but to the discretion extent in the total realm of managerial actions and choices. Thus, the principle of managerial discretion is premised on the following ideas:

(a) managers exist in an organisational and societal environment that is full of choices;

(b) managers' actions are not totally derived out of corporate procedures, formal job definitions, resource availabilities, or technologies; and

(c) managers are moral actors on the job as well as in other domains of their lives.

Despite the existence of certain corporate social responsibilities prescribed in various domains, managers have choices about how to fulfill many of these responsibilities. Further, the principle implies that because managers possess discretion, they are personally responsible for exercising it and cannot avoid this responsibility through reference to rules, policies, or procedures (see Berthoin Antal, 1985). In this context it is imperative to explore the conceptual understanding, attitude and behaviour of the individual managers in India toward corporate social responsibility.

In management literature, there has been growing interest in investigating the perceptions of top management toward CSR and the actions they take regarding social issues. The personal values of senior managers have a pervasive bearing throughout the strategic management process. Environmental forces (threats and opportunities), the firm's resources and capabilities (strengths and weaknesses), strategy evaluation and choice, as well as the implementation steps are screened and affected by management's values, (Sturdivant, Ginter and Sawyer, 1985). In fact Peters and Waterman (1982) base their bestselling book, '*In Search of Excellence*', on the so called McKinsey 7-

S Framework which is centred around 'shared values'. Steiner (1969) argues that:

> '. . . *The values of top managers are reflected in the network of aims of an enterprise. Whether written or not, these values have the profoundest impact on the direction in which a firm moves and the way it operates. . . .*'

Andrews (1980) reaches at a conclusion:

> '*We must acknowledge . . . that there is no way to divorce the decision determining the most sensible economic strategy for a company from the personal values of those who make the choice.*'

Thinkers advocate that CSR is "technology with a human face", and that the study of economics should be based on the assumption that ultimately it is the people who matter in the process of economic development. Along with the top managers the floor and middle level managers are also to discharge their social responsibility which in turn be reflected in the overall social behaviour of a firm.

Since the previous studies ignore these managers, a need arises to repeat similar studies to explore the perception of the managers that include the managers at all level of the organisation. Since the variables of such study are conditioned by the socio-organisational context a manager bears with, while operative, it is desirable to incorporate in this section the empirical researches on managerial notion on social responsibility undertaken earlier in different countries.

## Reviewed Literature on Managerial Notion about CSR

Krishnan (1973) conducting a survey of the managers from American companies points out that majority of the executives still believe in the profit maximization philosophy and the absoluteness of the prerogatives of management in operating the business organisation as they perceive it. The main trend noted from the study is that, although executives in general do not see evidence of changes in the attitude of managers in organisations towards exercising responsibility to groups other than stockholders, more executives as individuals believe that business should become more responsible to these other groups.

Buehler, and Shetty (1976) have conducted a survey(232 companies out of 1, 250 firms on Fortune's list of the largest U. S. industrial and nonindustrial firms)and found that the managers do perceive the CSR as important and a majority of them opine that urban development activities are to be prioritised followed by the environmental affairs and the consumers. Buehler and Shetty indicate "that many firms are apparently not prepared to make well-planned and integrated responses to the corporate social responsibility challenge" (1976, p. 77). At least three motives were cited in order to design corporate social policies:

(a) top management wanted to assure a strong commitment to provide a favorable climate for company activities;

(b) a positive and consistent response to social responsibility issues was desired throughout the company; and

(c) a need was perceived to do something visible to external and internal participants such as minority communities, consumer advocates, environmentalists, employees and others. Further analysis supports the notion that as a company grows in size, a greater degree of concern and commitment is expressed through a restructuring of the organisation to facilitate systematic responses to social issues. Their study supports a contingency perspective to social responsibility, namely, that a firm responds to perceived social demands based on the particular relevance of an issue and on a firm's resources and skills.

During the past two decades there has been a growing interest in CSR which suggests that increasing number of managers accept the relevance of CSR (Khan and Alkinson (1987). This study reveals that managers in USA are more conversant and thorough with broader objectives of CSR as compared to that of Britain and India.

Maclagan views CSR as a process in which managers take responsibility for identifying and accommodating the interests of those affected by the organisation's actions (Maclagan, 1998: 147). He supports Carroll's stakeholder view of CSR, arguing that all stakeholders are claimants on the moral direction of the company (Maclagan, 1999). According to sources cited in Carroll: (Johnson, 1971 in Carroll 1999: 273) "A socially responsible firm is one whose managerial staff balances a multiplicity of interests. Instead of striving only for larger profits for its stockholders, a responsible enterprise also takes into account employees, suppliers, dealers, local communities and the nation". This view signifies that it is manager who shall be finally sensitized regarding the value of CSR spectrum to business.

Tachizawa (2002) suggests that inculcation of values and its projection in managerial activities is all possible when the present executives are prepared for the challenge of harmonising several social concerns. Harmonisation of multiple stakeholders through innovative strategies of business will be rewarded, due to capable leadership influencing the ecology of the company. What does the new positioning of the society demands like; these managers shall know how to reconcile the economic objectives of the organisations with the social demands set forth? European Commission (2002) posits that managers have a crucial role to play in harmonising the social goals with that of the economic objectives with adequate justification using the words "Faced with a widening range of complex issues in areas such as labour practices and supplier relations, with implications across their organisations, businesses, regardless of sector, size, structure or maturity, would benefit from the inclusion of social and environmental issues into their daily operations. In this context, CSR management systems like-Total Quality Management Systems could allow enterprises to have a clear picture of their social and environmental impacts, help them to target the significant ones and manage them well". This leads to the survey into the Indian managers' attitudes towards the CSR whether they are equipped with the mindset to tackle the upcoming issues in near future.

As observed by Doane (2004) corporate leaders, of course, have an enabling role to play beyond what they seem prepared to currently accept. One of the primary barriers to government action is the fact that the business community is silent on matters of social and environmental regulation, even if it might further their long-term aims. APEC report (2005) mentions significant role of managers in shaping the corporations to meet the contemporary broader stakeholders' demand.

The Indian CSR is still in a confused state (Arora and Puranik 2004, 98).The findings of the survey by GDI (German Development Institute 2006) reveal a shift from a purely philanthropic approach (e.g. selective donations)to a more comprehensive CSR approach. This shift is apparent primarily in the perceptions of CSR, the professionalism of community development and the integration and organisation of CSR within a company. Irrespective of these aspects, the empirical results lead to the conclusion that CSR still has a philanthropic connotation because of its emphasis on external stakeholders, particularly communities. Where Indian companies' perceptions of CSR are concerned, the findings of the study paint an ambiguous and even contradictory picture. On the one hand, companies point out that CSR is now no longer philanthropic but an important aspect of a sustainable business strategy. On the other hand, they continue to feel a strong responsibility to "give something back to society". When expressing this responsibility, companies in India are thinking not of such internal stakeholders as employees but of surrounding communities. Accordingly, CSR can still be described as being in a "confused state". When Indian companies are asked what their understanding of CSR is, only a minority regard their own commitment as purely philanthropic. Interestingly, all the PSUs interviewed saw their CSR as philanthropic. About one third of Indian companies detect a recent change in their understanding of CSR, stating that "giving something back to society" is now no longer merely philanthropic. Half of the Indian companies and all of the foreign companies included in the survey consider CSR to be part of "sustainable business". Despite the Indian companies' assertion that CSR is seen as part of sustainable business rather than as philanthropy, the imbalance between internal and external CSR dimensions is huge. The vast majority of Indian companies include only the external dimension in their understanding of CSR. In contrast, less than 20 per cent of the Indian companies surveyed referred to such internal aspects as working conditions and environmental practices.

While ascertaining the attitude of Indian business towards its social responsibilities in the past has been hampered by the lack of systematic studies, two recent surveys provide insights into contemporary management views on corporate responsibility. Krishna (1992) undertook a survey of 539 top and middle level managers in private and public sector firms to examine their attitudes towards corporate social responsibility. It was observed that 87 per cent of the respondents believed that social concern was necessary for managers. Their reasons for acknowledging the importance of social concerns, which were predominantly pragmatic in nature, included the need to offset the negative image of business and the need to respond to the increased public demand for socially responsible behaviour (which, interestingly enough, they attributed in large part to the example of socially responsible behaviour demonstrated by several major business houses). The preferred response of the sample included projects which were perceived as easier to implement (for instance, consumer education) and related more directly to their economic activity (such as employment creation). They were much less inclined to take up rural development projects. In response to questions about obstacles firms face in assuming their social responsibilities, the major inhibiting factors were perceived to be poor profit performance, an ad-hoc approach to the issue by top management, a lack of consensus on priorities, problems of measurement and evaluation, and a lack of motivation and encouragement to executives. Subsequently, Partners in Change (PiC 1997) commissioned a survey of 647 firms (with follow-up interviews of the CEOs of a sample of the participating firms) on corporate involvement in social development. While many respondents acknowledged the example of major business houses such as the Tatas, it was generally felt that the concept of corporate social responsibility was a recent phenomenon, not previously given much attention in corporate circles in India. As in the survey by Krishna, the vast majority of respondents recognized the importance of firms accepting their social responsibilities, though there were some exceptions to this general trend. Among those few who dissented, the opinion was that fulfilling one's corporate social responsibilities only entailed conducting business honestly. Among the majority who accepted a broader understanding of corporate social responsibility, various conditions and limitations were held to exist with respect to these responsibilities. In terms of conditions, two caveats were commonly added. First, it was believed that such responsibilities were conditional upon the financial health of the firm (and its obligations to pay dividends to shareholders). Second, there was a general opinion that if firms were not likely to receive any benefits from social programmes, they should not undertake them.

With respect to the limitations placed upon corporate social responsibilities, there were varied opinions as to who should be the beneficiaries of such social programmes, both geographically (employees and their families, local communities, surrounding villages, the entire nation) and in terms of specific needs (women and children, Backward and Scheduled Castes, the ageing, the sick, etc.). While some corporations had an extremely narrow view (in which responsibilities extended only to employees and their families), most acknowledged wider social responsibilities (including many which could be categorized as having a development impact). Generally, however, most firms seemed to have a hierarchy of priorities which favoured first employees and their families and only then extended to the local community and (possibly) beyond. The question of other beneficiaries correlated closely in most instances with the nature of the corporation's activities and its geographic location.

With regard to the practice of social responsibility, there has been an increasing awareness on the part of corporations in recent years with respect to issues of corporate social responsibility. The PiC study offers some account of how this increased awareness translates into actual programmes. Of the 647 corporations that responded to the PiC study, 295 (46 per cent) reported that they had undertaken some form of social development work. The contributions of this latter number were registered in terms of the area in which they were involved, the beneficiaries of their contributions and the forms of their contribution. Of the 295 corporations, 50.5 per cent had made contributions in the area of health (family planning, AID[illegible] awareness, preventable disease prevention, malnutrition, [illegible] sanitation), 44.4 per cent in education (primary educ[illegible] literacy, vocational training), 14.2 per cent in n[illegible] management (wasteland development, conservation), 44.7 per cent in infrastructure (wells, roads, schools, clinics and hospitals, biogas plants), 19.7 per cent in the community (the elderly, drug/alcohol abuse, orphanages, shelter for the homeless), 32.9 per cent in employment promotion (arts and culture, sports), and 18.0 per cent in livelihood (farm based activities- employing disadvantaged people). In almost all areas of activity undertaken by firms, it was their employees who most frequently benefited (in anywhere from 41 to 58 per cent of the cases), the exceptions being natural resource management and livelihood projects (and even here employees were the second most represented group among the beneficiaries). Next to employees, rural people, women and children were the most frequent beneficiaries of these programmes. With respect to the type of contributions made by the corporations, 35 per cent made only monetary contributions while 27 per cent made monetary and other contributions, 12 per cent made only other contributions, and 19 per cent did not make any contribution. No information was available for the remaining 7 per cent.

The studies reviewed above not only present a conflicting and competing understanding of corporate social responsibility but also pose a diverse attitude of the corporate managers towards corporate social performance. The researchers in most of the cases have included the top managers or the CEOs that too from the top order of companies in their samples ignoring the fact that managers at middle and operational levels also matter in the exhibition of overall corporate social behaviour. In an increasingly participatory management process the policies are based on collective decision where the understanding, attitude and moral principles of all participating managers directly or indirectly regarded as contributing factors. Further, the surveys being conducted at a particular point of time provide us static result, the implications of which may not have future relevance. The trend that emerges from the chronological review of surveys in different cultural settings does not reveal the direction of managerial notion on CSR in a particular nation with unique socio-cultural values. The studies are silent with regard to variation in understanding or attitude on CSR across the socio-organisational characteristics of the individual managers. In the Indian context due to inadequate empirical studies to throw light on the above gaps, a comprehensive study on managerial perception on CSR is imperative.

To sum up it is observed that corporate social responsibility has attracted considerable attention during the past five decades. Conceptual developments have not been systematically integrated with one another, but usually have been treated as free standing, implicitly competing ideas-both at the level of concepts and theories. Thus, a vast, diverse, and interesting field of research and theory has been generated, but there is no means for assessing the relevance of all these works to some of the field's central questions. Therefore, management is hampered by the lack of a paradigm which addresses both the "what" and the "how" of social corporate activities and behaviour.

## Objective and hypothesis

The present paper is designed to explore the perception of Indian managers on corporate social reporting and analyze how the perception varies across their socio economic and company characteristics. Based on the above objective the following operational hypothesis is tested.

$H_0$. *The perception of the Indian corporate managers on corporate social responsibility and reporting does not vary across their socio-economic and corporate characteristics.*

## Methodology

Information used to study the above aspects has been collected from primary sources following a questionnaire based survey technique. The survey has been conducted with the managers at different levels participating various training programmes conducted by the most prestigious business school of India (IIMA) at its management development centre (KLMDC). The managers participating in different training programmes conducted by the institute during July-September2005 and the final year students of the PG programme of the institute then residing in various dormitories (referred as prospective or future managers) constitute the sample.

Altogether 300 questionnaires (150 for the managers at KLMDC, each consisting three parts-A, B and C as stated below and 150 for the PG students) were administered personally by the researcher. Another survey of this type administering the same questionnaire (sample constituting three batches of managers in KLMDC numbering 137 and 160 the then outgoing PGP students) had earlier been conducted exactly a decade ago i.e. in the year 1995 by another researcher. Since all the filled in questionnaires of that survey had remained unanalyzed and the present researcher could obtain them along with the relevant information regarding the design and administration, the data generated from the survey was used in this study particularly for comparison and visualizing the trend. The questionnaire designed to gather information pertaining to managerial notion and attitude consists of three parts : Part-A and B designed to capture the socio-organisational characteristics of the managers viz. name, age, educational qualification, gender, position in organizational hierarchy etc, and Part C to collect information regarding relevance of social responsibility, its outcome, and monitoring of social responsibility etc. Different types of questions have been asked in the questionnaire depending upon the purpose-in some cases the responses have been measured in nominal scale and some cases in interval scale (to reveal the order of agreement on a 7 point Likert scale with extreme anchors very large extent and very small extent. The questions appearing in Part B of the questionnaire were dropped while administering it to the perspective managers because of no organizational affiliation of the postgraduate students thus reducing the questionnaire to only two parts. Following (Table 6.1) is the break-up of responses obtained:

Responses thus obtained from the survey were statistically analysed by means of most commonly used statistical tools particularly Mean and Standard deviation. In order to determine the significance of variation in the mean scores obtained for the managers in various sub-groups according to their socio-organisational characteristics, F- test has been applied under the assumption that the population is normally distributed.

## Analysis and Discussion

In order to explore the managerial notion on the purpose, functions, accountability and transactional implications of a business enterprise a number of statements have been framed and managers' agreement on those statements has been obtained on a seven point Likert's Scale with the with extreme anchors very large extent and very small extent. The respondents under both the surveys have been asked to reveal their degree of agreement on seven statements.

At the first stage of analysis the mean scores against each statement and for each group of managers (according to their socio-organisational characteristics) have been computed along with their respective standard deviations, and subsequently a comparison has been made to disclose the mean difference between the surveys and across the groups. All the mean values along with their respective standard deviations and interpretation (according to the score range as stated in Table 6.2) are presented in Table 6.3 followed by a diagrammatic representation (Figure 6.1). Further to test the null hypothesis of no association between levels of

**Table 6.1**
**Response Rate of the Survey of Managers**

| Year of Survey | Managers | | | | Prospective Managers | | | |
|---|---|---|---|---|---|---|---|---|
| | Questionnaires Administered | Questionnaires Received | Response Rate | Questionnaires Finally Used | Questionnaires Administered | Questionnaires Received | Response Rate | Questionnaires Finally Used |
| 1995 | 137 | 62 | 45.25 | 57 | 160 | 79 | 49.37 | 71 |
| 2005 | 150 | 66 | 44 | 58 | 150 | 73 | 48.67 | 71 |

agreement for the managers in various socio- organisational characteristics, F-Test has been applied. Tables 6.4, 6.5 and 6.6 have been incorporated to present the result of the test.

To summarise the managerial attitudes towards outcomes of CSR, enhancement of goodwill is highly accepted by the Indian managers as one of the primary outcomes of CSR whereas moderate order of acceptance by them is found in favour of strengthening of social and economic system, and low order of acceptance in favour of the other possible outcomes *viz.* job satisfaction for managers and employees in general, enhancement of chance of corporate survival, attracting managerial talent, increase in long run profitability, investors' preference and customer loyalty. The magnitude of difference measured on a seven point scale between the mean scores of the two surveys being negligible for almost all the outcomes, it is observed that the interval of one decade has no material influence on the perception of Indian managers with respect to the outcomes of social responsibility performance of a firm.

**Table 6.2**
**Criteria for Interpreting the Mean Scores**

| Mean score between | Levels of Agreement |
|---|---|
| 1-2 | High Level of Disagreement(HLD) |
| 2-3 | Moderate Level of Disagreement(MLD) |
| 3-4 | Low Level of Disagreement (LLD) |
| 4-5 | Low Level of Agreement (LLA) |
| 5-6 | Moderate Level of Agreement (MLA) |
| 6-7 | High Level of Agreement (HLA) |

The managers and the prospective managers under both the surveys are found to have shown a moderate order of acceptance to the purpose of a Corporate firm as to sub-serve

**Table 6.3: Levels of Managerial Agreement on Purpose, Functions, Accountability and Transactional Implications of CSR**

| Statements | Managers Surveyed 1995 | | Managers Surveyed 2005 | | Prospective Managers 1995 | | Prospective Managers 2005 | | Overall Managers 1995 | | Overall Managers 2005 | |
|---|---|---|---|---|---|---|---|---|---|---|---|---|
| | Mean (S Dev) | Inter-pretation | Mean (S Dev) | Inter-pretation | Mean (S Dev) | Inter-pretation | Mean (S Dev) | Inter-pretation | Mean (S Dev) | Inter-pretation | Mean (S Dev) | Inter-pretation |
| Sole Function of business firm is to make profit and thus it is the most important social responsibility | 3.28 | **L L D** *(1.77)* | 4.36 | **L L A** *(1.86)* | 3.69 | **L L D** *(1.78)* | 3.85 | **L L D** *(1.89)* | 3.51 | **L L D** *(1.78)* | 4.08 | **L L A** *(1.89)* |
| Firms' purposes are significantly related to how their operations affect society and thus the firm has a purpose beyond profit making. | 5.53 *(1.54)* | **M L A** | 5.59 *(1.28)* | **M L A** | 5.56 *(1.17)* | **M L A** | 5.23 *(1.55)* | **M L A** | 5.55 *(1.34)* | **M L A** | 5.39 *(1.44)* | **M L A** |
| The company's objective of maximis ing profit should | 3.82 *(1.77)* | **L L D** | 4.14 *(1.47)* | **L L A** | 3.37 *(1.63)* | **L L D** | 3.83 *(1.66)* | **L L D** | 3.57 *(1.71)* | **L L D** | 3.97 *(1.58)* | **L L D** |

| | | | | | | | | | | | | |
|---|---|---|---|---|---|---|---|---|---|---|---|---|
| always take precedence over objective that seem to some people important for society | | | | | | | | | | | | |
| To become socially responsible a firm must give at least as much weight age to fair wages, fair prices, fair community practices , fair environmental practices as it does to fair return on investment. | 6.00 *(1.04)* | **H L A** | 5.78 *(1.09)* | **M L A** | 5.73 *(1.32)* | **M L A** | 5.70 *(1.39)* | **M L A** | 5.85 *(1.20)* | **M L A** | 5.74 *(1.26)* | **M L A** |
| In a broader sense of cost the socially conscious companies practically those who have earned reputation of being fair and acting in promoting welfare of the society do not suffer from higher unit costs for employees may accept lower wages and customers may pay higher price. | 3.51 *(1.73)* | **L L D** | 3.59 *(1.68)* | **L L D** | 3.80 *(1.54)* | **L L D** | 3.93 *(1.66)* | **L L D** | 3.67 *(1.63)* | **L L D** | 3.78 *(1.67)* | **L L D** |

*(contd.)*

| Statements | Managers Surveyed 1995 | | Managers Surveyed 2005 | | Prospective Managers 1995 | | Prospective Managers 2005 | | Overall Managers 1995 | | Overall Managers 2005 | |
|---|---|---|---|---|---|---|---|---|---|---|---|---|
| | Mean (S Dev) | Inter-pretation | Mean (S Dev) | Inter-pretation | Mean (S Dev) | Inter-pretation | Mean (S Dev) | Inter-pretation | Mean (S Dev) | Inter-pretation | Mean (S Dev) | Inter-pretation |
| Practice of efficient social reporting system can help a company to plan and monitor its social responsibilities. | 4.63 *(1.55)* | **L L A** | 5.21 *(1.10)* | **M L A** | 5.10 *(1.21)* | **M L A** | 5.31 *(1.33)* | **M L A** | 4.89 *(1.39)* | **L L A** | 5.26 *(1.23)* | **M L A** |
| There should be a three-tier social audit committee ( National level, Industry level, and individual corporate level) in India | 4.12 *(1.79)* | **L L A** | 4.48 *(1.71)* | **L L A** | 4.23 *(1.56)* | **L L A** | 4.11 *(1.81)* | **L L A** | 4.18 *(1.66)* | **L L A** | 4.28 *(1.77)* | **L L A** |

Index: Figures indicated in brackets are Standard Deviations against respective Mean , Level of Agreement (L A), or Level of Disagreement (LD), (H) for High, (L) for Low and (M) for Moderate, have been indicated by pre-fixing (H), (L) and (M) respectively.

societal welfare and to accomplish beyond profit maximisation and the degree of acceptance remain unchanged during the survey interval. They are further found to have revealed a high to moderate order of acceptance to the notion that social responsibility warrants the managers to balance the interest of the immediate stakeholders with the principle of justice.

Another finding that moves on the line with the instrumental theories propounded by Porter and Kramer (2002), Hart (1995), Litz (1996), Prahalad and Hammond (2002), Hart and Christensen (2002) and Prahalad (2002) is that the managers have a low order of resistance to accept that the cost per unit of a product is adversely affected by expenditure on social activities due to an offset effect with the associated benefits. The order of resistance remains unaltered between the managers and prospective managers and during the survey interval.

Regarding benefits of social reporting practice, both managers and prospective managers are found to have moderately endorsed the statement that social reporting practice helps planning and monitoring of social responsibility activities at the corporate level and the degree of agreement assumes an upward trend during the survey interval (mean score of later survey are greater than that of the former one). The managers have revealed a low order of acceptance to the policy of having a three tier social audit committee (national, industry and corporate level) and the degree of acceptance remains at the same level for both managers and prospective managers and also during the survey interval. It is also found that perceived managerial notion of purpose, relevance, stakeholders, functions, accountability, and transactional implications of corporate social performance is negligibly influenced by their socio-organisational characteristics. Thus, the findings of the study support the hypothesis ($H_o$) formulated under the study that *The perception of the Indian corporate managers on corporate social responsibility*

**Table 6.4: Results of Test (F) of Independence Between Working Managers' Response (1995 Survey) and their Socio-Organisational Characteristics**

| Significant Aspects of CSR | | Socio-Organisational Characteristics of Manager | | | | | | | |
|---|---|---|---|---|---|---|---|---|---|
| | | Age | Educational Qualification | Experience level | Level of Management | Department | Annual Turnover in Rs Crores | Fixed Assets in Rs Crores | No. of Employees |
| | df /df | 2, /54 | 3,/53 | 2 , /54 | 2 , /54 | 3,/53 | 2, /54 | 2, /54 | 2 , /54 |
| Sole Function of business firm is to make profit and thus it is the most important social responsibility | F<br>Sig | 1.947<br>*(0.153)* | 1.399<br>*(0.253)* | 2.127<br>*(0.129)* | 1.854<br>*(0.166)* | 0.471<br>*(0.704)* | 1.360<br>*(0.265)* | 0.167<br>*(0.847)* | 2.565<br>*(0.086)* |
| Firms' purposes are significantly related to how their operations affect society and thus the firm has a purpose beyond profit making | F<br>Sig | 0.747<br>*(0.479)* | 1.757<br>*(0.167)* | 0.180<br>*(0.836)* | 0.057<br>*(0.945)* | 0.417<br>*(0.742)* | 0.016<br>*(0.984)* | 0.926<br>*(0.402)* | 0.444<br>*(0.644)* |

| | | | | | | | | | |
|---|---|---|---|---|---|---|---|---|---|
| The company's objective of maximising profit should always take precedence over objective that seem to some people important for society | F<br>Sig | 0.341<br>*(0.713)* | 1.019<br>*(0.392)* | 0.666<br>*(0.518)* | 0.587<br>*(0.559)* | 0.117<br>*(0.950)* | 0.240<br>*(0.787)* | 0.036<br>*(0.965)* | 0.054<br>*(0.947)* |
| To become socially responsible a firm must give at least as much weight age to fair wages, fair prices, fair community practices, fair environmental practices as it does to fair return on investment. | F<br>Sig | 0.355<br>*(0.703)* | 1.508<br>*(0.223)* | 0.055<br>*(0.946)* | 0.446<br>*(0.642)* | 0.844<br>*(0.476)* | 0.641<br>*(0.531)* | 0.641<br>*(0.531)* | 0.635<br>*(0.534)* |
| In a broader sense of cost the socially conscious companies practically those who have earned reputation of being fair and acting | F<br>Sig | 1.423<br>*(0.250)* | 0.803<br>*(0.498)* | 0.474<br>*(0.625)* | 0.612<br>*(0.546)* | 3.734 *<br>*(0.017)* | 1.551<br>*(0.221)* | 3.348 *<br>*(0.043)* | 0.188<br>*(0.829)* |

(*contd.*)

| Significant Aspects of CSR | | Socio-Organisational Characteristics of Manager | | | | | | | |
|---|---|---|---|---|---|---|---|---|---|
| | | Age | Educational Qualification | Experience level | Level of Management | Department | Annual Turnover in Rs Crores | Fixed Assets in Rs Crores | No. of Employees |
| in promoting welfare of the society do not suffer from higher unit costs for employees may accept lower wages and customers may pay higher price. | | | | | | | | | |
| Practice of efficient social reporting system can help a company to plan and monitor its social responsibilities. | F<br>Sig | 0.466<br>*(0.630)* | 0.994<br>*(0.403)* | 0.758<br>*(0.474)* | 0.066<br>*(0.936)* | 1.694<br>*(0.179)* | 0.422<br>*(0.658)* | 1.985<br>*(0.147)* | 0.639<br>*(0.532)* |
| There should be a three- tier social audit committee ( National level, Industry level, and individual corporate level) in India | F<br>Sig | 0.986<br>*(C.380)* | 0.746<br>*(0.530)* | 1.716<br>*(0.190)* | 1.654<br>*(0.201)* | 0.375<br>*(0.771)* | 0.555<br>*(0.578)* | 0.521<br>*(0.597)* | 0.646<br>*(0.528)* |

Figures appearing in Brackets show the level of significance. df : degrees of Freedom. *Significant at 0.05 level of significance.

*and reporting does not vary across their socio-economic and corporate characteristics.*

This is in tune with theoretical synthesis of Duane Windsor (2006), who observed that an instrumental citizenship interpretation expands philanthropy as a strategic lever for increasing corporate reputation and market opportunities while retaining managerial discretion. An ideal citizenship interpretation restates ethical responsibility into voluntarism language intended to influence managerial discretion concerning universal human rights.

The mean scores computed to reveal the notion of the managers regarding objectives, functions, accountability and transactional implications of social performance not only vary across the statements in both the surveys but also between the surveys and the types of managers. But while capturing the magnitude of difference and making a relative comparison, the following observations are made:

1. Corporate firms' purpose is to sub- serve societal welfare and is beyond profit maximisation, is moderately acceptable to the managers and the prospective managers under both the surveys and the degree of agreement remains unchanged during the survey interval. This managerial notion gets reaffirmed when a low order of disagreement is observed against the first and third statement Table 6.7 framed in consonance with the traditional philosophy of the business as economic entity to make profit.
2. Managers have revealed a high to moderate order of acceptance to the notion that social responsibility warrants the managers to balance the interest of the immediate stakeholders with the principle of justice.
3. The managers have a low order of resistance to accept that the cost per unit of a product is adversely affected

by expenditure on social activities due to an offset effect with the associated benefits. The order of resistance remains unaltered between the managers and prospective managers and also during the survey interval.

4. Both managers and prospective managers endorse moderately that social reporting practice helps planning and monitoring of social responsibility activities and the degree of agreement assumes an upward movement during the survey interval ( mean score of later survey are greater than that of the former one).

5. The managers have revealed a low order of acceptance to the policy of having a three tier social audit committee ( national, industry and corporate level) and the degree of acceptance remains at the same level for both managers and prospective managers and also during the survey interval.

On performing F-Test it has been found that managers' socio- organisational characteristics have negligible influence on their degree of agreement or disagreement on the statements revealing purpose, functions, accountability, and transactional implications of social performance. Thus, managers irrespective of their socio-organisational characteristics conceive social responsibility under contemporary philosophy of business and are willing to be socially accountable through a social reporting system.

## Findings and Conclusion

Majority (94%) of the managers perceive corporate social responsibility as relevant to the present society and the response rate is observed to be higher in case of the young professional managers employed in relatively smaller companies. The favourable response changes negligibly from 93.75% to 93.80%

during the survey interval of ten years. Though, the response rate among the working managers have increased from 91.23% to 96.55%, combined response rate has remained almost static due to a decline registered in the response rate of the prospective managers by 4.23%.

The managers and the prospective managers under both the surveys are found to have shown a moderate order of acceptance to the purpose of a Corporate firm as to sub-serve societal welfare and to accomplish beyond profit maximisation and the degree of acceptance remains unchanged during the survey interval. They are further found to have revealed a high to moderate order of acceptance to the notion that social responsibility warrants the managers to balance the interest of the immediate stakeholders with the principle of justice. Another finding that moves on the line with the instrumental theories propounded by Porter and Kramer (2002), Hart (1995), Lizt (1996), Prahalad and Hammond (2002), Hart and Christensen (2002) and Prahalad (2002) is that the managers have a low order of resistance to accept that the cost per unit of a product is adversely affected by expenditure on social activities due to an offset effect with the associated benefits. The order of resistance remains unaltered between the managers and prospective managers and also during the survey interval.

Regarding benefits of social reporting practice, both managers and prospective managers are found to have moderately endorsed the statement that social reporting practice helps planning and monitoring of social responsibility activities at the corporate level and the degree of agreement assumes an upward trend during the survey interval (mean score of later survey are greater than that of the former one). The managers have revealed a low order of acceptance to the policy of having a three tier social audit committee (national, industry and corporate level) and the degree of acceptance remains at the

**Table 6.5 : Results of Test (F) of Independence between Working Managers' Response (2005 survey) and their Socio- Organisational Characteristics**

| Significant Aspects of CSR | | Socio-Organisational Characteristics of Manager | | | | | | | |
|---|---|---|---|---|---|---|---|---|---|
| | | Age | Educational Qualification | Experience level | Level of Management | Department | Annual Turnover in Rs Crores | Fixed Assets in Rs Crores | No. of Employees |
| | df/df | 2 /55 | 3 /54 | 2 /55 | 2 /55 | 2 /55 | 2 /55 | 2 /55 | 2 /55 |
| Sole Function of business firm is to make profit and thus it is the most important social responsibility | F | 2.050 | 0.210 | 0.839 | 0.274 | 0.223 | 2.633 | 2.378 | 0.756 |
| | Sig | (0.138) | (0.889) | (0.438) | (0.761) | (0.801) | (0.081) | (0.102) | (0.474) |
| Firms' purposes are significantly related to how their operations affect society and thus the firm has a purpose beyond profit making | F | 1.217 | 2.286 | 0.783 | 1.690 | 1.714 | 2.535 | 1.581 | 1.465 |
| | Sig | (0.304) | (0.089) | (0.462) | (0.194) | (0.190) | (0.088) | (0.215) | (0.240) |
| The company's objective of | F | 0.211 | 0.581 | 1.985 | 4.249* | 0.442 | 0.121 | 0.132 | 0.795 |
| | Sig | (0.810) | (0.630) | (0.147) | (0.019) | (0.645) | (0.886) | (0.877) | (0.457) |

| | | | | | | | | | |
|---|---|---|---|---|---|---|---|---|---|
| maximising profit should always take precedence over objective that seem to some people important for society | | | | | | | | | |
| To become socially responsible a firm must give at least as much weight age to fair wages, fair prices, fair community practices, fair environmental practices as it does to fair return on investment. | F<br>Sig | 0.256<br>(0.775) | 4.161*<br>(0.010) | 0.139<br>(0.871) | 0.590<br>(0.558) | 0.270<br>(0.765) | 0.082<br>(0.922) | 0.058<br>(0.944) | 1.049<br>(0.357) |
| In a broader sense of cost the socially conscious companies practically those who have earned reputation of being fair and acting in promoting welfare of the society do not suffer from higher unit costs | F<br>Sig | 0.023<br>(0.978) | 1.919<br>(0.137) | 0.141<br>(0.868) | 0.677<br>(0.512) | 0.588<br>(0.559) | 1.420<br>(0.250) | 0.454<br>(0.637) | 1.625<br>(0.206) |

(*contd.*)

| Significant Aspects of CSR | | Socio-Organisational Characteristics of Manager | | | | | | | |
|---|---|---|---|---|---|---|---|---|---|
| | | Age | Educational Qualification | Experience level | Level of Management | Department | Annual Turnover in Rs Crores | Fixed Assets in Rs Crores | No. of Employees |
| for employees may accept lower wages and customers may pay higher price. | | | | | | | | | |
| Practice of efficient social reporting system can help a company to plan and monitor its social responsibilities. | F<br>Sig | 5.485*<br>(0.007) | 3.970*<br>(0.013) | 0.677<br>(0.512) | 1.670<br>(0.198) | 1.242<br>(0.297) | 0.303<br>(0.740) | 0.415<br>(0.663) | 0.400<br>(0.672) |
| There should be a three-tier social audit committee ( National level, Industry level, and individual corporate level) in India | F<br>Sig | 1.708<br>(0.191) | 0.581<br>(0.630) | 0.188<br>(0.829) | 0.647<br>(0.528) | 0.238<br>(0.789) | 1.523<br>(0.227) | 0.850<br>(0.433) | 0.474<br>(0.625) |

Figures appearing in Brackets show the level of significance. df : degrees of Freedom , *Significant at 0.05 level of significance.

same level for both managers and prospective managers and also during the survey interval. It is also found that perceived managerial notion of purpose, relevance, stakeholders, functions, accountability, and transactional implications of corporate social performance is negligibly influenced by their socio-organisational characteristics. Thus, the findings of the study support the hypothesis *(H01)* formulated under the study.

Majority of the Indian managers under survey perceive CSR as relevant for relationship between business and greater society. They view social activities of a corporate firm as the product of the autonomous philanthropic or strategic choice of the management, not as the result of external pressure from the government or any social group. The time interval of one decade (1995-2005) has not significantly altered the relative importance assigned to various Social responsibility stakeholder groups in India. Both managers and prospective managers moderately endorse that social accounting practice helps planning and monitoring of social responsibility activities and the degree of agreement assumes an upward movement during the survey interval of ten years. The managers and perspective managers irrespective of their socio-organisational characteristics conceive social responsibility under contemporary philosophy of business and are willing to be socially accountable through a social reporting system.

In view of the findings it is suggested that Managers' training institutions and the B-Schools should compulsorily include and impart a course on applied CSR. The contents of the course may be designed to alter the managerial notion of CSR in the desired direction, particularly to lay more emphasis on their concerns for environmental responsibilities and societal needs of rural population. The survey results incorporated in this study lay down various aspects of CSR where the present and future managers' attitude needs a change. So that the

**Table 6.6: Test of Independence for Response of Prospective Managers and with Respect to Educational Background**

| Significant Aspects of CSR | | Socio-Organisational Characteristics of Managers | | | |
|---|---|---|---|---|---|
| | | Prospective 1995 | Prospective 2005 | Combined 1995 | Combined 2005 |
| | df /df | 1/69 | 1/69 | 3/124 | 3/125 |
| Sole Function of business firm is to make profit and thus it is the most important social responsibility | F<br>Sig | 2.298<br>(0.134) | 1.247<br>(0.268) | 0.624<br>(0.601) | 1.908<br>(0.132) |
| Firms' purposes are significantly related to how their operations affect society and thus the firm has a purpose beyond profit making | F<br>Sig | 2.202<br>(0.142) | 0.175<br>(0.677) | 1.356<br>(0.259) | 0.330<br>(0.803) |
| The company's objective of maximising profit should always take precedence over objective that seem to some people important for society | F<br>Sig | 0.016<br>(0.899) | 0.108<br>(0.743) | 0.125<br>(0.945) | 1.365<br>(0.257) |
| To become socially responsible a firm must give at least as much weight age to fair wages, fair prices, fair community practices, fair environmental practices as it does to fair return on investment. | F<br>Sig | 0.187<br>(0.667) | 0.089<br>(0.766) | 1.106<br>(0.350) | 0.329<br>(0.805) |

| | | | | | |
|---|---|---|---|---|---|
| In a broader sense of cost the socially conscious companies practically those who have earned reputation of being fair and acting in promoting welfare of the society do not suffer from higher unit costs for employees may accept lower wages and customers may pay higher price. | F<br>Sig | 0.919<br>(0.341) | 0.187<br>(0.667) | 0.309<br>(0.819) | 1.399<br>(0.246) |
| Practice of efficient social reporting system can help a company to plan and monitor its social responsibilities. | F<br>Sig | 1.825<br>(0.181) | 1.504<br>(0.224) | 0.316<br>(0.813) | 0.586<br>(0.625) |
| There should be a three- tier social audit committee( National level, Industry level, and individual corporate level) in India | | | | | F |
| 1.795 | 0.419 | 0.111 | 0.135 | | |
| | Sig | (0.185) | (0.519) | (0.953) | (0.939) |

Figures appearing in Brackets show the level of significance. df : degrees of Freedom ,

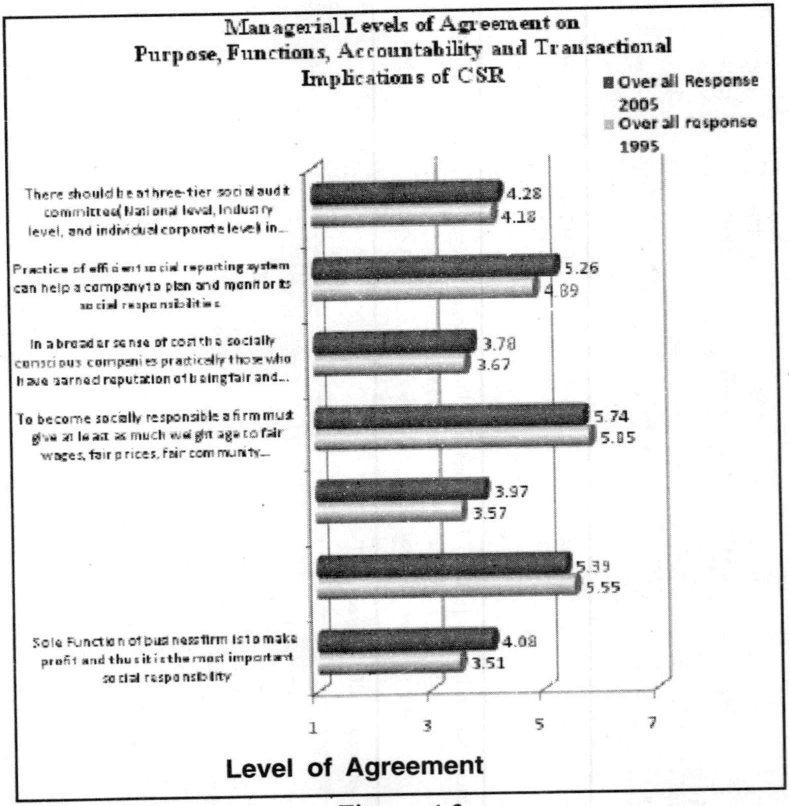


**Figure 6.2**

managers with inadequate CSR handling skills could be equipped to meet the routine CSR challenges.(Manikutty 1980). This has far reaching implication because ethical judgments and choices of social responsibility are soon becoming issues of survival, and accordingly the management of ethics and social responsibility programmes in a corporation will become a matter of strategic importance.

The results of this study seem to be in congruence with the theories of current acceptance. However, given the overall character of a rarity of Indian research in this area, the study may be regarded as a contribution to existing knowledge on corporate social responsibility.

## REFERENCES

Ackerman, Robert W. (1975), *The Social Challenge to Business* ,Cambridge, Massachusetts, Harvard University Press.Mass, USA.

Andrews, Kenneth R.(1980), *The Concept of Corporate Strategy,* (Rev. Edn). Richard D. Irwin, Inc., Homewood, IL, USA.

Antal A B (1985), Institutionalizing Corporate Social Responsiveness: Lessons Learned from the Migros Experiment, In: Preston, L. E. (Ed.)*Research in Corporate Social Performance and Policy*, Vol. 7, JAI Press: Greenwich, Conn, 229-249.

A-PEC (2005), *Corporate Social Responsibility in the A-PEC Region: Current Status and Implications*, The Asia-Pacific Economic Cooperation Secretariat, Singapore.

Arora, B. And R. Puranik (2004), A Review of Corporate Social Responsibility in India, in: Development *Journal of the Society for International Development*,47 (3), 93–100.

Aupperle, K E. Carroll,A B, and Hatfield J D (1985 ), An Empirical Examination of the Relationship between Corporate Social Responsibility and Profitability, *The Academy of Management Journal*,. 28( 2), 446-463.

Carroll A B (1979), A Three-Dimensional Conceptual Model of Corporate Performance, *The Academy of Management Review*, Vol. 4( 4) (Oct., 1979), pp. 497-50.

Carroll, A.B. (1999), Corporate Social Responsibility, *Business and Society,* 38 (3), 268-295.

Crawford, R. L., & Gram, H. A. (1978), Social Responsibility as Inter-Organizational Transaction , *Academy of Management Review*, 3, 880-888.

Deborah Doane (2004), Beyond Corporate Social Responsibility: Minnows, Mammoths and Markets, *Futures*, 37, 215-229, New Economics Foundation, 3 Jonathan Street, London SE11 5NH, UK.

European Commission(2002), *Corporate Social Responsibility: A Business Contribution to Sustainable Development*, Employment and Social Affairs, Industrial Relations and Industrial Change. EU.

GDI-(2007) , Corporate Social and Environmental Responsibility in India – Assessing the UN Global Compact's Role http://www.die-gdi.de accessed on 12-10-2008

Hart, S. L. and C. M. Christensen(2002), The Great Leap. Driving Innovation from the Base of the Pyramid, *MIT Sloan Management Review,* 44(1), 51–57.

Hart, S. L.(1995), A Natural-Resource-Based View of the Firm, *Academy of Management Review*, 20(4), 986–1012.

Johnson, H. L. (1971), *Business in Contemporary Society: Framework and Issues*, Wadsworth., Belmont, CA USA.

Khan A F and Alkinson A (1987), Managerial Attitudes to Social Responsibility: A Comparative Study in India and Britain, *Journal of Business Ethics*, 6, 419-432.

Krishna C G,(1992), Corporate Social Responsibility in India: A Study of Management Attitudes,: Mittal Publications, New Delhi.

Litz, R. A. (1996), A Resourced-Based-View of the Socially Responsible Firm: Stakeholder Interdependence, Ethical Awareness, and Issue Responsiveness as Strategic Assets, *Journal of Business Ethics*, 15, 1355–1363.

Maclagan, P.W. (1998), *Management and Morality*, London: Sage Publications

Maclagan, P.W. (1999), Corporate Social Responsibility as a Participative Process, *Business Ethics: A European Review,* 8 (1), 43-49.

Partners in Change (1997), *Report on Survey on Corporate Involvement in Social Development in India*, Partners in Change, New Delhi, India.

Peters, Thomas J. and Robert H. Waterman, Jr (1982), *In Search of Excellence*, Harper and Row, New York, USA.

Porter, M. E. and M. R. Kramer (2002), The Competitive Advantage of Corporate Philanthropy, *Harvard Business Review*, 80(12), 56–69.

Prahalad, C. K. and A. Hammond(2002), Serving the World's Poor, Profitably, *Harvard Business Review* 80(9), 48–58.

Prahalad, C. K.(2002), Strategies for the Bottom of the Economic Pyramid: India as a Source of Innovation, Reflections: *The SOL Journal* 3(4), 6–18.

Rama Krishnan(1973), Business Philosophy and Executive Responsibility ,*The Academy of Management Journal*,16(4), 658-669, Published by: Academy of Management

Steiner, George A.(1969), *Top Management Planning*, The Macmillan Company, London, UK.

Sturdivant, F D, Ginter, J L, and. Sawyer A G(1985), Managers' Conservatism and Corporate Performance, *Strategic Management Journa*l, 6 ( 1), 17-38 John Wiley and Amp Sons.

Tachizawa Takeshy. (2002), Environmental Administration and Corporate Social Responsibility, SãoPaulo: Atlas, 2002.

Vernon M. Buehle, and Y. K. Shetty (1976), Managerial Response to Social Responsibility Challenge, *The Academy of Management Journal*, 19(1), 66-78.

Richard E. Wokutch (1990) ,Corporate Social Responsibility Japanese Style, *The Executive*, Vol. 4, No. 2 (May, 1990), pp. 56-74. Pub: Academy of Management Stable URL: http://www.jstor.org/stable/4164948.

Duane Windsor (2006), Corporate Social Responsibility: Three Key Approaches, *Journal of Management Studies*, Vol 43 (01), pp 93-11

# 7

# 'Management Disclosure' in Annual Reports – Rambling Thoughts

**A. Bhowal**

**Abstract:** The chapter strives to look into the flow of disclosure practice under the heading "Management Discussion" disclosed in the Annual Reports by the corporate houses in India. And understand the reasons of such pattern in the context of the Theories of Disclosure. Paper concluded that existing Theories are not ample to grasp the reasons of such pattern, and, there is urgent need for Comprehensive Theory of Corporate Disclosure.

Disclosure of information in Annual Report is a necessity. Annual Report contains a section "Management Discussion". It discloses the management's perception of the business activities that were done, are being done and will be done. This is to provide in addition to the Director's Report which is provided along with the Annual Reports.

Given the above, to identify, generally, what is disclosed under the "Management Discussion", the 17th Annual Report and Audited Statements of Accounts of ONGC for the year ended 31stMarch, 2010 has been considered. ONGC as a Case deserves selection as it continues to achieve excellence in its core area of E & P sphere both in India as well as abroad and also continues to win accolades from various quarters.

- Finance Asia, Hongkong has ranked ONGC as Number-1 Top Blue Chip Company of India (for 2009).
- ONGC is ranked at Second Position in Financial Express FE500 listing of Indian companies both in terms of Net Worth and Overall Composite Ranking (March 2009).
- It has been ranked at 155th position in Forbes Global 2000 list of world's biggest companies for 2010 (April 2010).
- It retains number one rank among Indian companies and has been ranked 95th among the Forbes Global 2000 biggest companies as per profit.

From the self explanatory Table 7.1, it is discernible that Column 1 indicates the dimensions or pattern of information disclosed. These have been disclosed under 15 different Items as recorded in Column 2. The dimensions, disclosed in Column 1, can be classified in five categories as shown in column 3. These are:

[a] Antecedents i.e. the issues that have already taken place,

[b] Concurrent i.e the issues that are happening concurrently in the environment of the business of the ONGC,

[c] Intervention i.e. the issues or the drivers that the ONGC used to fulfil the objectives of the organisation,

[d] Consequent i.e the results or the happenings that resulted because of the effect and affect of the Antecedents, Concurrents, and Interventions, finally,

[e] Futures i.e. the issues that are likely to come up in the

near future and have substantial affect and effect on the interventions and Consequents.

The flow of arrangements of the information disclosed through "Management Discussions" [may be derived b comparing the column 1 and 2] deserve attention i.e how the various items from no.1 to no. 15 have been arranged to give birth to a particular pattern. Item 15 which deals with 'Liability Exclusion Clause' warns and restricts the user not to rely completely on the "Management Discussion" – stating differently, this document has to be used in consultation with other available information relating to the company and ts business environment for judicious decision making.

The reasons for the disclosure of above information can be traced in the theories of the Disclosure. It is argued that managers gain by disclosing information with discretion. **Full disclosure theory**[1] suggests that it can be quite counter-productive to hide information from shareholders, creditors, government regulators, and other venture Stakeholders. The stakeholders' trust in management decreases without the perception that "management is fully and fairly disclosing all relevant facts", and in such a situation, the perceived reliability of the information it communicates decreases. The prediction of full discounting, or full disclosure, was first derived (separately) by **Grossman**[2] (1981) and **Milgrom**[3] (1981).

There also exists **Discretionary Disclosure Theory**. **Verrecchia** [4]**(1983)** shows that cost of disclosure can preclude full discounting by investors, and therefore full disclosure by managers may be withheld resulting into Discretionary Disclosure. Investors are unable to determine if the news is withheld because it is unfavorable or because of the cost the firm will bear by disclosing it. **McNichols** [5]**(1988)** presents evidence the skewness of stock returns distributions at earnings and non-earnings announcement dates. Thus the study supports the disclosure predictions of Verrecchia (1983). The study **Scott** [6](1994), presents a prediction of voluntary disclosure by using financial statement announcement of defined benefit pension plan information. His prediction states that the incentive to disclose decreases as the cost of disclosure increases. Disclosure increases as the news becomes more favorable.

On the other hand, **Diamond[7] (1985)**, explains **Voluntary Disclosures** through information cost savings. The firm commits to a policy of revealing relevant news to preempt private information search by investors.

Still others believe that volume of disclosure is function of **Disclosure thresholds.** Discretionary disclosure models explain observations of nondisclosure by introducing confounding factors. These factors block the ability of uninformed parties to discount price fully. These confounding factors cause disclosure thresholds. Buyers (of shares) are unable to assume the lowest possible value because they are not unable to ascertain that the news or disclosure withheld is unfavorable. The disclosure threshold gives the manager disclosure discretion. It is argued that manager reveals private information only if the value of disclosure exceeds the threshold limit of the benefit, otherwise, manager withholds the information[8].

Buyer of shares of a company may face uncertainty; and, and end up in supporting a threshold of disclosure. If buyers are uncertain that the manager has received private information, they are unable to judge 'withheld news' as unfavorable[9].

**King and Wallin (1995)[10]** test a disclosure threshold that arises from cost of disclosure. Here, the cost of disclosure has been perceived as the profit lost when information release encourages an opponent to enter the firm's product market. **Wagenhofer[11]** [1990] defined this cost as **proprietary due** to its direct impact on firm profits. Managers disclose information

**Table 7.1**
**Pattern of disclosure in Annual reports under the Heading "MANAGEMENT DISCUSSIONS" for ONGC**

| Col no 1 | Col No. 2 | Col. No. 3 |
|---|---|---|
| Issues disclosed in annual reports under the heading "management discussion" | MANAGEMENT DISCUSSION | Nature of Information |
| • Global economy description –<br>• Global growth statistics – past and future and<br>• Country growth statistics of India. | ITEM NO 1 | CONCURRENT |
| • Global crude oil consuption statistics<br>• Statistics for crude oil demand in India<br>• Price of oil and gas scenario of world<br>• Declinning world field operation data<br>• Declinning discoveries of oil field<br>• Declinning world trend in oil and gas investment<br>• Emergence of bio fuel as an alternative<br>• New gas distribution technology and associated concern<br>• Off-shore drilling future restrictions likely to come | ITEM 2 | CONCURRENT / FUTURE |
| • Increase in consumption of crude oil in india –? | ITEM 3 | CONCURRENT/ |

| | | |
|---|---|---|
| • Use of technology for crude oil production enhancement by ONGC –<br>• Crude oil price [Indian to use of basket] and under recoveries of cost as per government directives for making the customer access to use of oil –<br>• Natural gas production in india, share of ongc and major field of production –<br>• Different sources of enerfgy and position of oil and gas [both India and world] –<br>• Impetous in oil production growth of the company for court decisions in favour of ONGC | | intervention |
| • Oil and gas production statistics – antecedent [fy'06 to fy'09] to consequent [fy'10] and<br>• Reserve for oil and gas statistics- – antecedent [fy'06 to fy'09] to consequent [fy'10] | ITEM 4 | antcedent / consequent |
| • Income from sales, other incomes, gross margin,<br>• Ebidta, pat,<br>• Eps, net worth, return on net worth, return on capital employed<br>• Both for ongc and the group – antecedent [ for fy09] and consequence [ fy,2010] | ITEM NO 5 | antcedent / consequent |
| • Opportunities and threats in the future the company is going to face – as set by the oil business environment of oil | ITEM NO 6 | future |
| • Risks and concerns –<br>• Technology investment,<br>• Off-shore drilling problem<br>• Health and safety and<br>• Environment issues | ITEM NO 7 | future |

| Col no 1 | Col No. 2 | Col. No. 3 |
|---|---|---|
| Strategic business pursuits adopted by ONGC like<br>• [a] Intensive exploration to locate new oil & gas assets.<br>• [b] Expeditious development of discoveries.<br>• [c] Arresting decline from the matured fields.<br>• [d] Leverage its position as a favoured partner globally for overseas energy projects.<br>• [e] Developing new sources of energy like-CBM, UCG, Shalegas, etc.<br>• [f] Establish alternate energy as commercially viable option.<br>• [g] Value-multiplication through integration in hydrocarbon and energy value-chains. | ITEM NO 8 & 9 | intervention/ |
| **Outlook** particularly the future covering the aspects like<br>• **Exploration acreage, Exploration programme, New field development,**<br>• **Plan expenditure** [For domestic operations; seismic survey; exploratory drilling; development drilling; capital projects and purchases; alongwith information for XI plan period,]<br>• Overseas E & P with countries involved, nature of operation | ITEM NO 10 | future |
| **INTERNAL CONTROL SYSTEM with focus on**<br>• Group -Performance Management and Benchmarking Group (PMBG),<br>• Revised the Book of Delegated Powers (BDP),<br>• Using latest ERP system ,<br>• Audit & Ethics committee of the Board, | ITEM NO 11 | intervention / |

| | | |
|---|---|---|
| • Whistle Blower policy, and<br>• Fraud prevention policy. | | |
| **Human Resource Development:** with initiatives towards<br>• Coaching & Mentoring scheme,<br>• Business Games,<br>• Employee Engagement Survey,<br>• HR Audit,<br>• Assessment Development Centre (ADC),<br>• Along with the institutionalize Multi Disciplinary Team (MDT) concept ; leading to the best company towork in core sector in India (Business Today; 7th Feb 2010 edition), | ITEM NO 12 | intervention / |
| Referring<br>• **Corporate Governance** [a part of the Annual report.], and<br>• **Corporate Social Responsibility (CSR)** [as detailed in Directors' Report] | ITEM NO 13 & 14 | intervention / |
| **Cautionary statement:**<br>• Statements in the management discussion [describing the company's objectives, projections and estimates,] are forward-looking statements and<br>• Progressive within the meaning of applicable laws and regulations.<br>• Actual results may vary from those expressed or implied, depending upon economic conditions, government policies and other incidental factors.<br>• Readers are cautioned not to place undue reliance on the forward looking statements. | ITEM 15 | LIABILITY EXCLUSION DISCLOSURE |

Source: Compiled from 17th Annual Report of ONGC

only if the benefit to the firm exceeds the proprietary cost resulting from opponent entry.

It was further argued by **Wagenhofer**[12] (1990) that the manager offsets the effect that disclosures have on investors and his opponent. The manager has incentive to disclose good news to capital markets to increase firm price. However, release of favorable news poses a risk of opponent entry and lost profit in the product market. If the opponent enters, the firm incurs an exogenously specified proprietary cost that reduces firm value. Another way of interpretation of the why of disclosure put by **Verrecchia** [2001][13]

[a] **Association-based disclosure** whose primary concern is how **exogenous disclosure** is associated with the change in the activities of investors who compete in capital market settings as individual welfare-maximizing agents. It explains the effects of exoge-nous disclosure on the aggregate or cumulative change in investors' actions. This is verified through the behavior of asset equilibrium prices and trading volume in stock exchanges.

[b] **Discretionary-based disclosure** examines how managers and/or firms exercise discretion with regard to the disclosure of information about which they may have knowledge, it treats disclosure as endogenous by considering managers and / or firms incentives to disclose information known to them. Here too the context is capital market setting in which the market is considered as a single representative consumer of disclosed information.

[c] **Efficiency-based disclosure** discusses the types of disclosure arrangements that are preferred in the absence of prior knowledge of the information. It examines un-

conditional disclosure choices. Here the context is that of a capital market setting in which the actions of individual, welfare-maximizing agents are endogenous.

But the behaviours of the Dominant Decision making managers are also capable of explaining the Disclosure related behaviour. This is indicative of **Applied Behavioral Dimension** which has the potential for answering the unexplained reasons using Antecedent-Intervention-Consequence mode [or with its potentials to be modified with **Concurrents** and **Futures**] of learning on the parts of the managers. Modern behavior analysis has also witnessed a massive resurgence in research and applications related to language and cognition, the development of Relational Frame Theory (RFT; described as a "Post-Skinnerian account of language and cognition").[14] In the context of the Corporate Disclosure, cognition of both the manager and the user of the "management discussion" receive attention to predict the unexplained disclosure dimensions. Modell [1996][15] states that a review of previous research reveals an undue over-emphasis on structural accounting implications at the expense of the behavioural side of accounting and control. Ray & Piper (1977)[16] states that the majority of these articles are concerned with how 'the behavioural variable' in relation to accounting information should be managed, and vice-versa. Thus, they are predominantly prescriptive. The prescription is sometimes presented as a set of guidelines for management action which have their bases on the references to other research studies.

MacDonald, Bath, & Booth [2011][17] tried to gain insight into managers' decision making practices vis-à-vis information behaviour in managers when these managers are challenged by inappropriate information quality. This study further tried to test frameworks developed from research to see if **information overload, information poverty and satisficing** apply to these managers. This paper suggests that existing definitions for the concepts of information poverty and information overload can be used to describe managers' experiences. Zhuang, Qiu, & Peng (2011)[18] endeavoured to uncover some empirical evidence on how prevalent the problem of information overload has become, how it has affected the performance of organisations. An exploratory study provides some empirical evidence to complement the growing body of anecdotal evidence demonstrating how information explosion especially through the internet is having an adverse impact on corporate performance.

Organisational politics too has something to contribute in the Disclosure episode. Gotsis & Kortezi [2011][19] aimed at critically exploring the behavioral assumptions of organizational politics with a conceptual research framework that integrates self-interest and constructive politics. The paper represents an attempt toward inferring positive political behavior through adopting an alternative view of established behavioral assumptions. Findings suggested the possibility of an inclusive, participative and welfare-enhancing political process, founded on the pro-social and reciprocating aspects of human interaction. Boundedly selfish organizational members are expected to demonstrate these qualities that are in position to transform the very nature of political activities to the direction of greater organizational well-being. Corporate disclosure function is not free from these.

Behavioral accounting research (BAR) paper of Birnberg [2011][20] offers a framework within which BAR literature that can be viewed as a whole rather than in segments (such as by accounting sub-areas or by research method). The framework classifies BAR by the focus of the research: the individual, group, organization, or the society within which accounting exists. The paper argued that Disclosure of Information without referring to 'Sustainability of the Business and Society" incomplete. Burritt, & Schaltegger (2010)[21] aimed to discuss the current development of sustainability accounting research, to identify the critical and managerial paths, and to assess the future of sustainability accounting and reporting. The paper concludes that both management decision making (through problem solving and scorekeeping) and a critical approach (through awareness raising) contribute to the development of **sustainability accounting and reporting**. They finally argued that the development of sustainability accounting and reporting should be orientated more towards improving management decision making.

Refering the underlying features of the multiple approaches to accounting research, Laughlin, (1995)[22] points out the need for choices to be made on the perspective to be adopted along three continuums concerning "**theory**", "**methodology**" and "**change**". Presenting a case for "middle-range" thinking for empirical research in accounting, **Luglin** [1995] [23] demonstrated that no one perspective can provide a complete picture of accounting reality. They also observed that choices on perspective have to be, and can be, made and that these choices are, and should be, contestable.

A discussion on Corporate Disclosure should also bring in within its fold the type of Corporate Disclosure which is regulated by Code Of Internal Procedure & Conduct And Code Of Corporate Disclosure Practies as envisaged under The SEBI (Prohibition Of Insider Trading) Regulations, 1992 as amended. Under its provisions, the Trading Window will be closed before specified days of the happening of the following events:-

(a) Declaration of Financial Results (Quarterly, Half Yearly and Annual)

(b) Declaration of Dividends (interim and final)

(c) Issue of Securities by way of public/rights/bonus issue etc.

(d) Any major expansion plan or execution of new projects.

(e) Amalgamation, mergers, takeovers and buy back.

(f) Disposal of whole or substantially the whole of the undertaking

(g) Any changes in policies, plans or operations of the Company

Similarly, Trading Windows shall remain closed up to specified days after the publication of the price sensitive information. Here, "price sensitive informations" include:

(i) Periodical financial results of the Company

(ii) Intended declaration of dividends (both interim and final)

(iii) Issue of securities or buy-back of securities

(iv) Any major expansion plans or execution of new projects.

(v) Amalgamation or mergers or take-overs.

(vi) Disposal of the whole or substantial part of the undertaking.

(vii) Any significant changes in policies, plans or operations of the Company.

But, not a single theory seems to bring within its fold the legal limits to the corporate disclosure while predicting Disclosure.

In final conclusion it is submitted that the findings are based on a single case study and are therefore an exercise in theory development rather than theory testing. More cases have to be studied before generalisations of the findings from the present study. But , it obviously calls for a search for the **Comprehensive Theory** of Disclosure. In this connection, **Verrecchia[24] (2001)** recommend **information asymmetry reduction** as one potential starting point for a comprehensive theory of disclosure. It was further argued for information asymmetry reduction as a vehicle to integrate the efficiency of disclosure choice, the incentives to disclose, and the endogeneity of the capital market process as it involves the interactions among individual and diverse investors. But, **Ball** [25](2006) argued that increased worldwide integration of both markets and politics (driven by reductions in communications and information processing costs) makes increased integration of financial reporting standards and practice almost inevitable. He further argued that there is little settled theory or evidence on which to build an assessment of the advantages and disadvantages of uniform accounting rules within a country, let alone internationally. The notion that uniform standards alone will produce uniform financial reporting seems naive. Given the above, the logical corrollary is that the **information asymmetry reduction** through Accounting Standard for Disclosure needs a new perspective perusal.

## REFERENCES

1. http://www.google.co.in/search?q=%22DISCLOSURE+THEORY%22+ filetype: pdf&hl= en &num= 10&lr =lang en&ft=i&cr=&safe=images&tbs=rl:1,rls:2 / 24/1/2011.
2. Grossman, S. (1981). The Informational Role of Warranties and Private Disclosure About Product Quality. *Journal of Law and Economics*, 24 (Dec.), 461-483.
3. Milgrom, P. (1981). Good News and Bad News: Representation Theorems and Applications. *Bell Journal of Economics*, 12 (Autumn), 380-391.
4. Verrecchia, R. (1983). Discretionary Disclosure. *Journal of Accounting and Economics*, 5, 179-194.
5. McNichols, M. (1988). A Comparison of the Skewness of Stock Return

Distributions in Earnings and Non-Earnings Announcement Dates. *Journal of Accounting and Economics*, 10 (July), 239-273.

6. Scott, T. (1994). Incentives and Disincentives for Financial Disclosure: Voluntary Disclosure of Defined Benefit Pension Plan Information by Canadian Firms. *The Accounting Review*, 69 (1), 26-43.
7. Diamond, D. (1985). Optimal Release of Information by Firms. Journal of Finance, 40 (Sept.),1071-1094.
8. http://www.csupomona.edu/~jis/1999/martin.pdf / 24/1/2011.
9. *ibid.*
10. King, R., & Wallin, D. (1995). Experimental Tests of Disclosure with an Opponent. *Journal of Accounting and Economics*, 19 (1), 139-167.
11. Wagenhofer, A. (1990). Voluntary Disclosure with a Strategic Opponent. *Journal of Accounting and Economics*, 12 (4), 341-363.
12. *ibid.*
13. Verrecchia, Robert E., Essays on Disclosure (June 2001). JAE Rochester Conference April 2000. Available at SSRN: http://ssrn.com/abstract=276699 or doi:10.2139/ssrn.276699.
14. Hayes, S.C., Barnes-Holmes, D., & Roche, B. (2001) *Relational Frame Theory: A Post-Skinnerian account of human language and cognition.* Kluwer Academic: New York.
15. Modell, Sven [1996] Management accounting and control in services: structural and behavioural perspectives, *International Journal of Service Industry Management* Volume: 7 Issue: 2 1996.
16. Ray G.H., Piper J.A. (1977) A Closer Examination of some Aspects of Behavioural Accounting Research, *Managerial Finance* Volume: 3 Issue: 3 1977.
17. MacDonald, J., Bath, P., and Booth, A. [2011],Information Overload and Information Poverty: challenges for healthcare services managers? *Journal of Documentation* Volume: 67 Issue: 2 2011.
18. Zhuang, L., Qiu,Y., and Peng, L.(2011),Is it the more the merrier?: An exploratory study into the growing problem of information overload, *Journal of Technology Management in China* Volume: 6 Issue: 1 2011.
19. Gotsis, G. N., and Kortezi, Z. [2011] Bounded Self-Interest: A Basis for Constructive Organizational Politics, *Management Research News* Volume: 34 Issue: 4 2011.
20. Birnberg, J. G. [2011] A Proposed Framework for Behavioral Accounting Research, *Behavioral Research in Accounting* 23 (1), 1 (2011) http://link.aip.org/link/BRIAXX/v23/i1/p1/s1.

21. Burritt, R. L., and Schaltegger, S. (2010) Sustainability accounting and reporting: fad or trend? *Accounting, Auditing & Accountability Journal* Volume: 23 Issue: 7 2010.
22. Laughlin, R. (1995) "Empirical research in accounting: alternative approaches and a case for "middle-range" thinking", Accounting, *Auditing & Accountability Journal*, Vol. 8 Iss: 1, pp.63 - 87.
23. *Ibid.*
24. Verrecchia, Robert E., *Essays on Disclosure* (June 2001) op.cit.
25. Ball, Ray, International Financial Reporting Standards (IFRS): *Pros and Cons for Investors. Accounting and Business Research*, Forthcoming. Available at SSRN: http://ssrn.com/abstract=92956.

# 8

# Reporting of Revenue Recognition Policy by Select Indian Companies – A Critical Study

**Sankar Thappa & H C Gautam**

Accounting is a financial-measurement discipline. Measurement is the assignment of numerals to objects or events according to certain rules or standards. Determination of financial position and operating results of an enterprise are the main purposes of measurement in financial accounting. To determine financial position, money value is assigned to all assets and liabilities of the enterprise. To determine operating results for a given period, accountants assign money value to economic transactions. These economic transactions are income received or earned on the one hand and the costs and expenses paid or incurred on the other. Money values of these two groups are compared at periodic intervals to determine operating results of these economic transactions. The operating result so ascertained is either surplus of income received or earned over the costs and expenses paid or incurred, or deficit.

Major accounting problems deal with aspects of income measurement. For measurement of income there shall be a clear-cut operational definition of 'income' based on a well-defined objective. Through the mechanism of accounting periodic net income, i.e. annual net income, is determined. In this context three basic expressions of income developed by the economists and accounting experts are worth mentioning. These are:

(i) Psychic income,

(ii) Real income and

(iii) Money income.

Psychic expression refers to the satisfaction of human wants. Real income is expressed in terms of units of purchasing power. Money income refers to the flow of utility over a period of time, measured in rupee terms. Due to accounting problem the first two concepts are not recognised for the purpose of determining business income and only the third is accepted. Business income which is generally called 'Net Income', and to be more specific, it is the income after tax (EAT) or profit after tax (PAT) is the final surplus from revenue. Therefore, 'Revenue Recognition' is considered as the primary concern in the process of net income measurement and reporting. Recognition of revenue is generally associated with specific accounting procedures, certain value base and assumed or implicit rules which are considered to measure and determine the timing when to report revenue.

Present study endeavours to examine the revenue recognition policy adopted by 30 Indian companies as evident from their reporting through Annual Reports. These companies are taken from various sectors, namely automobile, fast moving consumer goods, information technology, infrastructure, oil, pharmaceutical and health care. The companies are selected on the basis of judgment sampling. The companies publish their annual reports regularly. While selecting the individual company basically three factors have been kept in mind: sectoral representation, product variation and ownership.

Measurement of income of a business enterprise, which is founded and administered by set of statutory provisions and other administrative & professional bindings, is not an easy task. The concept of income is defined by various authorities in different ways. A business enterprise may have income from core activities as well as other non-core activities. The income disclosed in the Profit & Loss Account is the result of accounting measurement process. In arriving at 'income after tax' the accountant has to follow the basic accounting principles, statutory provisions and professional norms spelt out in the accounting standards. Companies have to follow the provisions of Section 209, 210, 211 etc of the Companies Act, 1956 as amended up to date, for the measurement and reporting of income. Moreover subjectivity also plays a role in the measurement of income. Further the reporting style of income and expenses by the companies are not uniform. These have been examined in the present study of the reported Profit and Loss Accounts and the related schedules of the sample companies. The findings of the study are listed below.

## Major Findings

1. The format for disclosure of profit in the Profit & Loss Account is not prescribed by the Companies Act. But broad guidelines have been provided. This has given the companies a scope to adopt their own style of preparing Profit & Loss Account within the limitation provided by those guidelines.

2. In regard to reporting of income it has been found that most of the companies have shown their income through net sales after deducting the excise duty except Hindustan Unilever Ltd, Tata Tea Ltd, ONGC, Wipro Ltd, Patni Computer systems Ltd, Mphasis Ltd, Glaxo Smithkline Pharmaceutical Ltd. Income or net income shown by some of the sample companies are shown below.

(i) **Colgate-Palmolive (India) Ltd:**

**Income** = Sales Less Excise Duty + Other Income

(ii) **Hindustan Unilever Limited:**

**Income** = Sales + Other Income

(iii) **ITC Limited:**

**Net Income** = Net Sales (Gross Sales Less Excise Duties and Taxes on Sales of Products and Services) + Other Income

(iv) **TATA Tea Limited:**

**Income** = Sales and Services (Net) + Other Income

(v) **Maruti Suzuki Ltd:**

**Income** = Gross Sales Less Excise Duty (Net Sales) + income from Services (Net) + Other Income

(vi) **Mahindra & Mahindra Ltd:**

**Net Income** = Sales (Traded and Manufactured Goods) Less Excise Duty on Sales (Net) + Income from Operations and Other Income

**3.** It is found that some of the Companies have shown excise duty separately and some have not shown it separately. In relation to reporting of excise duty it has been found that 21 companies (70%) have shown as deduction from gross sales in the income statement. Rests of the companies have shown it in the schedules as deductions from gross sales.

**4.** In similar ways, some of the companies have shown cost of goods sold, purchase of raw material, raw material consumed, consumption of stores and spare, Manufacturing and other expenses, Employees cost etc separately. These variations in the presentation some times create problems to the user of income information to take economic decision. Disclosure of these by the sample companies are summarised below:

(i) **Cost of Goods sold**: In relation to reporting of cost of goods sold it has been found during the study that only 3 companies have reported cost of goods sold in the income statement. Other companies have reported in the schedules along with other items of expenditures.

(ii) **Purchase of Raw material, Raw material consumed consumption of stores & spares**: With regard to reporting of purchase of raw materials, raw materials consumed consumption of stores & spares, 16 companies (53%) out of total sample have reported separately as an item of expenditure in the income statement. Rest 14 companies have shown it under different items of expenditure.

(iii) **Manufacturing and other expenses**: In relation to reporting of manufacturing and other expenses without showing the cost of goods sold it has been found that 15 companies (50%) out of the sample have reported in the income statement as item of expenditure. Rest 15 companies have reported the manufacturing expenses either individual item or with other item of expenditure.

(iv) **Depreciation/Depletion/ Amortisation**: With regard to reporting of depreciation and amortization of assets in the income statement it has been found that all the companies have reported depreciation/ depletion/amortization as a separate item of expenditure

(v) **Interest/Financial Expenses:** In relation to reporting of financial expenses it has been found that 21 companies (70%) out of the sample have reported the interest/financial expenses/financial charges as a separate item of expenditure in the income statement.

(vi) **Employees cost/expenditure/personnel cost :** With regard to reporting of employees cost/expenditure it has been found that 16 companies (53%) out of the sample have reported employees cost/ expenditure/personnel cost as a separate item of expenditure in the income statement.

(vii) **Profit before tax:** With regard to reporting of profit before tax all the companies have reported profit before tax in the income statement.

(viii) **Provision for tax:** In relation to reporting of tax it has been found that all the companies have shown properly the provision for tax in the name of current tax, deferred tax, fringe benefit tax in the income statement.

(ix) **Exceptional Items:** In relation to reporting of exceptional items it has been found that only 3 companies reported in the income statement.

(x) **Extraordinary items:** With regard to reporting of extraordinary items it has been found that only 2 companies have reported it in the income statement.

(xi) **Appropriation of Profit:** In relation to reporting of appropriation of profit it has been found that all the companies of the sample have reported properly appropriation of profit in the income statement properly.

**5.** None of the sample companies had given financial statements adjusted with price level changes.

**6.** Compliance report for Accounting standard as disclosed in the Annual Reports has revealed that each of the companies has followed all the mandatory standards in the preparation of accounts and financial statements. This fact has also been supported by the auditor's report attached in the annual report.

7. AS – 1 is followed by all the sample companies, since it is mandatory. The items stated under accounting policies or notes are more or less similar in all the concerns selected for the study but the treatment of some items was not similar among the companies. The requirement of AS-1 is only to disclose the material facts. What is the material or immaterial it would be decided by the organization, where the influence of personal judgement is expected in the absence of concrete guidelines. Therefore, the very purpose of AS-1 may not be fulfilled. The users may not be able to form a rationale judgement.

8. During the study it was found that 40 percent of the sample companies viewed Accounting Standard-9 as most useful, 50% useful and 10% not useful for recognizing revenue.

9. Most of the companies have adopted Weighted Average Cost Method (80% of the sample companies) and only 20% follows FIFO method. It was also found that during the study 50% of the respondents of sample companies viewed Accounting Standard-2 for valuation for inventory as most useful.

10. The study has found that the majority of the sample companies (80%) have followed written down value method for the computation of depreciation whereas, the remaining (20%) followed straight line method. It was also found that during the study 50 percent of the respondents viewed AS-6 as most useful for accounting depreciation.

11. 85% of the sample companies have disclosed the expenditure on research and development. All of these companies treated research and development expenditure

as revenue and capital both considering the nature and final effect of such expenditure.

**12.** The examination of 'Compliance to Accounting Standards' reveals that there is scope for applying alternative accounting treatment. There are inter-unit, intra-industry or inter-period variations in the adoption of methods. More frequently such variation is found in valuation of inventories, depreciation accounting, treatment of borrowing cost, foreign exchange fluctuation, construction contracts, R & D expenditure etc. This kind of variation creates problems in judging the quality and reliability of financial statements and impairs inter-unit, intra-industry or inter-period comparison. The lack of comparability makes the financial information less useful and creates confusion in the minds of the investing public. Therefore, in many cases, the accounting standards are looked only in the nature of disclosure.

## RECOMMENDATIONS

On the basis of the findings of the study the following recommendations are made:

A. Companies of a particular industry should follow similar pattern for disclosure of income, cost of goods sold and other expenditures. This will facilitate comparison of the companies by the present and prospective investor.

B. Industry wise format of Profit & Loss Account shall be provided in the Companies Act under Section 211 like the format of Balance Sheet. This will reduce the alternative choices for disclosure of income and expenses on the part of the companies.

C. The income earned from regular operations of a business firm should be segregated from various other elements of income, such as items resulting from unusual events and major holding gains and losses of the business.

D. The major holding gains or losses of a business firm should be segregated from the income from regular operations of the business.

E. The gains or losses arising from changes in the value of input factors should be disclosed.

F. The income statement of the business firm should provide an analysis of the significant factors that have contributed to and have affected the income for the period.

G. The provisions for compliance of Companies Act have provided scope for non-compliance. Companies Act requires to disclose the fact that accounting standards have been complied fully and for any variation there shall be proper discloser. Accounting Standards should narrow down the choice of alternative accounting practices. This will make fair disclosure of accounting and financial information. In case of the choice between alternative accounting practices in the areas like valuation of inventory, depreciation accounting and treatment of retirement benefits etc it is to be ensured that a shift from one accounting practice to other is genuine need for the business firm.

H. The Accounting Standards Board (ASB) in India in consultation with other professionals and regulatory bodies should develop some system to limit the scope of alternative methods available within an accounting standard. Thus, the use of uniform accounting standards would enhance the qualitative and comparability dimensions of financial statement and reporting.

I. Section 211(2AA) of the Companies Act requires that the directors shall disclose whether the Accounting

Standards have been followed and if there is any material departure that should also be disclosed. But for non-compliance of Accounting Standard the Companies Act is silent. There should be a proper guideline in this regard.

J. The users and preparers of the financial statement should be educated about the utility and significance of the accounting standards incorporated by financial reporting.

## Conclusion

The Companies Act 1956 under Section 211(1) and (2) requires that every balance sheet of a company shall give a true and fair view of the state of affairs of the company as at the end of the financial year and every profit and loss account of a company should give a true and fair view of the profit or loss of the company for the financial year. Thus, the income (net profit) as disclosed by the company should be 'true and fair view' and this is legal requirement.

A true and fair view of accounts is one which is such that directors or other persons in control are not deprived of knowledge which might have afforded them the opportunity to take remedial action or which might afford them the chance to incur liabilities to third parties on the basis of inaccurate accounts.

With the insertion of Sub-sections (3A), (3B) and (3C) in Section 211 the Profit & Loss Account and the Balance Sheet have to comply with the Accounting Standards and non-compliance with these Standards would lead to violation of Section 211 . This is on assumption that non-compliance with the Standards will result such accounts and state of affairs that can not be regarded as 'true and fair.'

But it is said that the spirit of the accounting standards to disclose a true and fair view is defeated when companies are allowed to deviate from the mandate of the standards. In this context two cases may be referred where it is decided whether a set of financial statements present the true and fair view of the financial position and performance of the company.

The Honourable Supreme Court in *JK Industries* v. *Union of India,* (2008) case observed that:

> "with the insertion of Sub-sections (3A), (3B) and (3C) in Section 211 the P & L a/c and the Balance Sheet have to comply with the Accounting Standards . . . non compliance with these Standards would lead to violation of Section 211 in as much as the annual accounts may then not be regarded as showing a "true and fair view."

On the other hand Bombay High Court in *Hindalco case,* (2009) observed that on conjoint reading of sub-sections (3A) and (3B) of Section 211, it necessarily follows that deviation from the accounting standards is permissible subject, however, to compliance of the requirement of disclosure in the profit and loss account and balance sheet of such deviation and the reasons for such deviation and financial effects thereof. In other words, deviation of accounting standards is not wholly prohibited, but it is regulated by the provisions of Section 211 of the Act.

In the context of income measurement a deviation from accounting standards is prima facie evidence that financial statements do not provide true and fair view. However, preparation of financial statements is not a mechanical exercise. In certain rare situations, compliance with accounting standards might distort the true and fair view and results in misleading information on income. In those situations it is necessary to deviate from the accounting standards.

## REFERENCES

1. Irving Fisher, The Theory of Interest (New York: The Macmillan Company, 1930), pp. 10-11.
2. G. Edward Philips, "The Accretion Concept of Income," The Accounting Review, XXXVIII (January, 1963), 16.
3. FASB concept no.3, 'Elements of Financial Statements of Business Enterprises," 1980 paragraph.
4. American Institute of Certified public Accountants, APB Statement No.4 'Basic concepts and Accounting principles Underlying financial statements of Business Enterprises'[ New York; AICPA,1970 par.134]
5. Annual Reports of Companies :
    1. Colgate Palmolive (India) Ltd.
    2. Hindustan Unilever Ltd
    3. ITC Ltd.
    4. TATA Tea Ltd
    5. Maruti Suzuki India Ltd.
    6. TATA Motors Ltd.
    7. Mahindra & Mahindra Ltd.
    8. Hero Honda Motors Ltd.
    9. Ashok Leyland
    10. TVS Motors Company Ltd.
    11. Reliance Industries Ltd
    12. Oil and Natural Gas Corporation Ltd.
    13. Numaligarh Refinery Ltd.
    14. Bongaigaon Refinery & Petrochemical Ltd.
    15. Indian Oil Corporation Ltd.
    16. TATA STEEL Ltd.
    17. Steel Authority of India Ltd.
    18. Bharat Heavy Electricals Ltd.
    19. ACC Ltd.
    20. Ambuja Cements Ltd.
    21. Grasim Industries Ltd.
    22. HCL Info system Ltd.
    23. Wipro Ltd.

24. Patni Computers System Ltd.
25. Mphasis Ltd
26. GlaxoSmithKline Pharmaceutical Ltd.
27. Sun Pharmaceutical Industries Ltd
28. Pfizer Ltd
29. Assam Carbon Ltd.
30. India Carbon Ltd

# 9

# Environmental Accounting: Its Nature and Significance in the Context of Corporate Information Disclosure in North-Eastern Region of India

**Bhaskarjyoti Bora & Jiban Upadhyaya**

**Abstract**: Protection of environment has become very essential to protect the civilization itself. A cohesive effort from each and every section of the society at global level can really make difference in the effort of protection of environment. As such, the corporate world also has to play its due role in this regard. The paper focuses on the nature and significance of environmental accounting *vis-à-vis* the corporate information disclosure in India. A total of 25 organizations are taken as sample which covers environmentally sensitive companies from areas such as paper mills, oil, iron and steel, cement and soft drink among others. It is found that 13 out of 25 such companies do not disclose environmental information in their annual report. Statutory provisions making it mandatory to include environmental information in the annual report of the corporate world can be of great use in ensuring corporate responsibility towards environment to a certain extent. Other measures may be devising appropriate accounting standards to guide the companies in this regard which will also ensure comparability of the environmental reporting by these companies.

Responsibility towards environment has become one of the most crucial areas of social responsibility. The concern for environmental degradation has witnessed a rising trend in the recent years. It is a worldwide phenomenon. It spoils human health, reduces economic productivity and leads to loss of amenities.

A careful assessment of the benefits and costs of environmental damages is necessary to find the safe limit of environmental degradation and the required level of development. But unless proper accounting work is done either by the individual firm or by the Government itself, it cannot be determined that both has been fulfilling their responsibilities towards the environment. Therefore, the need of environmental accounting has emerged.

Environmental Accounting is a process of economically recognizing the exhaustion of natural goods and services, analyzing the benefits rendered by the environment to a corporate citizen and the cost of benefits to the environment by the corporate citizen.

## Methodology

A corporate citizen utilizes both economic and natural (free) resources. Conventional accounting incorporates economic resources and ignores natural resources available free of cost. Environmental accounting is a rational attempt to value natural resources before incorporation for ascertaining the real profitability of the corporate citizen. In other words, environmental accounting envisages cost-benefit analysis from the point of view of both the corporate citizen and the environment.

## Environmental Budget

Environmental budget is allocation for environmental activities. It is the responsibility of the management to check whether such amount is spent on such activities.

## Profit and Loss Account

All revenue expenses incurred for the protection of environment have to be debited to the Profit and Loss account.

## Balance Sheet

All natural resources exhausted by the corporate entity are to be shown as asset in the Environmental Balance Sheet and the corporate entity is liable to the society for the effective utilization of natural resources without any adverse effect to the society. All capital expenditure incurred by the organization should be shown in the Balance sheet.

## Cost Benefit analysis

Benefits derived by the corporate citizen from the environment are:

1. Air
2. Water
3. Sunlight
4. Sand and clay
5. Oil
6. Minerals

7. Coal

Activities of corporate citizen which cost the environment

1. Ground water loss
2. Destruction of forest
3. Soil erosion
4. Air pollution
5. Water pollution
6. Loss of ozone layer
7. Acid rain

Environment imposes the following for indifferent attitude of corporate citizen

1. Extreme climatic condition
2. Famine and epidemics
3. Flood and drought
4. Natural fire accident
5. Human health hazard

Acts of corporate citizen, which benefit the environment

1. River purification system
2. Social forestry
3. Greening barren land
4. Installation of effluent treatment plant
5. Setting up of system of dust extraction

From the above, one can realize the dire need for and importance of environmental accounting.

## Corporate Environmental Accounting

At its simplest, corporate environmental accounting is about making environment related costs more transparent within corporate accounting system and reports. One of the major distinction within the field is whether the primary focus is to report environment related costs within internal management accounts, or external financial accounts or other public reports.

The benefit of undertaking a corporate environmental accounting initiative is that the identification and greater awareness of environment related costs often provides the opportunity to find ways to reduce or avoid these costs, while also improving environmental performance.

With the pressure on business to improve environmental performance, corporate environmental accounting can provide a valuable tool that enables business to respond to environmental challenges while retaining a focus on bottom -line imperatives.

The focus on the corporate or business entity makes corporate environmental accounting different to the environmental accounting undertaken by organizations, such as the Australian Bureau of Statistics, which attempt to develop monitors and physical statistics on the state of environmental and nature resources assets at the regional or national level.

Corporate environmental accounting is an emerging and dynamic field. Internationally the United Nations Division for Sustainable Development, national governments, professional accounting bodies and leading companies are undertaking a range of corporate environmental accounting initiatives. Most of these initiatives have to date looked at the area of Environmental Management Accounting.

Environmental Management Accounting has a focus on providing the management of an organization with better information on the actual private environmental costs already being incurred by the entity. Other directions being taken with corporate environmental accounting place greater emphasis on the external reporting of environmental expenditures and estimating the external environmental costs not recognized by the entity (external cost accounting). With external cost accounting, the estimation of external cost can be used to determine the profit that would remain if a provision or expenditure had been made to restore or avoid the external environmental impacts.

As already noted, corporate environmental accounting is an emerging and dynamic field that can be considered work-in- process. As a result, it is important to remember that the different streams of work that have greater or lesser emphasis on internal or external reporting, or private or external costs, are not mutually exclusive. Indeed corporate environmental accounting can also be closely linked to other corporate environmental management initiatives. In particular, corporate environmental accounting can be closely linked to the development or use of an Environmental Management System (EMS), or producing a corporate sustainability report. Determining a better understanding of environment related cost clearly requires a better understanding of the physical environmental impacts and performance of an organization, and this is often achieved through the development of an EMS or corporate sustainability report.

## Environmental Accounting - Practices

In many countries, the disclosure of environmental information has been mandatory. Companies, all over the world, have also started reporting on the matter voluntarily, but it is found that these disclosures do not provide sufficient ground for celebration. One needs to go deeper and examine the silence in those successful stories in order to understand the motives of such disclosures. A recent study by D.M. Patten (2002) which was published in the journal "Accounting organization and society" reports a significant negative relation between environmental performance and related disclosure in annual report. The findings support the argument that companies with worst environmental performance records provide most extensive environmental disclosure.

In the wake of growing legal and social pressures many companies in India have also made attempts to disclose their concern for environment in the annual report or by some other media, like environmental statements.

With the pressure on business to improve environmental performance, corporate environmental accounting can provide a valuable tool that enables business to respond to environmental challenges while retaining a focus on bottom-line imperatives.

## Recent Developments

The UN Statistical Office (UNSO designed a system of integrated environmental and Economic accounting (SEEA). Under SEEA all assets have been divided into three categories.

(i) Produced Assets

(ii) Non produced Assets.

(iii) Other Non produced Environmental assets required to be mentioned in SNA (System of National Accounts) for SEEA; the following are further required to be disclosed separately under SEEA.

1. Depletion of other non produced environmental assets,
2. Degradation of produced assets not reflected in the market value,
3. Degradation of other non produced assets, and
4. Other accumulation of produced and non produced

assets with additional separate disclosure of accumulation in other non produced environmental assets have been shifted to a section prior to consumption of fixed capital after degradation on non produced assets reflected in market value of assets under SNA for SEEA.

With the help of information available under SNA for SEEA, Assets accounts and balances are prepared.

As far as SEEA's model is concerned, it's particularly focused on National level accounting. The scope of environmental accounting is very wide. It includes corporate level, national level and international level.

## Issues

The major issues and challenges before the accountants are as follows-

1. How cost, revenues, depreciation and values of natural resources should be accounted for in the books of accounts in the organization?
2. What criteria should be evolved to assign monetary value to environmental changes?
3. How to depreciate an environmental asset?
4. How can one assess the impact of business organization on the environment?
5. How to estimate the remaining natural resources?
6. How can one measure the extent of damages suffered by the environment because of the activities of a corporate entity?
7. How can one compute the cost of benefits to the corporate entity and the cost of damages to the environment?

## How to Account?

How environmental accounting is being done varies in a number of respects, notably the magnitude of the investment required, the objectivity of the data, the ability to compare different kinds of environmental impacts, and kinds of policy purposes to which they may be applied. Some of the methods currently in use are Natural Resource Accounts, Emission Accounting, Desegregation of Conventional National Accounts and Green GDP.

## Towards Consensus on Method

Environmental accounting would receive a substantial boost if an international consensus could be reached in it on methodology. The UN statistics Department has coordinated some of the ongoing efforts towards this end since the 1980's. In 1993, the UN published the System of Integrated Economic and Environmental Accounting (SEEA) as an annex to the 1993 revisions of the SNA. SEEA is structured as a series of methodological options, which include most of the different accounting activities described above; users choose the options most appropriate to their needs.

No consensus exists on the various methods that the UN recommended. In fact, SEEA is now undergoing revision by the so-called London Group comprised primarily of national income accountants and statistician from OECD countries. The group's work will be an important step toward consensus on accounting methods, but the process will be lengthy. Development of the conventional SNA took some forty years.

## Towards Widespread Use

A number of steps can be taken now towards the goal of ensuring that environmental accounting is well established as the SNA. First, information must circulate freely about existing environmental accounts and how they are contributing to economic and environmental policy. Ongoing work needs to be identified and systematically reviewed and analyzed to learn lessons, which may form the design and implementation of future accounting activities. The Green Accounting Initiative of the world Conservation Union has embarked on this effort, and a number of other organizations are calling for similar activities.

Second, development of a core of internationally standardized methods will contribute to willingness to adopt environmental accounting. Experts in the field- including economists, environmentalists, academics, and others outside of the national statistical offices - should take a proactive role in tracking the work of the London Group and insist that the standard- setting process involves participants representing a spectrum of viewpoints, countries and interested stakeholders. An opportunity exists for research institutes to take a lead in identifying the financial resources needed to facilitate a broader standard setting process, and to illicit a full range of voices to build a consensus on methodology.

Finally, and perhaps most importantly, the more countries institutionalize construction of environmental accounts, the greater the momentum for more for the same.

Their construction will require sustained institutional and financial commitment to ensure that the investment lasts long enough to yield results. But the experiences of Norway, Namibia and the Philippines show that such a commitment can pay off: it is a commitment that more countries around the world need to make.

## Nature and Extent of Environmental Information Disclosure in North Eastern Region of India

The disclosure of Environment Information (EI) is a way through which a company can demonstrate its concern for environment. The information is disclosed on several issues and matters like pollution control, energy conservation, waste management, safety measures, environmental hazards and accidents, production research etc.

There are 25 companies selected for detailed study which are present in the north-eastern region of India. All these companies are environmentally sensitive companies although the level of sensitiveness may vary. The areas covered are paper mills, oil, iron and steel, electronic, cement, soft drink, biscuits, pipes and tubes. Hence, the study presents a fair representation of the environmentally sensitive population of organisation. Moreover, the sample represents the type of companies that are existent in the north-east region of India. As such, the study is expected to be useful in formulating a well thought out policy in this regard.

Table 9.1 shows the pattern and type of Environmental Information disclosure in selected companies and PSUs. Out of these companies two are paper mills, three are oil companies, three are iron and steel companies, four are electronic companies, four are cements companies, three are soft drink companies, three are biscuit factories and three are pipes and tubes companies in the North Eastern Region of India.

**Table 9.1**
**Form of EI Disclosure Adopted by Sample Companies**

| Type/Nature of Disclosure | No. of Companies |
|---|---|
| Descriptive type | 9 |
| Pictorial type | 2 |
| Quantitative type | Nil |
| Financial type | 1 |
| Graphical type | Nil |
| Not disclosed | 13 |
| Total | 25 |

Table 9.1 shows that out of 25 organizations taken into consideration for this study, 13 organizations do not have any concern for EI disclosure. Out of the organizations disclosing this information, 9 disclosures are of descriptive type covering a space from ¼ of a page to 1 page only. Two of the organizations present this information pictorially along with a brief note of description. Graphical and quantitative type information is not furnished or published by any of the concerns.

One company, namely Oil India Ltd., headquartered at Duliajan, Assam publishes not only descriptive information but also some sort of financial information in regard to environment. Oil India Ltd., which is a leading public sector oil company in the country, is the only company which incorporates environmental information in its Social Accounts' statements presented in the form of Additional Statements in the Annual Report.

**Table 9.2**
**Different aspects of EI Disclosure by Sample Companies**

| Aspects of Disclosure | No. of Companies |
|---|---|
| Pollution control | Ten companies |
| Environmental Hazards | Five companies |
| Protection of Surrounding | Almost all the companies |
| Energy conservation | Almost all the companies |
| Raw Material conservation | Three companies |
| Wastage management scientific | Six companies |
| water management and disposal etc. | Four companies |
| Two or three aspects on Multiple aspects together | |

Table 9.2 above shows the nature and issues of disclosure by the sample companies. From the table, it can be observed that information in respect of energy conservation is published

by almost all companies since it is statutorily required under section 217(1) (e) of the Companies Act, 1956. Among other aspects of disclosure, pollution control secures the first place followed by waste management water management disposal etc., environmental hazards and raw material conservation. One interesting point to be noted here is that almost all the organizations including PSUs publish some sort of declaration and description in regard to their commitment towards protection of surrounding.

A study of the annual reports in respect of 'Energy' revealed that almost all the companies disclosed the qualitative and financial information in detail in respect of various issues like energy conservation, technology absorption and foreign exchange inflows and outflows. The extent of disclosures covered half of a page to two pages. On the contrary, on other environmental matters, the extent of disclosure did not exceed even one-quarter of a page and in most cases the information were in one or two sentences. Except Oil India Ltd., none of the companies has so far taken up any comprehensive policy in regard to the accounting treatment of environment issues.

## Form of Disclosure

"Form of disclosure" means whether the information disclosed is quantitative, qualitative, analytical, financial, pictorial or graphical. Some of the sample companies (a very few) have been adopting one or more forms of disclosure like OIL, ONGC and the IOC. Majority of the companies disclosing EI adopted descriptive form of general statements (in Director's Report) as follows:

(a) Your company continued to maintain excellent safety records.

(b) Your company has continuous efforts in reducing the waste load discharge from the effluent treatment plant.

(c) Your company is committed to provide safe working conditions to the employees and to maintain ecological balance and protection of the environment in its operational activities. For planning, monitoring, auditing, developing environment indices and keeping a liaison with external agencies and the Ministry of 'Environment and Forest', a corporate set up for Safety and Environment Management (SEM) exists.

(d) Special emphasis on pollution control and safety measures have been undertaken to prevent environmental degradation and to avoid unsafe acts and practices for the prevention of accidents. Various activities undertaken during the year include safety and environment trainings, safety audit and inspections, accident data analysis, hazard and risk analysis, periodical medical examination of employees, tree plantation and green belt development.

(e) Your corporation is committed to environmental protection and maintaining the ecological balance. All sub-units fully meet the prescribed standards and sustained efforts are being made to further improve their performance in this area by incorporating cleaner state of the art technologies.

(f) During the year under review, through effective monitoring and co-ordination, substantial abetment of pollution from the company's various operations was achieved.

Except these types of descriptive statements in the Directors Report, majority of the companies don't have any mention in regard to environmental issues except three or four organizations which publish certain pictorial information. The Oil India Ltd., along with the descriptive/qualitative statements incorporate these information in social Income Statement and Social Balance

Sheet. The expenditure in "Environmental improvement" is shown as Social Benefits to Community and investment in Energy conservation along with expenditures is shown as 'Social Benefits to Society', both of which are a part of Social Income Statement in Annexure.

## Observation and Conclusion

1. Environmental Information (EI) disclosure by majority of the companies in the North Eastern Region of India like the rest of the country is confined only up to the making of certain generalized statements with reference to protection of environment, pollution control, conservation of energy and raw materials. Qualitative and pictorial types of disclosure are the two widely used forms and financial information concerning environment is totally absent in the annual reports. Moreover, the quality of the disclosed information is of so poor standard quality that users of these information cannot have a 'decision-feedback' based on these.

2. Business entities, especially Industrial houses with manufacturing plants are not much aware of the pros and cons of 'Environmental Information' disclosure through 'Environmental Accounting' so far. Under this circumstance, the concerned authorities in charge of Corporate Governance should make it mandatory for the companies to strictly go for maintaining, regulating and monitoring environmental standards laid down under various Environmental Acts and Rules like 'The Water (Prevention and Control of Pollution) Act, 1974, The Air (Prevention and Control of Pollution) Act, 1981, The Environment Protection Act. 1986, the Public Insurance Act, 1991. Besides, these, the companies, on their own part, can go for fiscal incentives in the form

of exemption from income tax, depreciation allowance, investment allowance, exemption from tax on capital gain etc. by adopting measures that encourage control of pollution and preservation of environment.

3. The national income accounting should be supplemented with an additional report showing 'Environmentally Adjusted Net National Product' sector-wise. There must be time bound reporting system on environmental issues of all major economic activities.

4. Protection and improvement of environmental resources is a must for sustained development of all including the business entities. So it should not be considered only a matter of social responsibility, but a part of day-to-day business operation to preserve and improve the environment.

   There being no direct relationship between environmental expenditure and revenue, business entities are least bothered to incur such expenditures. Hence there is a need for making statutory provisions: (a) for mandatory disclosure of environmental protection measures adopted through annual plan, and (b) to examine by proper authority whether the measures are in proportion to the damage caused to the environment.

5. The Indian Companies Act should be amended suitably requiring the companies for full disclosure of environmental information regarding effluents, emissions, pollution level, damage to agriculture and community health etc. and the steps taken on these issues.

Another provision may be added to the Companies Act requiring the companies to conduct Environmental Audit and to include the report thereof in the Board of Directors' Report and to the Ministry of Environment and Forests. A proforma of the Audit Report may be prepared in this regard in consultation with the expert group. Besides these, an Accounting Standard on the disclosure of environmental information may be formulated and the Institute of Chartered Accountants of India may be requested to do the needful in this respect.

## REFERENCES

1. Bojom Jan, Major Karl-Goran and Unemo Lena, 1990, *Environment and Development, An Economic Approach*, Kluwer Academic Publisher, London.
2. Centre for Environmental Education, (North East) *Reading Materials for Workshops on Industry and Environment*: 28 January, 1994.
3. Field, Barry C., 1994, *Environmental Economics. An Introduction*, McGraw Hill International Edition.
4. Pachauri R. K., Economic Cost of Eco-damage. *The Economic Times*, 14 December, 1996, Calcutta.
5. Repetto, Robert, William Magrath, Michael wells, Christine Beer and Fabrizio Rossini, 1989. *Wasting Assets: Natural Resources in the National 66 Accounts*: Washington D.C. World Resource Institute.

# 10

# Financial Inclusion - An Experimental Study over Kukurmara Village of Kamrup District

SUJIT SIKIDAR & PURNASHREE DAS

Financial Inclusion is the delivery of financial services at affordable cost to vast sections of disadvantaged and low-income groups. Unrestrained access to public goods and services is the sine qua non of an open and efficient society. The term gained importance from the beginning of 21$^{st}$ century, and is a result of findings about financial exclusion and its direct correlation to poverty.

The Committee of Financial Inclusion (the Rangarajan Committee) has defined 'financial inclusion is the process of ensuring access to financial services and timely and adequate credit when needed by vulnerable groups such as weaker sections and low income groups at an affordable cost.' Financial inclusion is, thus, an all embracing strategy encompassing several issues such as:

(a) Opening a bank account for those who so far remain excluded and bringing banking to unbanked areas;

(b) Provide access to credit;

(c) Provide affordable insurance and remittance facilities;

(d) Credit counseling and financial education.

The Great Britain was one of the first countries of the world to realise the significance of financial inclusion. As a result, it brought out a report entitled: ***Promoting Financial Inclusion***, which was part of the ***2004 pre-budget report***. A financial inclusion fund of *120 million pounds* and a task force was launched on 21 February, 2005.

In India, a step towards the end was set in with bank nationalisation. which pushed up domestic savings in the household sector from 9.5% of GDP in 1070-71 to 22.6% of GDP in 2008-09. Formally, the term financial inclusion first featured in 2005, when it was introduced from a pilot project in the Union Territory of Pondicherry by K.C.Chakraborty, the then Chairman of Indian Bank. Mangalam village became the first village of the country where all households were provided banking facilities.

In its platinum jubilee year, the RBI's vision is to connect every Indian to the country's banking system. In tune with this objective, it has permitted commercial banks to make provisions for 'no-frills' account as well as to use the services of NGOs/SHGs, micro-finance institutions and other civil society organizations as intermediaries for providing financial and banking services from January, 2006. Moreover, it has also asked the commercial banks in different regions to start a 100% financial inclusion campaign on a pilot basis as a result of which states or U.T.s like Puducherry, Himachal Pradesh and Kerala have already announced 100% financial inclusion in all their districts.

But despite its heightened focus on financial inclusion, Indian banks still somewhat failed to bring the under and unbanked into the mainstream banking fold. India has, in 2010, the second highest number of financially excluded households in the world.

The extent of Financial Exclusion in India has been severe. According to the first-ever Index of Financial Inclusion to find out the extent of reach of banking services among 100 countries, India has been ranked 50. After 40 years of nationalization of banks, over 60% of the country's population does not receive banking services and nearly 90% do not have credit access.

The picture of the NE region is far more dismal. According to statistics, the North East, Eastern and Central regions contain most of the financially excluded population. Out of 100 people only 59 have been brought under the mainstream banking network till August, 2010. Whereas, in the NE region, only 34 out of 100 citizens have been brought under the formal banking network.

According to a McKinsey report in March 2010, it was estimated that more than 65% of the population has limited or no access to a bank, whereas one out of two persons owns a mobile phone or a TV. Here 10,000 people share one bank branch and ATM, but collectively own 5,100 mobile phones.

Some pertinent facts about banking operation are indicated below as in March 2010:

| | 2000 | 2009 |
|---|---|---|
| No. of ATMs | 3,000 | 44,000 |
| No. of mobile banking users | 1 lakh | 5 crores |
| No. of Internet banking users | 5 lakhs | 2.2 crores |
| No. of Internet users | 50 lakhs | 8.1 crores |

(Source: The Economic Times dated 21 September, 2010)

Financial Exclusion is not only peculiar in India, rather it has been prevailing in other developed economies of the world as well. In Sweden, 2% of the adult population does not have a bank account, whereas in India 41% of the population does not have a bank account. It was roughly estimated that 5% of the population of the USA does not have bank accounts.

The term Financial Inclusion was coined when the direct correlation between financial exclusion and poverty was discovered. Thus, to have a better picture of what financial inclusion is, we ought to understand fully the meaning of financial exclusion first, which has been discussed hereunder.

## Financial Exclusion

The *Millennium Development Goals* (MDG) to be achieved by 2015 embraced achieving economic growth for all. It witnessed a social divide between those who are enjoying the fruits of development and those who are left outside the ambit, i.e. , those who are excluded. Hence, came the programme of inclusive growth. Similarly in the area of financial services sector, it is noticed that a sizeable portion of our total population are outside the mainstream of banking operation. Similar is the scenario of insurance sector. Thus, the agenda was raised for financial inclusion as a mandate to bring all those who are excluded to be brought within the mainland of banking services.

The financially excluded sections largely comprise marginal and landless farmers, unorganised sector enterprises and their employees, ethnic minorities, senior citizens, women, urban slum dwellers and laborers engaged in different activities like construction work, fruits vending, vegetables vending, etc. While recognising the huge extent of financial exclusion, the RBI Report entitled: Trend and Progress of Banking in India 2009-10, released on November 8, 2010, has attributed the reason for financial exclusion not as a deliberate design, but their ***lack of necessary input*** to be a part of it.

After considering the theoretical framework of financial exclusion, we now seek to examine the reasons for such exclusion.

## Reasons for Exclusion

The reasons for exclusion have been analyzed hereunder:

1. **Self exclusion:** It has been gathered from an NSSO Report, 2009 that there are around 80 million urban poor that lack access to basic banking services - savings account, credit facility, remittances and payment services, financial advisory services and the like.
2. **Stipulated Conditions:** Urban financial exclusion has been noticed owing to stiff conditions, loss of wage earnings for visiting a bank branch, negative experience, perceived absence of benefit.
3. **Pricing:** Banks and financial institutions levy penalty on accounts not maintaining minimum balance and on non-operative accounts. Banks have to incur huge cost also on these matters.
4. **Establishing identity proof:** Inability to fulfil KYC norma; KYC non-compliance occurs in the following cases.
5. Migration from the same state or other states;
6. Living in ghettos and groups (4-5 individuals living in one room) with no independent references.
7. People employed in unorganized sector.
8. **Loss of wage earning:** Persons in unorganized sector, in wage related jobs cannot visit the bank branch and cannot get access to banking services. For them technology savior arrangements would be most appropriate. Time involved in banking activities means

time lost in earning livelihood. Doorstep banking on a periodic basis can be a panacea and at the same bring earnings to the productive use of national economy.

The All India Rural Credit Survey in 1954 indicated that the credit needs of the financially excluded (FE) households are met by informal, non-institutional sources, unorganised agencies and private money lenders. The formal institutional sources could not penetrate and outreach the excluded segment of the society. FE varies from state to state in terms of occupation, landholding and other socio-economic characteristics.

Having considered the nature and extent of financial exclusion, it may be said that what is urgently needed is the use of sophisticated technology as used in banks with a view to connecting men-machine-money –method together into a comprehensive unit. Hence, the technologies useful for the purpose are discussed hereunder.

## Technologies Needed to Achieve Inclusion

The RBI's approach to Financial inclusion aims at 'connecting people' with the banking system and not just opening accounts. This includes meeting the small credit needs of the people, giving them access to the payments system and providing remittance facilities. High and sophisticated use of technological devices have been implemented in this regard which have been discussed hereunder:

i) Offer a basic banking **'no-frills'** account with low or zero minimum balances and minimum charges.

ii) The 'Know Your Customer' (KYC) procedure for opening accounts was simplified for those accounts with balances not exceeding Rs 50,000 and credits thereto not exceeding Rs.1, 00, 000 in a year.

iii) Use of Business Correspondents (BC) supported by service provider with on line connectivity linked with the server of the concerned bank.

iv) Extension counters and mobile banking services.

v) Biometrics and hand held collection devices.

vi) Smart cards for opening bank accounts with biometric identification which would help the customers get banking services near their doorstep.

vii) The Unique Identification Authority of India (UIDAI) and National Payment Council of India (NPCI) are in a position to solve the problem arising from KYC. UIDAI has two core objectives; to provide a unique ID to every Indian citizen on the basis of biometrics and to authenticate any citizen based on this UID.

viii) The NPCI has been mandated with creating the financial infrastructure on several major projects; managing the National Financial Switch (NFS) for domestic ATMs; creating a National Automated Clearing House (NACH) System; a switch for mobile to mobile payments called India Pay Mobile Switch; creating an infrastructure to enable UID to UID micro payments.

ix) The aim is to link the UID to a bank account and a mobile number in a central database. Once this mapping is done, a payment can be initiated through any bank or mobile phone. This would enable a Business Correspondent (BC) to identify the account holder and he would route the transaction to the beneficiary's UID or mobile number; and the money will be automatically credited to the bank account linked to that UID. UID based payment facility coupled with mobile payments switch is going to be a major toolkit for achieving financial inclusion.

## PAYMENT SYSTEM UNDER POST UID

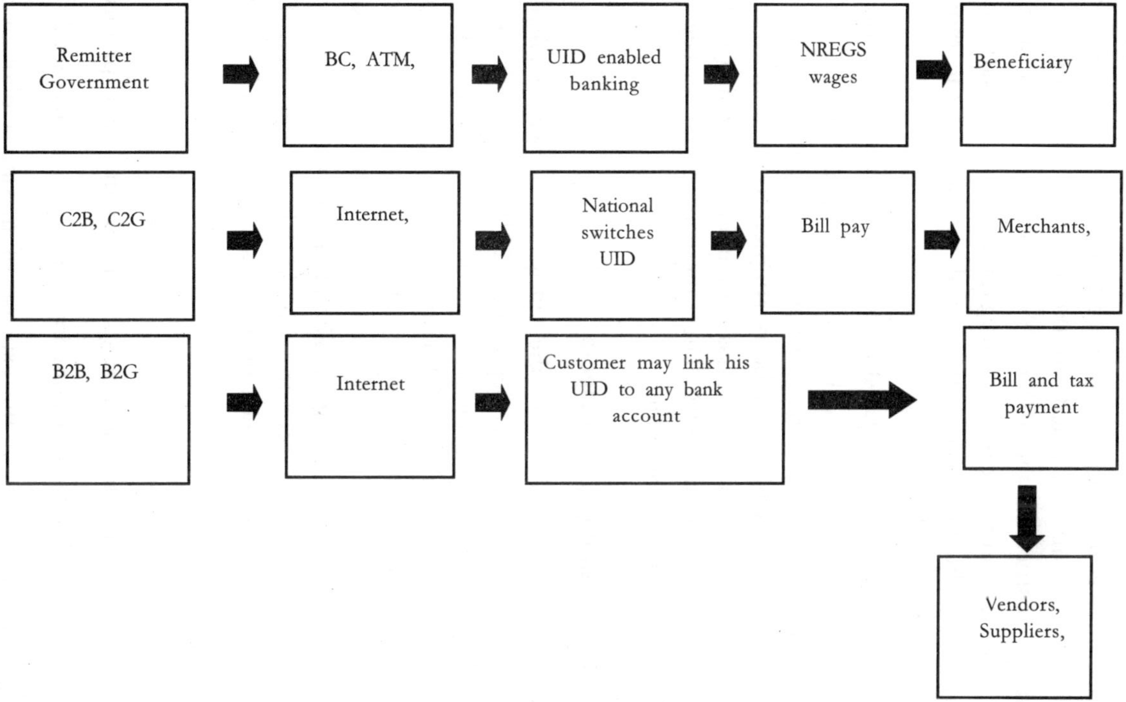


(**Source**: Rana Kapoor, Financial Inclusion: Game changer for urban renewal, The Economic Times dated 20 September, 2010.)

Having considered the theoretical framework of financial inclusion, we may now conveniently consider the outcomes of the field survey carried on the village of Kukurmara in Kamrup District on the 10th of November, 2010, and another field survey carried on the unorganized urban construction workers in the Guwahati city carried throughout the month of October, 2010.

Outcome of Field Survey Conducted In Kukurmara Village, Kamrup District

A survey was conducted by the present paper writers jointly on the 10th of November, 2010 in the Kukurmara village of Kamrup District which has been adopted as a model village for financial inclusion by the Assam Gramin Vikas Bank(AGVB) under the aegis of the RBI. The outcome of our survey has been deliberated hereunder.

## Coverage among the villagers

The survey revealed that the village has a total population of 552 households. Up to September, 2010, the bank's efforts have yielded 88.59% financial inclusion in the village. To be more precise, a total of 489 families have been financially included, whereas only 63 families(11.41%) have been excluded from the purview of banking services. By financial inclusion it is meant the number of families(at least one person from each family) having account with AGVB, Kukurmara. The survey also revealed that such financial exclusion could be mainly attributed to:

- Illiteracy,
- Shyness of the villagers to come to the Bank premises,
- Lack of substantial income to open an account,
- Inability to meet the expense of making a photograph,
- Inability to comply with KYC norms.

Even though the bank offers 'no-frills' account, the excluded population has not shown much eagerness to open accounts with the Bank. However, for the purpose of making a photograph, a digital camera was provided to the Local Gaon Panchayat, but still it could not be utilised for the purpose.

The Bank is currently pursuing the Business Facilitator(BF) Model, whereby the BF acts as middleman for mobilising deposits and opening accounts for the villagers who are relieved from the duty to personally come to the Bank branch for opening accounts or depositing money. Thus, their valuable time and conveyance cost is saved. However, the RBI has directed all the banks to adopt the Business Correspondent(BC) model and the AGVB hopes to get the BC model streamlined by 2012 which would go a long way in mobilising more resources and extending more credit services to the village of Kukurmara, thereby guaranteeing it 100% financial inclusion in the near future.

## Extension of Credit Facilities:

The credit delivery system adopted by AGVB as observed by the present researchers has been deliberated hereunder. The AGVB has done an excellent work in the village by extending credit facilities to around 400 families, constituting approximately 72% percent of the population. The different types of credit facilities offered by the bank are:

a. **Loans under SGRY:** 25 Self Help Groups(SHGs) have been identified and given credit under the Swarojgar Gramin Rojgar Yojana(SGRY) whereby Rs10000-20000 is initially given to them as direct loan, and after its repayment another sum of Rs 25,000 is given as credit. Out of this, Rs 10,000 is a subsidy on which no interest is also required to be paid. It is basically a Revolving Fund loan where interest is charged @8.5% p.a. on the balance Rs 15000.

b. **Piggery Loan:** A total number of 13 persons have been given loans for raising piggery which is quite an attractive business in the locality. An amount of Rs20000 is given to each person getting credit under this scheme.

c. **Weaving Activity Loan:** 3 SHG groups have been identified and given credit under this scheme of DRDA whereby an amount of Rs 2,50,000 is released in a span of 3 years. Here, again, Rs.1,25,000 is subsidy.

   The village essentially being a Scheduled Caste village, is eligible for 50% subsidy for all forms of financial accommodations.

d. **General Credit Card (AGVBGCC):** Such credit cards have been distributed to 42 people in the said village. These cards have been issued under the Government of India's instruction to the Bank.

   The landless farmers or those villagers who do not have any property to keep as mortgage so as to obtain loans, qualify for this scheme of the AGVB, whereby up to Rs 25,000 credit limit is given to the assisted persons on no security basis.

e. **Kisan Credit Cards:** 8 Kisan Credit Cards have been distributed till date by the bank, whereby a total of Rs 1,48,800 has been disbursed.

f. **Retail Trade Loans:** Such loans have been given for starting retail shops, etc. to a total of 7 persons amounting to a total of Rs 40,000.

g. **Loans to Joint Liability Groups(JLGs):** Such loans have been given to 3 groups for raising Piggery. A total of Rs 3,00,000 have been provided under this scheme.

h. **Overdraft:** The overdraft facility has been given against 'no-frills' account also whereby the customers enjoy a zero balance account. An overdraft of Rs 500 has been given to 11 persons each for miscellaneous small activities. This is, indeed, an innovative credit arrangement by the Bank.

i. **Handloom Loan:** 1 Handloom Weaver Group has been identified consiting of 5 weavers and an assistance of Rs 1,00,000 has been extended without any form of security. However, this loan does not qualify for any subsidy.

We have also visited the Ziakur village under the same survey. It may be mentioned here that Ziakur village has also been adopted by the AGVB. The Bank is also actively performing similar work in the Ziakur village, but not with so much success.

The level of financial inclusion achieved in Ziakur village is much less than that of Kukurmara village. In course of our survey, we met the officials of AGVB, including the Branch Manager Sri Bratajit Das who furnished us with all the relevant information necessary for our survey.

We are beholden to the people in the branch of the AGVB. It has also been revealed during our survey that Ziakur village is also under the coverage of the AGVB , Kukurmara Branch.

We, therefore, find that if the money circulated among the income earners in the unorganised sector can be brought into the proximity of financial sector, then:

1. the income can be banked;
2. regular interest income could be fetched to the workers;
3. the money can be converted into white or made transparent; and the same can be put to productive use in the banking sector.

## CONCLUSION

It is apparent from our discussion that the RBI as well as the banks under its purview have fully appreciated the fact that financial inclusion is a win-win opportunity for the poor, for the banks and for the nation as well. And in tune with this, the RBI has made conscious attempts to redress the problem in the form of various technological moves and at the same time encouraging and supporting the banks in their financial inclusion endeavours by way of information dissemination, sharing of best practices and regulatory incentives.

## REFERENCES


1. R.Kamath, A.Mukherji, M.Sandstorm, Accessing Institutional Finance: A demand side story for rural India, *Economic and Political Weekly*, Vol XLV No.37, Sept 11, 2010, Mumbai, pp 56-58.
2. Rana Kapoor, Financial Inclusion: Game changer for urban renewal, *The Economic Times* dated 20 September, 2010.
3. Speech by Dr. Duvvuri Subbarao, Governor, Reserve Bank of India at the Bankers' Club in Kolkata on December 9, 2009.
4. Prabhakar Kulkarni, *Compulsory dedication for financial inclusion*.
5. Rajesh Shukla, Desultory financial inclusion drive, *The Economic Times* dated 1 November, 2010.

# 11

# Internet Banking in India: Challenges and Opportunities

**Elangbam Nixon Singh**

**Abstract**: Internet banking has gained wide acceptance internationally and seems to be fast catching up in India with more and more banks entering the fray. Online banking using internet was pioneered by Security First Network Bank in October 1995. In India, ICICI bank and Citibank can lay claim to be the first players to offer internet banking in 1996. Other banks such as HDFC bank, IndusInd and Times Bank followed and usage picked up 1999 onwards with increased PC penetration and arrival of ISPs. The present paper tries to evaluate the evolution of internet-banking and its existing scenario in India. An attempt has also been made to analyse the challenges and opportunities of Internet Banking in India.

***Key Words:** online banking, risks, customer service*

Internet banking has gained wide acceptance internationally and seems to be fast catching up in India with more and more banks entering the fray. With cybercafés and kiosks springing up in different cities and even in small towns, access to the Net is going to be easy. Internet banking (also referred to as e-banking) is the latest in this series of technological wonders in the recent past involving use of internet for delivery of banking products and services.

The term internet banking or e-banking are used as supplement. E-banking is the one of the major part of e-financing. Hertzum *et al* (2004) defined e-banking as web-based Banking. However, more comprehensive and well-established definition is given by the United Nations Conference on Trade and Development (UNCTAD). This definition covers almost all areas of E-Banking.

Internet banking refers to the deployment over the Internet of retail and wholesale banking services. It involves individual and corporate clients, and includes bank transfers, payments and settlements, documentary collections and credits, corporate and household lending, card business and some others (UNCTAD, 2002).

## Literature review

Since the late 1990s E-Banking has developed from virtual insignificance to tens of millions of users worldwide (OECD, 2001). For e-banking users, it facilitates current information and 24-hours-a-day access to banking services. The main purpose served by e-banks are transferring money among one's own accounts, paying different bills, and checking account balances. Loans, brokering, share trading, service bundling, and a host of other financial services are being added to these primary services (Dewan & Seidmann, 2001).

E-Banking is widely used in, among other places, the Nordic countries. In 2001, E-Banking was used by more than 25% of the population in Norway, Sweden, and Finland, and by 15% of the population in Denmark (OECD, 2001). In 2004, E-Banking usage in Denmark had grown to 45% (Statistics Denmark, 2004). Jeevan (2000) notes that with rigid controls giving way to deregulation, banks are gearing up their communications infrastructure to obtain a competitive edge from E-Banking, which is fast becoming a reality in India. Nair (1999)[8] points out that E-Banking is fast becoming a strategic necessity for most commercial banks, as competition increases from private banks and NBFIs.

Furthermore, factor analysis results indicate that 'utility request', 'seçurity', 'utility transaction', 'ticket booking' and 'fund transfer' are major factors responsible for internet banking. Out of total respondents' more than 50 % agreed that internet banking is convenient and flexible ways of banking and it also has various transaction related benefits. Thus, Providing Internet banking is increasingly becoming a "need to have" than a "nice to have" service (Divya Singhal and V. Padhma-nabhan, 2008).

## Objectives

Internet banking has been shaking and shaping the financial sector worldwide. Thus it has become imperative to know the issue of internet banking in-depth: evolution, challenges and opportunities in India. Thus the objectives of the study are to

- To identify with the evolution of internet-banking.
- To assess the existing internet banking scenario in India and its challenges.
- To explore the opportunities of Internet Banking in India.

## Evolution of internet banking

Banks, generally, used to harness the technology to improve their products, services and efficiency. They have, over a long time, been using electronic and telecommunication networks for delivering a wide range of value added products and services. The delivery channels include direct dial – up connections, private networks, public networks etc and the devices include telephone, Personal Computers including the Automated Teller Machines, etc. With the popularity of PCs, easy and cheaper access to Internet and World Wide Web (WWW), Internet is increasingly used by banks as a channel for receiving instructions and delivering their products and services to their customers. This system of banking is generally known as Internet Banking, although the range of products and services offered by different banks vary widely both in their content and sophistication.

Broadly, the levels of banking services offered through INTERNET can be categorized in to three types:

(i) The Basic Level Service is the banks' websites which disseminate information on different products and services offered to customers and members of public in general. It may receive and reply to customers' queries through e-mail,

(ii) In the next level are Simple Transactional Websites which allow customers to submit their instructions, applications for different services, queries on their account balances, etc, but do not permit any fund-based transactions on their accounts,

(iii) The third level of Internet banking services are offered by Fully Transactional Websites which allow the customers to operate on their accounts for transfer of funds, payment of different bills, subscribing to other products of the bank and to transact purchase and sale of securities, etc.

The present format of internet is the outcome of US Department of Defence project ARPANet (Advanced Research Project Administration Network), developed in the late 1960s and early 1970s as an experiment in wide area networking. The major advantage of ARPANet was that the network would continue to operate even if a segment of it is lost or destroyed since its operation did not depend on operation of any single computer. Initially it was designed as a defence network, but over the years it was used predominantly in areas of scientific research and communication. It moved out of Pentagon's control and more autonomous networks from US and outside got connected to it in the 1980s. In 1986, the US National Science Foundation (NSF) established a national network based on ARPA protocol using commercial telephone lines for connectivity. The NSFNet was easy to get to by a much larger scientific community, commercial networks and general users and the number of host computers grew rapidly. Ultimately, NSFNet became the framework of today's Internet. Interestingly, ARPANet was officially decommissioned in 1990.

## The entry of Indian banks into internet banking

A number of banks have either adopted internet banking or are on the threshold of adopting it. Private and foreign banks have been the early adopters of e-banking in India while the public sector banks are also beginning to hold on to the competition. The banks started internet banking initially with simple functions such as getting information about interest rates, checking account balances and computing loan eligibility. Then the services were extended to online bill payment, transfer of funds between accounts and cash management services for corporate. Recently, banks have started to facilitate payment for e-commerce transactions by directly debiting bank accounts or through credit cards.

Online banking using internet was pioneered by Security First Network Bank in October 1995. In India, ICICI bank and Citibank can lay claim to be the first players to offer internet banking in 1996. Other banks such as HDFC bank, IndusInd and Times Bank followed and usage picked up 1999 onwards with increased PC penetration and arrival of ISPs (Rajiv Rai, 2010).

The Government of India enacted the Information Technology Act, 2000, generally known as IT Act, 2000, with effect from the October 17, 2000 to provide legal recognition to electronic transactions and other means of electronic commerce. RBI had set up Working Group on Internet Banking to examine different aspects of internet Banking. The group had focussed on three major areas of Internet banking viz. (i) technology and security issues, (ii) legal issues and (iii) regulatory and supervisory issues. The RBI had accepted the recommendations of the Working Group and accordingly issued guidelines on Internet banking in India for implementation by banks (Reserve Bank of India, 2001).

The ISP market has been in disarray, even though there has been a considerable popularity of internet in India. At present, there were around 150 operational ISPs in the country, after a period of market rationalisation, but, despite the large number of providers, 10% of the ISPs have 90% of the subscribers. In fact, 5% have 85%. The state-owned – BSNL and MTNL – are the only major players, holding first and second place in terms of Internet subscribers. Cybercafés have certainly been playing a major role in fuelling Internet development in India. About 30% of the total Internet subscriber base has broadband access. Even with this relatively high proportion, usage of broadband Internet in India has been particularly slow. The following (Table 1.1) takes a look at the wider Internet and e-services market as the country moves slowly towards the New Internet Economy.

Further conforming with the above data available on internet usage in India, it becomes pertinent to study a report published by the Internet and Mobile Association of India [IAMAI] and market research leader IMRB that has claimed that 71 million people have used internet in 2009 (IAMAI, 2010). E-banking is still a big challenge for India as internet access is a must for e-banking. Active users, those who use internet at least once

**Table 11.1**
**Internet Usage and Population Statistics in India**

| YEAR | Users | Population | % Usage | Usage Source |
|---|---|---|---|---|
| 1998 | 1,400,000 | 1,094,870,677 | 0.1 % | ITU |
| 1999 | 2,800,000 | 1,094,870,677 | 0.3 % | ITU |
| 2000 | 5,500,000 | 1,094,870,677 | 0.5 % | ITU |
| 2001 | 7,000,000 | 1,094,870,677 | 0.7 % | ITU |
| 2002 | 16,500,000 | 1,094,870,677 | 1.6 % | ITU |
| 2003 | 22,500,000 | 1,094,870,677 | 2.1 % | ITU |
| 2004 | 39,200,000 | 1,094,870,677 | 3.6 % | C.I. Almanac |
| 2005 | 50,600,000 | 1,112,225,812 | 4.5 % | C.I. Almanac |
| 2006 | 40,000,000 | 1,112,225,812 | 3.6 % | IAMAI |
| 2007 | 42,000,000 | 1,129,667,528 | 3.7 % | IWS |
| 2009 | 81,000,000 | 1,156,897,766 | 7.0 % | ITU |

**Source:** www.internetworldstats.com/asia/in.htm

a month according the international standards of reckoning, rose from 42 million in September 2008 to 52 million in September 2009 according to the study, registering a year on year growth of 19%. The 'claimed users' is an important category for understanding future trends in active user base.

This surge in number may be primarily due to the increased numbers of the users in the remote urban pockets (small metros and towns) and among lower socio-economic classes (SEC C, D &E). This development has been more striking this year as the combined usage of these geographies and classes have overtaken top cities and higher socio-economic classes in numbers. This finding clearly indicates that the Internet has reached to remote masses in urban India.

The reason for this should be attributed to innovative content delivery, better applications and its increased use for entertainment purposes, which comprises downloading music or videos, socializing through social networking sites and expressing one's own opinions and views through micro-blogging and user-generated content sites (Chart 11.1).

The report further states that Internet usage has gone up from 9.3 hrs/week to 15.7 hrs/week i.e. a steep 70% rise (Chart 11.2).

Numerous factors such as competitive cost, customer service, and demographic considerations – are motivating banks in India to evaluate their technology and assess their electronic commerce and e-banking strategies. Two main factors are important-customers wanting to be in control of their finances and banks trying to reduce cost. The challenge is to convince the bank customers that the savings from internet banking technology more than offset the costs and risks associated with conducting business in internet.

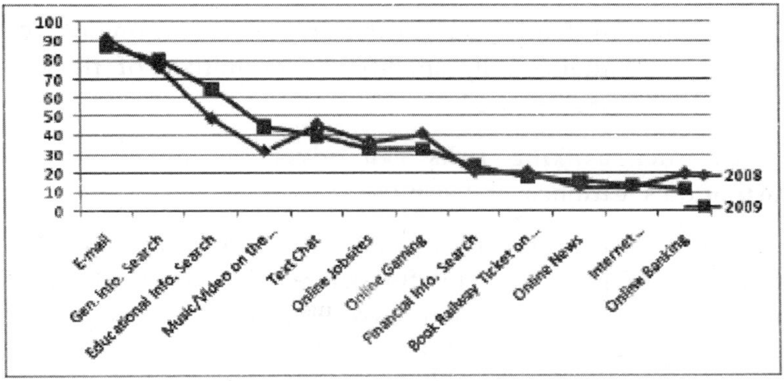


Source: IAMAI, 2010

**Chart 11.1: Purpose of Internet Access**

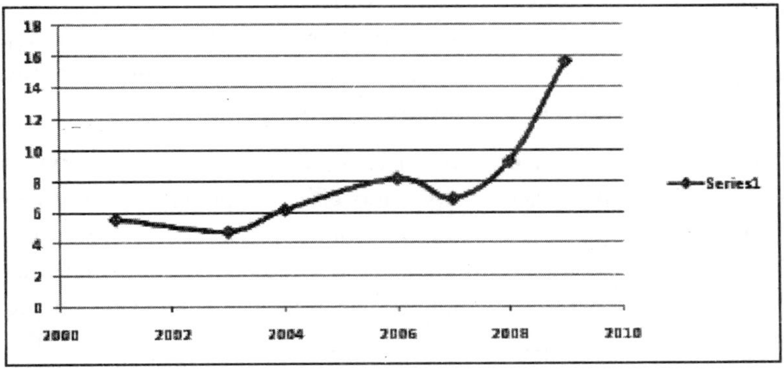


Source: IAMAI, 2010

**Chart 11.2: Internet Usage in hours/week**

## Internet banking risks

The past few years have been characterized by rapid changes in technology and the introduction of corporate and retail banking services through the Internet. The unprecedented speed with which new technologies are being adopted, the ubiquitous and global nature of electronic networks, the integration of e-banking platforms with legacy systems and the increasing dependence of banks on third party information service providers, all dramatically amplify the magnitude of risks to which banks are exposed.

Internet banking risks can adversely impact on an institution's earnings and capital.

For instances, more than 15,000 online ticket of Kingfisher Airline were purchased by fraudsters who got credit card information of Indian and foreign nationals. The loss to the carrier was Rs.17 Crores (Business News, 2007).

Ajay Sood and others (Operators of a placement agency involved in head-hunting), composed and sent emails to third parties in NASSCOM's name in order to obtain personal data. They agreed to pay Rs 1.6 Million to NASSCOM as damage for violating NASSCOM trademark right a compromise in the suit proceedings (Titus and Roy, 2005).

Therefore, an institution offering Internet banking services is required to implement proper and effective policies, procedures and controls to protect information and ensure its integrity, availability and confidentiality. It requires stringent methods of educating customers and regular review of security related information of individual customers (Singh, N. P., 2007). Internet banking risks can be categorised as follows:

- ***Strategic risk (Ramakrishnan, Ganesh, 2001)***

  It is the risk which is related with inappropriate business decision and/or incorrect implementation of decisions. An institution may incur substantial loss/wastage of its resources as a result of incorrect choices or decisions regarding its Internet banking strategy.

- ***Operational risk***

  Operational risk is also referred to as transactional risk. It is the most common form of risk associated with e-banking. It takes the form of inaccurate processing of transactions, non enforceability of contracts, compromises in data integrity, data privacy and confidentiality, unauthorized access / intrusion to bank's systems and transactions etc.

- ***Reputation risk***

This risk occurs when systems or products do not work as expected and cause widespread negative public reaction. Internet banking systems that are poorly managed would present this risk. An institution's reputation may also be affected if its internet banking system is unreliable or inefficient or the products and services offered are not presented in a fair and accurate manner.

- ***Traditional banking risk (Bank of Mauritius, 2001)***

An institution offering Internet banking services is faced with the same types of traditional banking risk such as credit risk, interest rate risk, liquidity risk, price risk and foreign exchange risk. The internet may, however, heighten some of these risks.

- ***Legal risk***

These risks arise from violation of, or non-conformance with laws, rules, regulations, or prescribed practices, or when the legal rights and obligations of parties to a transaction are not well established. Given the relatively new nature of Internet banking, rights and obligations in some cases are uncertain and applicability of laws and rules is uncertain or ambiguous, thus causing legal risk.

- ***Money laundering risk***

As internet banking transactions are conducted remotely banks may find it difficult to apply traditional method for detecting and preventing undesirable criminal activities.

Application of money laundering rules may also be inappropriate for some forms of electronic payments. Thus banks expose themselves to the money laundering risk. This may result in legal sanctions for non-compliance with "know your customer" laws.

- ***Cross border risks***

  Internet banking is based on technology that, by its very nature, is designed to extend the geographic reach of banks and customers. Such market expansion can extend beyond national borders. Then, there arises these risks. It includes legal and regulatory risks, as there may be uncertainty about legal requirements in some countries and jurisdiction ambiguities with respect to the responsibilities of different national authorities. Such considerations may expose banks to various legal risks associated with non-compliance of different national laws and regulations, including consumer protection laws, record-keeping and reporting requirements, privacy rules and money laundering laws.

## CHALLENGES OF INTERNET BANKING IN INDIA

Regulatory barriers in many countries are on the wane (Sathye, 1998). As the Internet gains momentum, governments are under pressure to reduce the barriers to competitive activity in the financial sector still further, to allow existing banks to remain competitive with their newer rivals (Carew, 1998). It is evident that banks can obtain an advantage by exploiting their existing, E-Commerce-ready infrastructure, through leveraging it on the Internet, but this opportunity must be seen in the context of a highly competitive, rapidly-moving market-place in which new rivals are emerging from many directions.

Several studies including Dourish and Redmiles (2002) suggest that security measures that are inconvenient for users may weaken E-Banking prospect, for example because of lack of user acceptance or outright resistance. They propose a distinction between theoretical and effective security. Theoretical security concerns the level of security that is technically possible; whereas effective security concerns the level of security achieved in practice, and is typically lower than theoretical security. Several studies including Jih et al. (2005) indicate that user adoption of E-Banking is affected by perceived security. This supports a view of security as crucial to the overall usability of E-Banking systems.

Developing countries like India are facing challenges in gaining acceptance for internet banking, which have been embraced by the tech savvy younger generation in certain parts of the country. There are some key barriers to achieving mass acceptance in India:

- **Convenient and powerful Internet banking systems**

  While foreign and private banks are aggressive in providing value services to customers through internet banking, state-owned banks have been a bit slow and have got their act together in recent years. Many a customers are still in dilemma whether to go for online or not. 'Risks are too high for it' seems by them.

- **Infrastructure constraints**

  Availability and access to internet is still a challenge in India. The deficiency of bandwidth and computing is slated to be there for a while. Bandwidth internet access is widely recognized as catalysts for economic and social development of a country. Serious efforts for availability of broadband services at affordable price levels will contribute to higher GDP growth rates, provide for a larger and more qualified labor force, and make that labor pool more efficient. Countries, like the US, are nowadays speaking of delivering "universal, affordable access to broadband" for all of their citizens. India also needs to endeavor an environment of higher access to internet and broadband connectivity for stimulating explosive initial growth. It is universally accepted that widespread broadband adoption accelerates GDP growth (Arunachalam, et al., 2007).

- **Absence of incentives**

  Internet banking is cheaper for banks internationally and this cost advantage has been passed on to the customers in the form of lower charges for transactions on the internet or higher charges if the transaction is carried out by visiting the branch. With rare exceptions (like Citibank Suvidha), we have not seen this policy being implemented in India.

- **Psychological factor**

  The primary reason preventing PSU banks from introducing online banking services has been the absence of a legal framework to bank up and regulate internet banking operations in the country. Though the IT Act, 2000 attempted to address a number of e-commerce related issues, there are still several grey areas which have neither been spelt out properly, nor have the courts suggested workable modes of implementation. The RBI in its report, 'Trend and Progress of Banking in India, 2001-02', says that internet banking has failed to take off due to a combination of psychological, technological and socio-economic factors. Further, the report says that additional hurdles relating to legal and infrastructure problems have also affected growth of internet banking.

## Opportunities of internet banking in India

Internet banking basically depends on a person's usage of access to a computer with an internet connection either at home or in the office. It is possible to use computers with internet connection in some of the self-service branches. The research of online shopping has pointed out that prior to web experience has had an influence on the person's beliefs about computers and technology. Consumers who are at ease with computers find it convenient to start banking over the internet. The above challenges notwithstanding, the future of internet banking is very bright in India.

Some specific factors need to be emphasised when looking at possible future growth of internet banking which can be seen as its potential opportunities. Such as:

- **High cost of real estate**: Real estate is becoming very costly in big metropolitan cities as well in smaller towns in India. Comparing the cost of opening branches and doing face-to-face banking, internet banking is turning out to be very cost effective. Door delivery system of services which has become very popular in Mumbai can be a good example of ultimately leading to promotion and acceptance of internet banking.
- **Congested road networks**: India being the second largest populated country in the world is finding it hard to come up with its ever increasing rate of population. The ultimate result of it is the congested road networks available in all major cities and towns. Internet banking can be a viable option for all banking customers to do their regular transactions online which can save them from all sorts of traffic jams and long queues at the bank branches.

- **Value-conscious Indian customer:** It is a fact that Indian customers are becoming value-conscious as far as banking services are concerned. For example, online railway ticket booking has been happily embraced by them even with low penetration of credit cards and computers. If we can give the customer a strong value proposition, he will surely adopt it. A recent RBI directive phasing out high-value cheques in favour of the electronic RTGS (Real Time Gross Settlement) is a welcome step in this direction.

- **Convenient way of operating banking transactions**: Online banking is a highly profitable channel for financial institutions. It provides customers convenience and flexibility and can be provided at a lower cost than traditional branch banking (Williamson, 2006). The advantage of online banking is helping people gain greater control of their finances and contributing to changing ways in cash withdrawal and day to day money management (Beer, 2006). Online banking users say that convenience is the most important factor; online banking lets them access their accounts from anywhere and at any time (IAMAI, 2006).

- **Flexible virtual banking system:** Financial institutions have spent a great deal of time and money developing online banking functionality to allow customers an easy and convenient way to manage their money (Williamson, 2006). A customer can check balance by logging into banks website through a user name and password. In this way he can enquire balance, status of cheques, perform funds transfers, order drafts, request issue of cheque books etc (Srivastava, 2009). Liu and Arnett in their study identified time factor as one of the prime factor that in Internet banking service quality feature for the customers. Saving time is an importance factor which influences the customers prefers to use e-banking. (Beer, 2006). Banks can make the information of products and services available on their site, which is, an advantageous proposition. Prospective customer can gather all the information from the website and thus if he comes to the branch with queries it will be very specific and will take less time of employee (Srivastava, 2009).

- **Trustworthiness:** Jun and Cai (2001) identified one of the very important service quality dimensions of e-banking service quality is trustworthiness. The online banking environment has grown tremendously over the past several years and will continue to grow as financial institutions continue to strive to allow customers to complete money transfers, pay bills, and access critical information online. During this same time, online banking has been plagued by Internet criminals and fraudsters attempting to steal customer information. Phishing, harming, and other types of attacks have become well known and are widely used as a means for fraudsters to obtain information from customers and access online banking accounts. As a result, authenticating customers logging onto their online banking service has become a crucial concern of financial institutions (Gregory D. Williamson, 2006).
- **Saving transaction cost:** Internet banking services improve customer service, market reach and reduce costs of transaction. If consumers are to use new technologies, the technologies must be reasonably priced relative to alternatives. Otherwise, the acceptance of the new technology may not be viable from the standpoint of the consumer (Suganthi et. al, 2001). Internet banking

offers advantages for both banks and customers. It enables the banks to deliver products and services to customers at a cost that is lower than any existing mode of delivery. Same is the case of customer. It helps them in cost reduction. In Internet banking, two types of costs are involved. First, the normal costs associated with Internet access fees and connection charges and secondly the bank fees and charges (Suganthi et. al, 2001). These two types of costs shape the perception of the customers.

- **On-line bill payments**: One of the most popular online transactions through internet banking is funds transfer/ bill payment (Beer, 2006). Of the twenty-two million users in US, twenty percent or 4.6 million people regularly used online bill payment services offered by the top ten financial institutions. This report also highlighted that the usage of online bill payment services increased by thirty-seven percent at the end of the first quarter of 2004.
- **Digital signature for security**: In a survey conducted by the Online Banking Association, member institutions rated security as the most important issue of online banking. There is a dual requirement to protect customers' privacy and protect against fraud (Mishra, 2009). Digital signature is a precautionary measure to prevent malpractices and tampering the information. It is a form of enhanced authentication (Williamson, 2006). Nearly one in 5 customers was victims of identity theft and fraud (TriCipher, 2007).
- **Easy to use and user friendliness**: Ease of use is another important determinant for the customer preferring the internet banking (Beer, 2006). In a study

conducted by Cooper (1997); reported that eases of use of innovative product or service as one of the three important characteristics for adoption from the customer's perspective. The user friendliness of domain names as well as the navigation tools available in the web-sites is an important determinant for ease of use. The design of the web-sites with appropriate use of graphical user interface is also considered as an important determinant. It is also worth noting that proper navigation attributes and search facility will also certainly be helpful to consumers when they surf the Internet. In addition, the level of interactivity of the site will certainly have an effect on the consumers' perception of the user friendliness of the Internet (Suganthi et. al, 2001). Another important factor that contributes the framework of the perception is the faster transfer of fund. The fundamental advantage of the internet banking is the transfer of the information about the money's worth to any place at any time with a mouse' clicks distance.

## CONCLUSION

India's 400 million un-banked represent an outstanding opportunity for financial institutions and telecommunications companies interested in serving the underneath of the pyramid. Serving this market requires the management of high volumes of low value transactions which is precisely what robust e-banking systems are designed to do. Indeed, profitable e-banking systems are dependent on managing large volumes of transactions, since it is these transactions that drive the majority of their revenue. With significant and growing penetration of internet connections (7% of the total population), linked to the potential tech-savvy youths, and the low cost of internet banking in India, one can only hope that e-banking will be allowed to play a significant role in achieving financial inclusion. Policy makers in India are clearly committed to optimising financial inclusion whilst maintaining the integrity of the financial system, securing depositors' savings and suppressing money laundering. This is a balancing act that will continue to challenge regulators worldwide. However, even with the most enabling of regulatory environments, e-banking solution providers are only going to be successful in the short term if they concentrate on areas where cash is inconvenient and the e-banking solution can do things that cash cannot.

The future of internet banking will be one in which customers can address most of their needs through self-directed means and the key differentiator will be how effective a bank is in getting its customers online and deriving measureable value from this presence by:

- Looking forward to and prepare for regulatory change.
- Focus on identifying core competence and migrate to a business model of choice.
- Build an optimal operating model by understanding which activities to retain collaborate and outsource.
- Go beyond compliance to use risk management as a critical decision support tool.
- Create and sustain customer, investor and regulator confidence by adopting international accounting standards and improving corporate governance.
- Ease and reliably play a vital role in switching from the traditional banking system to modern 24/7 net banking.

To do this effectively, banks in India need to spend more time on understanding the market and edifice the value proposal and business case. The technology is ready and available!

## REFERENCES

Arunachalam, L and Sivasubramanian, M (2007), 'The future of Internet Banking in India', *Academic Open Internet Journal*, ISSN 1311-4360 Volume 20, 2007

Bank of Mauritius, (2001): '*Guidelines on Internet Banking*' under Bank of Mauritius Act and the Banking Act 1988 effective from 2 April.

Beer Stan (2006). *Customers Preference on Internet Banking, Survey* (Retrieved from http://www.itwire.com/content/view/4570/53 on 20 March 2009)

Business News (2007). *India in the list of 10 top countries hosting* phishing websites, http://in.news.yahoo.com/070216/203/6c73r.html

Carew, E. (1998), *Fast money 4: the bestselling guide to Australia's financial markets* (New Soth Wales: Allen Unwin).

Cooper, R.G. (1997). Examining Some Myths About New Product Winners in Katz, R. (Eds),*The Human Side of Managing Technological Innovation*, Oxford, pp.550-60. (Retrieved from www.ebsco.com)

Dewan, R., and A. Seidmann (eds.) (2001), "Communications of the ACM," *Current issues in E-Banking* (Special section), 44(6): 31-57.

Dourish, P. and D. Redmiles, D. (2002), "An approach to usable security based on event monitoring and visualization," in *Proceedings of the 2002 Workshop on New Security Paradigms* (New York: ACM Press): 75-81.

Divya Singhal and V. Padhmanabhan (2008), 'A Study on Customer Perception Towards Internet Banking: Identifying Major Contributing Factors', *The Journal of Nepalese Business Studies*, Vol. V, No. 1, Dec.

Ganesh Ramakrishnan (2001), 'Risk Management for Internet Banking', *Information Systems Control Journal*, Volume 6.

Gregory D. Williamson (2006). Enhanced Authentication In Online Banking, *Journal of Economic Crime Management*, Volume 4, Issue 2, http://www.utica.edu/academic/institutes/ecii/publications/articles/51D6D996-90F2-F468-AC09C4E8071575AE.pdf on 18 March 2009

Hertzum, M., N.C. Juul, N. Jørgensen, and M. Nørgaard (2004), "Usable Security and E-Banking: Ease of Use vis-à-vis Security," *Technical Report*. Available at URL: http://www.ruc.dk/~nielsj/research/papers/E-Banking-tr.pdf.

IAMAI, (2010) Press release '**71 Million People Claimed to have used Internet in 2009' April** http://www.iamai.in PRelease_detail.aspx?nid=2045 &NMonth=4&NYear=2010.

Jeevan M T. (2000), "Only Banks - No Bricks", *Voice and Data*, November 11 th, Available [online] www.voicendata.com/content/convergence/trends_01.

Jih, W. J., S. Y. Wong and T. B. Chang (2005) "Effects of perceived risks on adoption of Internet banking services: an empirical investigation in Taiwan," *International Journal of E-Business Research*, 1(1): 70-88.

Jun, M. and Cai, S. (2001). The key Determinants of Internet Bank Service Quality: a Content Analysis, *International Journal of Bank Marketing*, 19(7): 276–291

Mishra A. K. (NK) (2009), *Internet Banking in India - Part I.* Retrieved from http://www.banknetindia.com/banking/ibkg.htm on 18 March 2009

Nair, A (1999), "Indian Internet banking still nascent," *Asia Internetnews*, May 12th; Available [online] www.asia.internet.com/asia-news/print/0,,161_648221,00.html

Organization for Economic Co-operation and Development (OECD) (2001) "Electronic Finance: Economics and Institutional Factors," *Occasional Papers No. 2*, Financial Affairs Division, OECD, Paris.

Rajiv Rai (2010), 'Power of being Online', Swagat, Air India, April, p.68-69.

Reserve Bank of India, 2001, Report on Internet banking, June 22, http://www.rbi.org.in/index.dll/21?sectionhomepage?secid=9999&s2secid=9999.

Sathye, M. (1998), "Internet Banking in Australia," *Journal of Internet Banking and Commerce*, 2(4); Available [online] at http://ww.arraydev.com/commerce/JIBC/articles.htm; Accessed on 7 January 2001.

Singh, N. P., (2007), Online Frauds in Banks with Phishing, Journal of Internet Banking and Commerce, *August, vol. 12, no.2, An open access Internet journal http://www.arraydev.com/commerce/jibc/)*

Srivastva Saurabh (2009). *Internet Banking - A Global Way to Bank*, Retrieved from http://www.indianmba.com/Faculty_Column/FC908/fc908.html on 18 March 2009

Statistics Denmark (2004), "Information Society Denmark. ICT Status 2004," available at http://www.dst.dk/infosamfundet2004.aspx.

Suganthi, Balachandher, and Balachandran, (2001) Internet Banking Patronage: An Empirical Investigation of Malaysia. *Journal of Internet Banking and Commerce*, 6 (1). Retrieved from http://www.arraydev.com/commerce/JIBC/0103_01.htm

Titus, D. and Roy, S. (2005). Phishing on the Net, http://www.asialaw.com/default.asp?page=14&ISS=16853&SID=518004

TriCipher Consumer Online, Banking Study, *Tri Cipher Solution Series*. March 2007.

UNCTAD (2002), *E-Commerce and Development Report 2002* (New York & Geneva: United Nations).

# 12

# Priority Sector Advances by Commercial Banks: A Diagnostic Study in Barak Valley Region of Assam

Jaynal Ud-din Ahmed

**Abstract**: The priority sector advance is mainly intended to ensure that the assistance from the banking system in an increasing manner to those sectors of the economy which have not received adequate support of institutional finance. The attainment of the socio-economic priorities of the government like growth of agriculture, promotion of small entrepreneurs and development of backward area etc is the major responsibility of commercial banks. Since seventies, RBI and government of India have stipulated guidelines for priority sector lending by banks. The same was revised on April 30, 2007 and overall priority sector lending target was fixed at 40 per cent for domestic banks and 32 per cent for foreign banks. However, the banks are not able to reach the prescribed target of lending to priority sector. The small entrepreneurs and farmers are continued to be both credit and demand constraints. Thus, it can be observed that the demand for funds for priority sector viz., small entrepreneurs and agricultural sector is enormous. With this backdrop, the present discourse is an attempt to identify the factors affecting priority sector lending by banks in the area under consideration in the context of national scenario.

The concept of priority sector was evolved in the late sixties in order to focus attention on the need to ensure adequate credit facilities to certain neglected sectors of the economy particularly in the rural areas. The involvement of banks in priority sector lending (PSL) has grown considerably with special emphasis on opening branches in un-banked areas. The diversification of a large fraction of bank credit from the traditional sector to the priority sector is a remarkable feature of credit deployment in the post nationalization era. The PSL is mainly intended to ensure that assistance from the banking system in an increasing manner to those sectors of the economy which has not received adequate support of institutional finance. Since seventies, Reserve bank of India (RBI) and government of India have stipulated some guidelines viz, financing in the priority sector on an increasing scale 40 per cent of total bank credit, more deployment of credit to backward regions, preparation and implementation of district credit plan (DCP) and measures for enhancing productivity, employment and economic growth with social justice (Narasimham, 1994)[1].

The commercial banks, without maintaining adequate security, have supplied advances to priority and other neglected sections of the society at a concessional rate of interest. The banking statistics revealed that, this designated priority sector as well as neglected sections received about 15 per cent of the total bank credit at the time of bank nationalization (weblink, 2010)[2]. On the later period, proportion of advances to the priority sector has increased from 15.0 per cent to 33.3 per cent in 1974 and further to 40.0 per cent in 1980. The commercial banks have achieved the target and even surpassed it in quantitative terms. But in qualitative terms, there is an apprehension among the bankers that the advances to priority sector resulted in a loss of interest income due to highly subsidized lending rates. As a result, the profitability of banks has been adversely affected besides maintaining additional manpower requirements for supervision of small loans, mounting over dues, poor recovery of advances and raising volume of non performing assets (NPAs) (Niranjana and Anbumani, 2002)[3].

The Narasimham Committee (1991)[4] on financial sector reform had drawn attention to the problem of low and declining profitability and stated that 'there is need for gradual phasing out of the directed credit programme, i.e. the stipulations that 40 per cent of all credit should go to the priority sector should be scrapped. The priority sector should be redefined and the proportion shall be fixed at 10 per cent of the aggregate credit'. The committee (1998)[5] indicated that timely and adequate availability of credit rather than its costs is very indispensable for intended beneficiaries. The impact of Narasimham Committee recommendations with regard to lending to priority sector has not been encouraging (Majumdar, 2001)[6]. It emerges that there is a growing anxiety that the process of financial sector reforms has by-passed the priority sector. In this respect, Y. V. Reddy (February 3, 2001)[7], Deputy Governor of RBI, remarked that the flow of credit to priority sector/ rural areas has not been up to the mark owing to accumulation of losses in public sector banks on account of mounting NPAs. The internal working group was set up by RBI under the chairmanship of C.S. Murthy to examine the need of continuance of PSL prescriptions. On the basis of the recommendations of the working group, the guideline for PSL were revised on April 30, 2007 and overall PSL target was fixed at 40 per cent for domestic banks and 32 per cent for foreign banks (RBI, 2009)[8].

The banks are not able to reach the prescribed target of lending to priority sector. The small entrepreneurs and farmers are continued to be both credit and demand constraints. The bankers have the excuse that the constraints faced by them with regard to deployment of credit to priority sector are lack of viable credit products, implying lack of demand for credit etc (Shete, 2002)[9]. On the other hand, there exists an informal sector which provides credit to priority sector particularly agricultural credit at higher rates of interest, which indicates that there are no demand constraints. Thus, it can be observed that the demand for funds for priority sector viz., small entrepreneurs and agricultural sector is enormous. The present paper is an attempt to diagnose empirically the factors affecting priority sector advances by banks in the area under consideration in the context of national scenario.

## Review of Related Literature

There have been many researches and studies on PSL by banks in India and abroad. A brief review of these studies is made in the following paragraphs to highlight the significance of the present study.

There exist cross-country studies on asset quality and PSL of banks. Radelet and Sachs, (1998)[10] found that the Asian crisis was caused by a boom in international lending followed by a sudden withdrawal of funds. At the core of the Asian crisis were large-scale foreign capital inflows into financial systems that became vulnerable to panic. The recessions cause banking crisis which resulted recycling problems of banks studied by Hardy and Pazarbasioglu (1999)[11] and Kaminsky and Reinhert (1999)[12]. Salas and Saurina (2002)[13] established the significant role of economic slump in increasing loan problem in Spanish banks. Meyer and Yeager (2001)[14] found that the loan quality of local banks in U.S. is affected by local economic slowdowns. Gambera (2000)[15] used a bivariate VAR technique and found that firm income and annual product have significant influence on bank loan quality and deployment of bank credit in US. Recently some studies investigated the feedback effect from the banks to the real economy. Marcucci and Quagliariello (2005)[16] validated the cyclicality of write-offs to total loans for Italian banks. Hoggarth, Sorensen and Zicchino (2005)[17] observed cyclicality of aggregate write-offs in UK banks. Baboucek and Jancar (2005)[18] found no corroboration of the cyclicality of NPAs in priority sector but conform pro-cyclicality for banks in Czech economy. Rikta (2006)[19] in a policy note on institutional lending and financing policy for small sector in Bangladesh examined the effectiveness of financial, fiscal, and related policies for financing the small sector. The study suggested that the financial institutions need to have the financial capacity to accept the lending risks along with access to appropriate funding which fulfill the clients' requirements. The bank's lending program in support of private sector development consists of the SME to the National Bank of Egypt as observed in the progress report (2009)[20] of Egypt. The mid term review on portfolio performance has underscored the main problems as programme implementation were delays in lapse of time between approval, effectiveness and first disbursement; non-adherence to bank procurement and disbursement rules and procedures; non-compliance with reporting requirements; weak capacity etc. The banking sector in Egypt remained less affected by the global financial crisis as the Central Bank of Egypt was successful in reforming the sector since 2004 by consolidating the small banks into larger banks; strengthening bank supervision; restructuring bank management; and cleaning up NPAs.

In Indian milieu, Joshi (1972)[21] proposed the RBI to give clear and specific definition of different component of priority sector as some of the bankers are not clear about the precise scope of agricultural lendings. Chawla (1979)[22] examined the dimension of credit flow to the priority sector during seventies and observed that the purpose of PSL by banks is not available for which it is meant for. Angadi (1983)[23] observed the concentration of PSL in general and agricultural advances in particular in some state because of rapid branch expansion, deposit mobilization, privileged cropped area, adoption of high yielding variety etc. Joshi (1986)[24] in his study identified weak fund management capacity of banks due to statutory liquidity ratio (SLR), cash reserve ratio (CRR) and PSL. He found that the low yield rate and rising cost contributed a lot to the declining trend in profitability of banks. Singh (1987)[25] identified many exogenous and endogenous factors for the strains and stresses of banking system. The major of them being continuous increase in the SLR, CRR, persistent emphasis on social goals, growing incidence of industrial sickness, rapid branch expansion in the under banked areas, unfavorable change of deposit mix and growing incidence of financial disintermediation.

Muhammed Yunus (1988)[26] strongly underlined that credit without discipline is nothing but charity and charity in the name of credit will only destroy the poor, instead of helping them. He, however, stressed on the loan recovery mechanism rather than blaming the defaulters. Rangarajan (1991)[27] pointed out that improving the quality of loan assets is the true test of improved efficiency of banking system. The Narasimham Committee (1991)[28] has stated the need for gradual phasing out of the directed credit programme. Krishnaswamy (1992)[29] criticized the recommendations of the committee on financial system. He pointed out the Committee's report considered only the interest of industrialist and it essentially concerned with reducing govt. regulations and improving profitability. Rajagopal (1994)[30] studied on the consequences of PSL in Indian banking and remarked that concessional credit should be restricted only to the poorest of the poor and to the under privileged sections of the society. Commercial rate of interest should be charged from those who can afford it. Patel (1996)[31] in his paper realised that the traditional banking ethics were not compatible with the needs of economic development and that the balanced development was not possible without strengthening the hold of commercial banks in the backward and neglected areas. With a view to bring the down-trodden, hitherto neglected sector households to the mainstream, fundamental changes in the traditional banking norms were called for to move away from security based credit towards programme oriented credit.

The Narasimham Committee (1998)[32] pointed out that the sufficient credit to priority sector is very indispensable for intended beneficiaries. Kohli (1997)[33] observed the existence of significant linkages between bank credit and investment in both agriculture and industries in India. He suggested that although directed credit programme for PSL is effective in India, affirmative support to small-scale units is required. Ajit (1997)[34] examined the issue of para banking activities and suggested that bank should be allowed to undertake these activities, particularly use of capital as risk, from the experience of other countries like USA.

Department of Banking Supervision (1999)[35] studied the impact of priority sector advances on NPAs and found that the incidence of NPAs in priority sector is much higher in view of the fact that priority sector advances constitute 30-32 per cent of the gross bank credit. Vyas Committee (2001)[36] also observed that commercial banks seem to have shied in extending rural credit as they are dealing vast number of small accounts. Niranjana and Anbumani (2002)[37] observed that there is anxiety among the bankers that the advances to priority sector resulted in a loss of interest income due to highly subsidized lending rates. In the context of enormous demand for funds for priority sector, Shete (2002)[38] examined priority sector advances by PSBs during the post reform years and found that the PSBs are not able to reach the prescribed target of lending to priority sector.

The World Bank (2004)[39] in its report, 'Sustaining India's Service Revolution' highlighted that government ownership of banks in India stifles competition and raises the cost of lending to the public. The World Bank has blamed RBI's stiff PSL norms for foreign and domestic banks for the weak financial health of commercial banks. The report has indicated that largest government ownership in the banking sector led to insufficient competition in the Indian banking system and hence, led to increased cost of intermediation, lowering capital allocation efficiency and under-lending to the private sector. RBI (2005)[40] draft technical paper of internal working group identified the issues relating to necessity of PSL. The working group recommended the need for PSL prescriptions, the composition of priority sector which includes agriculture, small industries, small road and water transport operators, small business, professional and self-employed persons, education, housing etc. The existing system of computation of priority sector obligations in relation to NBC is based on the outstanding advances of banks. Linking the priority sector obligations to outstanding advances has its shortcomings as outstanding tend to decline as a result of better recovery, write-offs, etc. Moreover, a portion of outstanding comprises NPAs, which continue to get reflected in the achievement of banks in lending to priority sector. The disbursement during a given period is, therefore, a better indicator of banks' lending. In order to improve the flow of credit to the priority sector and to ensure that a certain proportion of funds out of the total bank credit flows to this sector, the computation of PSL obligations of banks could be linked to the total disbursements made by banks during the previous year. Ahmed (2005)[41] in a diagnosis observed that commercial banks together have gradually increased the quantum of advances to small industries but the proportion in which total bank credit in priority sector has expanded, the relative share of small sector has not grown in the same ratio during the reform regime. The weak infrastructure facilities may have prevented the greater flow of credit. The industrial campaign, awareness programmes and industrial training to the prospective entrepreneurs from the appropriate authority may be the remedy in this respect.

Bhati (2006)[42] examined the lending climate for banks in emerging economies like India. The study found that due to the government policies, banks in India undertake many additional risks when they lend. This study focused on one specific aspect of lending relationship between branch manager and loan officer of bank branches in India and recommended social risk evaluation is therefore more appropriate for risk evaluation and reduction by banks in India. An assessment on the causes and consequences of NPAs of commercial banks, by Rajesham and Rajender (2007)[43], concluded that a strong political will only be able to find satisfactory solution to the problem of mounting NPAs. Narasaiah and Naik (2007)[44] observed that although great strives have been made in the last decade to ensure finance for micro enterprises, rare initiative has been taken to help small sector. As a result, small enterprises have been constrained to seek loans for new ventures from commercial banks. Sooden and Kumar (2007)[45] analysed the PSL in the post reform period and suggested for a balanced approach as development agent and sustainability of directed lendings keeping in view the quantum of NPA in priority sector advances. Paramjit and Priyanka (2007)[46] in their comparative study on PSBs and private banks relating to NPA level in PSL during 1997- 2005 found that priority sector had been contributing lion's share of total bank's NPA in India.

In order to review the efficacy of existing framework of money lending a technical group, constituted under the chairmanship of S.C. Gupta, submitted its report in July 2007 and recommended measures pertaining to the institutional reform, alternative avenues of credit dispensation such as micro finance institutions (RBI, 2007)[47]. Roy (2008)[48] observed that the agriculture is one of the so-called priority sectors to which banks are mandated to channel 40 per cent of their net credit. The agricultural lending is highly technical; it has to be crop-specific and time-bound. The under-lending does not serve the purpose, over-lending also invites trouble. The farmer eventually has to return the money. The Economic Survey Report, 2008-09 expressed that the government should allow trading of directed credit obligations among banks and other financial institutions. This will allow and encourage the development of financial institutions that can specialize in and exploit economies of scale and scope in un-banked and low-banked areas and sectors.

RBI (2010)[49] observed that certain scheduled commercial banks are extending short-term loans of tenure ranging from six months to one year to housing finance and classifying the same as priority sector advances. Since housing loans are generally medium to long-term loans taken by the individuals, these loans are considered to be not eligible as PSL. The banks should now ensure that the end use of the funds strictly as per the guidelines on lending to priority sector. Hence PSL constitutes a loan amount of less than Rs 20 lakhs. RBI in this connection reiterated the guidelines that banks have to lend 40 per cent of their lending to areas like farm sector, small and medium sector, and weaker sections among others, which are collectively called priority sector.

Verma and Antony (2010)[50] viewed that the priority sector loan portfolio of banks tradable is likely to be neglected. After consultation with various stakeholders, the internal working group set up by the central bank has said that implementing this proposal could redirect the attention of most banks from actual lending to buying credits from a few banks that more than meet the targets. The banks short of meeting their priority sector targets could meet their requirements by buying the priority sector lending certificates (PSLCs) from other banks in the open market

From the above review of earlier studies it is revealed that not many studies based exclusively on the PSL by banks. Most of the studies relate to the institutional financing, nature and problems of PSL by banks. However, the studies relating to the factors affecting the PSL by commercial banks remained un-researched in the study area.

## Priority Sector lending by Commercial Banks: An Overview

The commercial banks have been playing an important responsibility of channelizing the funds with most important sectors to fulfil the pre-determined objectives. There is a rapid expansion in banking network, deposit mobilization and credit deployment due to which there is change in the scope of banking operations. The banks were especially concerned with financing the priority sector of agriculture, small scale enterprises and small transport operators. In course of time, other priority sectors were also added, such as retail trade, professional and self-employed persons, education, housing loans for weaker sections and consumption loans. The rationale of PSL was one of the causes for nationalization of the top 14 banks in 1969. However, it was the working group on the PSL and the 20 point economic programme which clearly indicated the concept of PSL is mainly intended to ensure that assistance from banking system should flow in an increasing manner to those sectors of the economy which though accounting for a significant proportion of the national product, have not received adequate support of institutional finance in the past.

## Deployment of Bank Credit to Priority Sector in India

The commercial banks played a significant role among the institutional sources of credit for priority sector in India. The significance of bank credit in the priority sector can be observed against the backdrop of increasing quantum of such credit to this sector. The deceleration in bank credit growth is reflected in the fact of slowdown in real economy as also cautious approach adopted by banks against the backdrop of growing uncertainties. The data suggested that growth rate of bank's lending to small enterprises, and agriculture and allied activities increased substantially during 2000-09. Table 12.1 presents total bank credit and the deployment of bank credit to priority sector in India during 2000-2009.

The outstanding bank credit of small scale sector increased from Rs. 52,814 crores in March 2000 to Rs. 2, 59,998 crores in March 2009 recording around 5 fold increases but the percentage share to total bank credit has declined from 13.2 per cent to 10.0 per cent. During the same period, the amount of bank advances to agriculture sector increased from Rs. 44,381 crores to Rs.3, 38,656 crores. There is a sudden jump of bank credit deployed to other priority sectors during the period under consideration. The same has recorded an increase from Rs. 34,632 crores in March 2000 to Rs.2, 03,154 crores in March 2009. It can be argued that the growth of advances to other priority sector in absolute figure has gone over the growth of bank credit to small sector although the percentage share has remained lower throughout the period. This signifies that the banking system is doing some appropriate and practical strategies in assisting to those sectors of the economy which have not received adequate support of institutional finance.

However, there exists a close relationship between total bank credit and fund available for priority sector. Thus in order to assess inter-relationship between the total bank credit and

**Table 12.1**
**Deployment of Bank Credit to Priority Sector in India (March 2000 to March 2009)**

(Amount Rs. in crores)

| Sl No | Priority Sectors | March 2000 | March 2001 | March 2002 | March 2003 | March 2004 | March 2005 | March 2006 | March 2007 | March 2008 | March 2009 |
|---|---|---|---|---|---|---|---|---|---|---|---|
| 1 | **Total bank credit** | 4,00,818 (100) | 4,69,153 (100) | 5,36,727 (100) | 6,69,534 (100) | 7,64,383 (100) | 10,40,909 (100) | 14,45,837 (100) | 18,48,187 (100) | 22,47,289 (100) | 26,48,501 (100) |
| 2 | **Agriculture & allied** | 44381 (11.1) | 51922 (11.0) | 60761 (11.3) | 73,518 (10.9) | 90,541 (11.8) | 1,25,250 (12.0) | 1,72,279 (11.9) | 2,30,377 (12.8) | 2,75, 342 (12.5) | 3,38,656 (13.0) |
| 3 | **Small scale industries** | 52814 (13.2) | 56002 (11.9) | 57199 (10.6) | 60,394 (9.0) | 65,855 (8.6) | 74,588 (7.2) | 90,239 (6.2) | 1,23,987 (8.7) | 2,04,892 (9.3) | 2,59,998 (10.0) |
| 4 | **Other priority sector** | 34632 (8.6) | 46490 (9.9) | 57299 (10.7) | 77,697 (11.6) | 1,07,438 (14.0) | 1,81,638 (17.4) | 2,47,379 (17.1) | 1,60,343 (8.9) | 1,91,878 (8.7) | 2,03,154 (7.8) |

Figures in the parentheses indicate percentages to total bank credit deployed.
Source: *Reserve Bank of India, Report on Currency and Finance, Various issues*

credit available to the priority sector, we have calculated correlation coefficient (r) between total bank credit (x), bank credit to agricultural sector ($x_1$), bank credit to small sector ($x_2$) and bank credit to other priority sector ($x_3$) during 2000 to 2009. The matrix of 'r' value is presented in Table 12.2.

**Table 12.2**
**Matrix of Correlation Co-efficients**

| Variables | X | $X_1$ | $X_2$ | $X_3$ |
|---|---|---|---|---|
| **X** | 1.00 | | | |
| **$X_1$** | 0.999** | 1.00 | | |
| | (19.80) | | | |
| **$X_2$** | 0.951** | 0.954* | 1.00 | |
| | (8.68) | (8.70) | | |
| **$X_3$** | 0.798** | 0.788** | 0.627* | 1.00 |
| | (3.74) | (3.62) | (2.78) | |

**Source:** *Self-calculated by the present investigator.*
$\mathbf{t}_{0.05}$( 8 d f ) =2.306, $\mathbf{t}_{0.01}$( 8 d f ) =3.355

The above econometric analysis manifests that positive correlation coefficients (r) values are statistically significant at 5 per cent and 1 per cent level of significance except r value between small scale sector and other priority sector (0.627) is significant at only 5 per cent level of significance but not at 1 per cent level. This indicates that with the expansion of total bank credit, the outstanding credit to priority sectors have increased in the same proportion with the exception of other priority sector. This indicates that the credit expansion in other priority sector are not alike others viz., small sector and agricultural sector.

## Priority Sector Advances: Bank Group-wise Comparisons.

The bank group wise distribution of priority sector advances and percentage share to total bank credit in India are furnished in Table 12.3. It is clear that over the years percentage share of priority sector advances of public sector banks (PSBs) has remained around 43 per cent of total bank advances although in absolute term, the priority sector advances increased from 1,07,200 crores in 1999-00 to 7,20,083 crores in 2008-09. The PSBs achieved the priority sector target of 40 per cent throughout the period under study. The private sector banks were also able to meet priority sector lending norms of 40 per cent throughout the period except 2000-01. The 32 per cent target fixed for priority sector lending has been met by foreign banks over the years. Further, the reality is that the PSBs position in lending in priority sector is higher than the foreign banks operating in India. This indicates that these banks, private banks in particular, lent larger amount of money to the priority sector in recent years though the volume of advances are meagre than that of PSBs.

In order to examine the prospect of priority sector advances of bank groups, an analysis of skewness was undertaken. It is found that the highly positive skewness value 2.605 of private sector banks indicates an asymmetric appendage of priority sector advances encouraging and liquidating more in years to come. The negative skewness value -0.0487 indicates a reverse situation in extending towards additional fund to this sector.

## Level of NPAs in Priority Sector Advances of Banks

Any analysis on priority sector will remain incomplete if the issue of sustainability of advances is not considered. This depends upon how efficiently the credit is recycled in the priority sector and the issue is directly linked with the level of priority sector NPAs. The priority sector NPAs of banks are presented in Table 12.4. The sector-wise analysis of NPAs of public sector commercial banks revealed that priority sector added up a large proportion 44.5 per cent of total advances in March 2000 and increased to 63.6 per cent in March 2008. This however declined to 55.2 per cent in March 2009. In the non-priority sector, the

**Table 12.3**
**Priority Sector Advances by Bank Groups in India**

(Amount Rs in crores)

| As on March | Public Sector Banks | Private Sector Banks | Foreign Banks |
|---|---|---|---|
| 1999-00 | 107200 (43.5) | 14155 (41.4) | 8270 (37.0) |
| 2000-01 | 127807 (43.6) | 10819 (38.7) | 9699 (34.5) |
| 2004-05 | 307046 (42.8) | 69886 (43.6) | 23843 (35.3) |
| 2005-06 | 409748 (40.0) | 106586 (42.8) | 30439 (34.4) |
| 2006-07 | 521376 (39.7) | 143768(42.7) | 37835 (33.4) |
| 2007-08 | 610450 (44.7) | 164068 (42.5) | 50254 (39.5) |
| 2008-09 | 720083 (42.5) | 190207 (46.8) | 55483 (34.3) |
| **Skewness** | -0.0487 | 2.605 | 0.052 |

Figures in parentheses indicate percentage to total bank credit.

**Source**: *RBI, Statistical tables Relating to Banks in India. IBA Bulletins*

**Table 12.4**
**NPAs of Priority Sector Vis-A-Vis Other Sector**

(Amount Rs. in crores)

| Year (End March) | Priority Sector | | Non-Priority Sector | | Public Sector | | Total |
|---|---|---|---|---|---|---|---|
| | Amount | Per cent | Amount | Per cent | Amount | Per cent | |
| 2000 | 23715 | 44.5 | 28524 | 53.5 | 1055 | 2.0 | 53294 |
| 2001 | 24156 | 45.4 | 27307 | 51.4 | 1711 | 3.2 | 53174 |
| 2002 | 25150 | 46.2 | 28405 | 52.2 | 903 | 1.7 | 54458 |
| 2003 | 24939 | 47.2 | 26781 | 50.7 | 1087 | 2.1 | 52807 |
| 2004 | 23841 | 47.5 | 25698 | 51.2 | 610 | 1.2 | 50149 |
| 2005 | 21926 | 48.1 | 23249 | 51.0 | 444 | 1.0 | 45619 |
| 2006 | 22374 | 54.1 | 18664 | 45.1 | 341 | 0.8 | 41378 |
| 2007 | 22954 | 59.5 | 15158 | 39.3 | 490 | 1.3 | 38602 |
| 2008 | 25287 | 63.6 | 14163 | 35.6 | 299 | 0.8 | 39749 |
| 2009 | 24318 | 55.2 | 19251 | 43.7 | 474 | 1.1 | 44043 |
| *Cgr* | 4.12 | | 9.76 | | - 1.31 | | 7.24 |

**Source:** *Reserve Bank of India, Trend and Progress of Banking in India, Various issues*

same has been decreased to 43.7 per cent in March 2009 from 53.5 per cent in March 2000. The public sector NPAs remained at minimum level throughout the period.

The compound growth rate (cgr) of NPAs in non-priority sector is comparatively higher (9.76%). The 'cgr' became negative in the public sector. This exposes that the commercial banks have not considered loan to the public sector due to further NPAs menace over the years. Moreover, the overall 'cgr' of NPAs during 2000-2009 of PSBs was 7.24 per cent while non-priority sectors cgr (9.76%) overweighs the priority sector (4.12%). Thus the non-priority sector is also considerably adding fresh NPAs over the years. On the other hand, the higher NPAs in priority sector advances have pushed up the overall proportion of NPAs. The reasons of higher proportion of NPAs in priority sector advances at the national level may be attributed to the directed and pre-approval nature of loans sanctioned under sponsored programmes, lack of effective follow up due to large number of small accounts, non-cost effective legal recovery measures, vitiation of the repayment culture consequent to the loan waiver schemes, willful defaulters and so on.

## Background of the Study Area

The Barak valley is the southernmost region of Assam and covers an extensive area of 6922 sq. kms in 4 sub-divisions of three districts (Cachar, Karimganj and Hailakandi) of southernmost part of Assam (GoA, 2007)[51]. The topography of the valley is heterogeneous composed of high hills, low lands and level plains dotted with low ranges isolated hills. The climatic condition of the valley is characterised by high temperature and heavy rainfall. The economy of the valley had been a periphery to the economic mainstream of Bengal during the British rule. The partition of the country in the wake of independence and the consequent emergence of East Pakistan (now Bangladesh) not only had shattered the traditional cheapest and quickest lines of transport and communication but also had snapped the age-old channels of trade, commerce and transactions. The post independence phase did not adequately compensate the valley for al the loss exacted on it by partition.

The valley is characterized by thickly populated area with density of 360 persons per sq. km. About 49 per cent of the geographical area is under agriculture and 36.9 per cent are under forest[52]. As per govt records, the number of existing small and micro industries in the valley constituted about 10 per cent[53] of the total number of industries of the State of Assam during the period 2000-2009. The District Industries Centres (DICs) are imparting training to the rural artisans in trade, leatherwork, tailoring, bamboo work, carpentry etc. Only 4.3 per cent of the workers are engaged in manufacturing, processing etc.

The institutional finance is essential for the development of industries in a particular area. The commercial banks play a very crucial role in the process of economic development and so the availability of banking infrastructure is considered as one of the prerequisites for rapid and balanced development of the country. But unfortunately, the rate of growth of banking infrastructure in the valley has not shown significant rise. The valley has 12.5 per cent of the total bank offices of state Assam (UBI, 2009)[54]. At present, 12 PSBs, 1 RRBs and 3 private banks are operating with a net work of 147 branches. As on 31.12.2009 there are 147 numbers of branches of commercial banks operating in the valley. The district Cachar is bestowed with 72 branches (51 PSBs, 19 RRBs and 2 private banks) while the district Karimganj got 52 branches (32 PSBs, 17 RRBs and 3 private banks) and 12 branches (13 PSBs, 8 RRBs and 2 private banks) in the district of Hailakandi are taking the care of banking activities.

The analysis of the aforesaid indicators revealed that the valley is economically and industrially backward. The socio-economic backwardness of the valley is discerned by the symptoms like under and un-utilization of resources, prejudice of agrarian economy, industrial backwardness, weak infrastructure, slow entrepreneurial zeal, peculiar nature of clientele and rising incidence of unemployment. Thus, the economic development of this region is urgently needed in the direction of industrial and agricultural development for overall development of the districts under study.

## Objective of the Study

The foregoing discussions relating to the PSL of banks at the national level revealed that there are a number of serious issues relating to the PSL which became great concern of the policy makers. Now the doubts relating to the sustainability of PSL may be studied in the backward area particularly to identify the actual factors. In this respect, we have conducted an empirical study over fifteen commercial banks operating in the study area. The RRBs will remain outside the purview of the present study. The major objectives are –

1. To examine the status of priority sector lendings by commercial banks in the area under study.
2. To study the recovery performance against the priority sector advances of banks over the years.
3. To examine the level of NPAs in priority sector advances of commercial banks in the area under study.
4. To identify the determinants of priority sector lending by commercial banks over the years.

## Hypotheses

The following operational hypotheses have been framed to meet the objectives of the study-

1. There exists a wide variation between deployment of bank credit and priority sector loans in the area under study.

2. The mounting overdue has significantly restricted the bank's lending capacity to priority sector over the years.
3. The priority sector advances have direct bearing on increasing quantum of NPAs of banks in the study area.

## Methodology

The secondary data collected from RBI Trend and Progress of Banking in India, RBI Report on Currency and Finance, RBI Annual Reports, RBI, Statistical tables Relating to Banks in India, IBA Bulletins, Regional offices of banks and Lead bank office of the study area has been considered for the purpose of the study. The entire study is subjected to statistical techniques like correlation analysis, regression analysis, skewness, growth rate analysis, parametric tests etc. The extent of credit channelization has been tested with the correlation matrix analysis. Linear growth rate and compound growth rate analysis have been used to assess the growth of bank credit in the area under study. A comparison of credit targets and actual achievements has been made to judge the credit performance in priority sector. Besides this the analysis of skewness, simple tabulation, and percentage analysis has been used. The banks lending capacity has been studied with the percentage of recovery in priority sector. Regression model has also been fitted to study the determinants of PSL by identifying independent variables which are mentioned in appropriate places.

## The Empirical Analysis

### *Sector-wise Break up of Commercial Bank Credit*

The socialization of bank credit has been the subject matter of PSL by the banks. The attainment of the socio economic priorities of the government like growth of agriculture, promotion of small entrepreneurs and development of backward area etc is the major responsibility of commercial banks. Table 12.5

**Table 12.5**

**Sector-wise Break-Up of Bank Credit in Barak Valley (2000-2009)**

(Amount Rs in lakhs)

| Year (End Dec.) | Karimganj district | | | Cachar district | | | Hailakandi district | | |
|---|---|---|---|---|---|---|---|---|---|
| | Priority Sector | Non-Priority Sector | Total | Priority Sector | Non-Priority Sector | Total | Priority Sector | Non-Priority Sector | Total |
| 2000 | 2022 (63.4) | 1167 (36.6) | 3189 (100) | 4025 (57.0) | 4200 (43.0) | 8225(100) | 1682 (51.3) | 1595 (48.7) | 3277(100) |
| 2001 | 2038 (50.8) | 1975 (49.2) | 4013 (100) | 4987 (52.5) | 4511 (47.5) | 9498(100) | 1695 (49.8) | 1705 (50.2) | 3400(100) |
| 2002 | 1875 (58.6) | 1324 (41.4) | 3199 (100) | 5595 (49.0) | 5821 (51.0) | 11416(100) | 1945 (53.5) | 1688 (46.5) | 3633(100) |
| 2003 | 2159 (60.9) | 1386 (39.1) | 3545 (100) | 5294 (47.0) | 6060 (53.0) | 11354(100) | 2300 (49.8) | 2314 (50.2) | 4614(100) |
| 2004 | 2980 (60.7) | 1873 (39.3) | 4853 (100) | 6432 (48.9) | 6934 (51.1) | 13366(100) | 2430 (50.8) | 2393 (49.2) | 4823 (100) |
| 2005 | 3421 (64.0) | 2309 (36.0) | 5730(100) | 6890 (51.2) | 6700 (48.8) | 13590 (100) | 2751 (45.6) | 3024 (54.5) | 5775 (100) |
| 2006 | 2653 (50.8) | 2510 (49.2) | 5163 (100) | 7534 (48.0) | 7890 (52.0) | 15424 (100) | 3230 (52.0) | 3129 (480) | 6359(100) |
| 2007 | 3120 (57.9) | 2751 (43.1) | 5871 (100) | 7834 (49.1) | 7908 (50.9) | 15742 (100) | 3904 (56.6) | 3079 (43.4) | 6983 (100) |
| 2008 | 3452 (53.1) | 3048 (46.9) | 6500 (100) | 7980 (49.9) | 8001 (50.1) | 15981 (100) | 4109 (56.9) | 3110 (43.1) | 7219(100) |
| 2009 | 3760 (55.4) | 3020 (44.5) | 6780 (100) | 8562 (51.6) | 8020 (48.4) | 16582 (100) | 3908 (51.6) | 3658 (48.4) | 7566(100) |
| agr | 4 | 2.2 | 3.3 | 3.4 | 14.7 | 8 | 6.1 | 5.6 | 3.8 |

Figure in the parentheses indicate percentage to total credit of the respective district.

**Source:** *Lead Bank office, UBI, Cachar, Karimganj and Hailakandi districts*

**Table 12.6**
**Bank Credit Deployment Under Annual Credit Plan in Barak valley**

(Account in Nos. and Amounts Rs. in thousands)

| Year (As on March) | Agriculture and Allied activities | | Small Sector and Rural Artisans | | Trade and Services | | Total | |
|---|---|---|---|---|---|---|---|---|
| | Account | Amount | Account | Amount | Account | Amount | Account | Amount |
| **Karimganj district** | | | | | | | | |
| 2000 | 4132 | 21132 | 784 | 21285 | 1290 | 24832 | 6206 | 67249 |
| 2001 | 2496 | 24349 | 817 | 23541 | 1393 | 20800 | 4706 | 68690 |
| 2002 | 2560 | 26965 | 743 | 15833 | 1638 | 27754 | 4941 | 70602 |
| 2003 | 2189 | 26565 | 773 | 16954 | 1624 | 34393 | 4586 | 77912 |
| 2004 | 1444 | 15419 | 484 | 8771 | 1448 | 30339 | 3376 | 54529 |
| 2005 | 1238 | 15977 | 565 | 10571 | 1836 | 45026 | 3639 | 71574 |
| 2006 | 1453 | 16530 | 462 | 10923 | 1983 | 46312 | 3780 | 73765 |
| 2007 | 1762 | 18756 | 643 | 21789 | 1867 | 49032 | 4272 | 89577 |
| 2008 | 1460 | 19870 | 548 | 23470 | 1795 | 53219 | 3839 | 96559 |
| 2009 | 1981 | 28764 | 890 | 22841 | 2310 | 52380 | 5181 | 103985 |
| **Cachar district** | | | | | | | | |
| 2000 | 2369 | 14673 | 624 | 14019 | 1635 | 31118 | 4628 | 59810 |
| 2001 | 2159 | 19609 | 952 | 20090 | 2022 | 40784 | 5133 | 80433 |

| | | | | | | | | |
|---|---|---|---|---|---|---|---|---|
| 2002 | 2255 | 29517 | 648 | 19839 | 2869 | 65709 | 5772 | 115065 |
| 2003 | 2136 | 34412 | 796 | 24190 | 2965 | 79623 | 5890 | 135323 |
| 2004 | 2350 | 32378 | 1265 | 37584 | 3126 | 94407 | 6741 | 164369 |
| 2005 | 2450 | 33478 | 1528 | 39281 | 3028 | 83408 | 7006 | 156167 |
| 2006 | 2590 | 32598 | 1674 | 40965 | 3210 | 97502 | 7623 | 171065 |
| 2007 | 2457 | 32967 | 1290 | 36095 | 3100 | 87207 | 7847 | 156269 |
| 2008 | 2709 | 35097 | 1873 | 41230 | 3490 | 103980 | 8072 | 180507 |
| 2009 | 2983 | 38602 | 1932 | 43096 | 3109 | 104382 | 8024 | 186080 |
| **Hailakandi district** | | | | | | | | |
| 2000 | 2639 | 21862 | 613 | 24139 | 1123 | 23689 | 4106 | 69690 |
| 2001 | 2416 | 18674 | 580 | 21017 | 1359 | 12536 | 4355 | 52227 |
| 2002 | 1938 | 26312 | 728 | 12829 | 1439 | 18390 | 4105 | 57913 |
| 2003 | 1539 | 22392 | 791 | 15312 | 1408 | 17890 | 3738 | 55594 |
| 2004 | 2560 | 21831 | 865 | 18316 | 1506 | 27831 | 4931 | 67978 |
| 2005 | 1961 | 14326 | 871 | 15109 | 1458 | 26091 | 3490 | 55526 |
| 2006 | 1980 | 23564 | 901 | 16534 | 1643 | 27325 | 5424 | 67423 |
| 2007 | 2690 | 19740 | 987 | 18652 | 1894 | 29034 | 5571 | 67426 |
| 2008 | 2381 | 26932 | 870 | 19056 | 1705 | 31983 | 4956 | 77971 |
| 2009 | 2984 | 25094 | 1093 | 22092 | 2091 | 34210 | 6168 | 81396 |

**Source:** *Lead Bank Office, United Bank of India, Cachar, Karimganj and Hailakandi Districts*

presented the data on the total bank advances to the priority and non-priority sector for the period between December 2000 and December 2009 in the districts of the valley.

The percentage share of priority sector advances of banks in the region is much higher than the national level during the period. The banks in the study area are able to maintain the priority sector lending prescription of 40 per cent as per revised guidelines. It is exposed from the table that the share of priority sector advances to total advances has declined in the area under study except Karimganj district while the same has increased at the national level. It has also been observed that the average annual growth (agr) of priority sector advances was 4.0 per cent, 3.4 per cent and 6.1 per cent in the Karimganj, Cachar and Hailakandi district respectively during 2000-2009. This indicates a wide gap between deployment of bank credit to priority sector and the development of the backward regions. It is imperative to take appropriate strategy for financing priority sector like micro and small sector, agriculture etc in backward regions.

## *Deployment of Bank Credit under Annual Credit Plan*

The banks operating in the study area, keeping in view their aim and objectives for the economic development under the lead bank schemes, have made an effort in providing financial support to agriculture and small scale sector. The sector-wise bank credit deployment under annual credit plan in the districts is shown in Table 12.6.

Table 12.6 reveals that agriculture is one of the single dominant sectors that absorbed major portion of the credit outstanding. In March 2000, credit outstanding for agriculture was Rs 21,132 thousands, Rs 14,673 thousands and Rs. 21,862 thousands for Karimganj, Cachar and Hailakandi districts respectively. The same has increased to Rs 28,764 thousands for Karimganj district and Rs. 38,602 thousands for Cachar district in March 2009. The district Hailakandi, however, experienced a marginal increase of Rs. 25094 thousands in March 2009. The total amount of PSL stands at Rs. 1039.85 lakhs with 5181 number of accounts in Karimganj district, Rs. 1060.80 lakhs with 8024 number of accounts in Cachar district and Rs. 813.96 lakhs with 6168 number of accounts in Hailakandi district as on March 2009. The bank credit deployed to small sector and service sector in absolute term has increased throughout the period in the districts. The service sector has experienced relatively more deployment of credit in terms of quantum. The growth of bank credit in different sectors may be assessed by compound growth rate (cgr) of bank credit sanctioned during the period. The results obtained are displayed in Table 12.7.

**Table 12.7**
**CGR of Bank Credit Deployed**

| District | Agriculture and Allied | SSI and Rural Artisans | Trade and Service | Total Credit |
|---|---|---|---|---|
| Karimganj | 0.26 | 2.45 | 8.23 | 11.27 |
| Cachar | 3.24 | 13.08 | 11.58 | 14.08 |
| Hailakandi | 1.29 | 0.32 | 6.05 | 4.71 |

The inter-sectoral growth rate analysis reveals that there is an increase in respect of credit sanctioned in agriculture and allied activities (cgr = 0.26), small scale sector (cgr=2.45) and trade and service (cgr = 8.23) in Karimganj district. In the same manner, district Cachar and Hailakandi experienced a positive growth rate of credit sanctioned in small sector (cgr = 13.08), agriculture and allied activities (cgr = 3.24) and trade and service (cgr = 11.58). It is therefore evident from the growth rate analysis that the priority sector guidelines implemented from time to time had a positive impact on the sectoral credit deployment in the area under consideration. The inter-district growth rate analysis shows that the small enterprises and agriculture sector received comparatively less attention than that of trade and services during the period. This may be due to the negative attitude of banks towards the proposals submitted by small entrepreneurs and the farmers. As they had bitter experience of sanctioning more loan to these sectors since the volume of overdues have mounted over the years.

## Recovery Performance of Banks in Priority Sector Lending

The liquidity of banks largely depends on the recovery of advances. The recovery position of banks in the area is, quite unsatisfactory, presented in Table 12.8. It has been observed that the recovery position was very much poor in almost all the sectors in the area under study. At the end September 1996, the recovery rate was 27.0 per cent in agriculture and allied activities followed by 31.6 per cent in small sector and 22.6 per cent in trade and service sector for Karimganj district while 17.7 per cent, 15.8 per cent and 49.7 per cent in the respective sectors for Cachar district as on end December 1994. The recovery position in agriculture and allied activities is relatively discouraging to other priority sectors in three districts under consideration.

The lower recovery indicates erosion of banks' profitability and blocking up bank credit from developmental project of the area. The gravity of the situation will be clear when we found Rs. 243.2 lakhs (37.1%) was realized against the total outstanding dues of Rs. 655.5 lakhs under agricultural sector in Karimganj district as on 30-03-10. While in Cachar district Rs. 432.3 lakhs (38.5%) was realized against the total dues of Rs. 1123.6 lakhs in 30-12-09 and in Hailakandi district Rs. 456.0 lakhs (35.3%) was realised against total dues of Rs. 1290.4 lakhs in 30.03.10. The similar trend was noticed in small sector and service sector in the districts. However, in Hailakandi district, the recovery position of small sector (43.9%) is relatively better than that of agriculture

(35.3%) in March 2010. The service sector has experienced a recovery of 51.7 per cent as on March 2010.

A significant feature of banks lending is that, despite mounting over dues in each year, the agriculture and allied sectors enjoyed relatively major portion of bank credit. The agriculturists and poor people of the area could not repay the loans because they spend their loan on consumption purposes rather than productive purposes without bothering the liability of making repayment because of illiteracy. Further, in the perspective of economic development, there have been many disparities in the area in the distribution of resources. The flow of institutional loans has particularly benefited the richer section. In that context, the priority sector lending provides privileges to the poor people in order to lift their economic structure and condition. They are provided loans for buying buffaloes, cows, and pigs, to buy auto-rickshaw, to rear chicken and different machines for small scale industries. Indeed, they get subsidy by government on this loan. But they do not use the loan in the proper way for productive exercise. So, the loanee can not return loan. The constant failure of monsoon, natural calamities as famine flood etc, willful default, deficiencies in lending policies are the chief reasons for non-recovery of loans. The reasons for poor recovery may also be attributed to various other factors such as lack of supervision of end use of fund owing to lack of vehicle and paucity of staffs, defective processing of loan applications, political interference's, communication gap between banker and customer etc. The loans sanctioning authority begins to take undue advantage from such people. No effort is made for recovery of such loan. The local leaders do not encourage them to pay it back. They assure them that government will exempt it. Consequently the loan is never recovered in future; it becomes difficult to pay it back due to heavy amount. As a result the mounting over-dues restricted the banks' lending capacity. Therefore, an immediate action

## Table 12.8
## Sector-wise Recovery Position of Banks in Barak Valley

(Amount Rs. in Lakhs)

| Year | Agriculture & Allied | | | Small Sector & Rural Artisans | | | Trade & Service | | |
|---|---|---|---|---|---|---|---|---|---|
| | Demand | Recovery | Overdue | Demand | Recovery | Overdues | Demand | Recovery | Overdues |
| **Karimganj District** | | | | | | | | | |
| 30-09-96 | 363.2 (100) | 98.2 (27.0) | 265.0 (73.0) | 143.0 (100) | 45.2 (31.6) | 97.8 (69.4) | 1530.8 (100) | 345.6 (22.5) | 1185.2 (77.5) |
| 30-03-99 | 458.8 (100) | 115.8 (25.2) | 343.0 (74.8) | 206.3 (100) | 92.6 (44.8) | 113.7 (55.2) | 1960.3 (100) | 558.2 (28.4) | 1402.1 (71.6) |
| 30-03-05 | 543.2 (100) | 231.1 (27.9) | 320.9 (72.1) | 245.7 (100) | 110.8 (43.6) | 134.2 (56.4) | 2134.0 (100) | 602.8 (27.6) | 1432.0 (72.4) |
| 30-03-08 | 599.1 (100) | 250.0 (35.4) | 349.1 (65.6) | 287.4 (100) | 140.2 (45.8) | 147.2 (55.2) | 2359.0 (100) | 879.0 (29.9) | 1480.0 (70.1) |
| 31-03-10 | 655.5 (100) | 243.2 (37.1) | 412.3 (62.9) | 329.8 (100) | 139.3 (42.3) | 190.5 (57.7) | 2765.5 (100) | 1090.1 (39.4) | 1675.4 (60.6) |
| **Cachar District** | | | | | | | | | |
| 31-12-94 | 638.3 (100) | 113.0 (17.7) | 525.3 (82.3) | 299.2 (100) | 45.8 (15.8) | 253.4 (84.7) | 853.2 (100) | 424.6 (49.7) | 428.6 (50.3) |
| 31-03-98 | 758.6 (100) | 215.6 (28.4) | 543.0 (71.6) | 345.2 (100) | 96.2 (27.8) | 249.0 (72.2) | 1022.8 (100) | 511.2 (49.9) | 511.6 (50.1) |
| 31-03-05 | 875.9 (100) | 298.7 (27.9) | 576.5 (72.1) | 398.5 (100) | 100.5 (32.1) | 298.0 (67.9) | 2563.9 (100) | 1263.8 (48.1) | 1300.1 (51.9) |
| 30-03-08 | 915.8 (100) | 314.7 (32.7) | 601.1 (67.3) | 450.5 (100) | 210.2 (35.1) | 240.3 (64.9) | 3290.3 (100) | 1687.0 (50.9) | 1603.3 (49.1) |
| 30-12-09 | 1123.6 (100) | 432.3 (38.5) | 691.3 (61.5) | 549.1 (100) | 270.5 (49.3) | 278.8 (50.7) | 4309.3 (100) | 1980.6 (45.9) | 2328.7 (54.1) |

**Hailakandi District**

| | | | | | | | | | |
|---|---|---|---|---|---|---|---|---|---|
| 31-03-94 | 258.3 (100) | 45.0 (17.4) | 213.3 (82.6) | 85.3 (100) | 41.6 (48.7) | 43.7 (51.3) | 512.6 (100) | 213.9 (41.7) | 298.7 (58.3) |
| 31-12-99 | 482.9 (100) | 102.9 (21.3) | 380.0 (78.7) | 90.6 (100) | 45.2 (49.8) | 45.4 (50.2) | 418.2 (100) | 219.0 (52.3) | 199.2 (47.7) |
| 31-03-05 | 879.6 (100) | 278.6 (25.3) | 601.0 (74.7) | 201.6 (100) | 95.3 (47.4) | 106.3 (52.3) | 657.2 (100) | 321.1 (49.1) | 336.1 (50.9) |
| 30-06-08 | 970.8 (100) | 290.1 (26.5) | 680.7 (73.5) | 234.8 (100) | 103.5 (46.0) | 131.3 (54.0) | 879.4 (100) | 432.1 (49.8) | 445.3 (50.2) |
| 31-03-10 | 1290.4 (100) | 456.0 (35.3) | 834.4 (64.7) | 342.3 (100) | 150.3 (43.9) | 192.0 (56.1) | 1097.3 (100) | 567.3 (51.7) | 530.0 (48.3) |

Figure in the parenthesis indicates percentage to total demand.
Source: *Lead Bank Statements (LBS), Lead Bank Office, Cachar, Karimganj and Hailakandi Districts of Assam*

from appropriate authority to accelerate the recovery position in all sectors is necessary.

## Interrelationship between Priority Sector Advances and Non-Performing Assets

Due to non-availability of information relating to priority sector NPAs in the area under study, an attempt has been made hereunder to study the relationship between NPA and priority sector advances to identify with contribution of the same to total NPA. Table 12.8 shows the position of the variables relating to NPAs and priority, non-priority sector advances per bank branch.

For this purpose, we have calculated 'r' between NPAs per branch (a) and priority sector advances per branch (b) and non-priority sector advances per branch (c) during the period 2000-09. The results are summarized here under:

| | 'r ' value | 't ' value (cal) | 't ' value (tab) at 8 d.f. |
|---|---|---|---|
| $r_{ab}$ | 0.864 | 4.858 | 1 per cent = 2.306 |
| $r_{ac}$ | 0.926 | 7.431 | 5 per cent = 3.355 |

The analysis reveals that the positive correlation 0.864 is statistically significant at 1 per cent and 5 per cent level of significance at their respective degree of freedom for priority sector advances. Since calculated value of 't' is greater than the critical value, the relationship between PSL and NPAs is not due to change. The 'r' value 0.926 for non-priority sector advances is also significant at 5 per cent level and 1 per cent level of significance. Hence there is a positive relationship between NPAs and non-priority sector advances. This implies that with the increase of priority sector lending, there has been corresponding increase in the volume of NPAs. However, it can not be argued that priority sector lending is the sole factor in enhancing the volume of NPAs in the area under study. The non-priority sector advances are also responsible for the current quantum of NPAs.

## FACTORS INFLUENCING PRIORITY SECTOR LENDING BY COMMERCIAL BANKS

The above analysis, therefore, shows that the bank credit support to priority sector lending is not satisfactory. Thus, it is very important at this juncture to identify the factors affecting bank financing of priority sector. For this, we have used regression analysis considering independent variables like percentage of overdue in priority sector, interest rate, performance of banks measured with credit-deposit (C/D) ratios, credit delivery centers, ie, branch expansion of banks and volume of business (deposit plus advance) per bank branch. Table 12.9 presents the position of the variables relating to the identification of variables of PSL by banks.

The following multiple regression model has been employed for this purpose.

$$Y_t = \beta_1 + \beta_2 X_1 + \beta_3 X_2 + \beta_4 X_3 + \beta_5 X_4 + \beta_6 X_5 + U_t$$

where,

$Y_t$ is the deployment of bank credit to priority sector.

$X_1$ is the percentage of overdue to total demand in priority sector.

$X_2$ is the interest rate

$X_3$ is the performance of credit delivery institution ie. C/D ratio

$X_4$ is the bank branch expansion.

$X_5$ is the volume of business (deposit plus advances) per bank branches.

**Table 12.9**
**Position of variables of NPAs of Commercial Banks**

(Amount Rs in Lakhs)

| Year | NPAs (Rs.) | Priority sector advances (Rs.) | Non-priority sector advances (Rs.) | NPA per branch (Rs.) | Priority sector advances per branch (Rs.) | Non-priority sector advances per branch (Rs.) | No. of Branches excluding RRBs | Volume of Business per branch (Rs.) | Percentage of Overdues in Priority sector | Credit Deposit Ratio |
|---|---|---|---|---|---|---|---|---|---|---|
| 2000 | 761.8 | 8310 | 4608 | 5.8 | 89.3 | 49.5 | 92 | 1202.6 | 64.6 | 36.9 |
| 2001 | 829.9 | 8720 | 6412 | 5.5 | 91.7 | 67.5 | 94 | 1032.9 | 69 | 32.3 |
| 2002 | 1154.9 | 9135 | 6644 | 12.1 | 96.2 | 69.9 | 94 | 1320.8 | 61.6 | 22.3 |
| 2003 | 1016.2 | 9753 | 8466 | 10.6 | 102.7 | 89.1 | 94 | 1387.3 | 59.4 | 20.8 |
| 2004 | 1997.5 | 9980 | 9754 | 22.0 | 105 | 87.9 | 95 | 1298.2 | 63.2 | 19.0 |
| 2005 | 3686.9 | 12780 | 9831 | 30.6 | 132.9 | 121.0 | 97 | 1324.8 | 58.6 | 20.7 |
| 2006 | 2976.2 | 14328 | 10895 | 28.5 | 186 | 113.9 | 99 | 1450.9 | 57.9 | 18.6 |
| 2007 | 5143.0 | 16453 | 11342 | 48.4 | 166.2 | 128.6 | 99 | 1659.4 | 60.1 | 19.6 |
| 2008 | 5239.1 | 15541 | 14159 | 37.5 | 156.9 | 143.0 | 99 | 1570.7 | 56 | 17.0 |
| 2009 | 5540.7 | 16230 | 14698 | 42.0 | 163.9 | 148.5 | 99 | 1874.2 | 62 | 18.6 |

$U_t$ is the error term.

$\beta_1$ is the intercept.

$\beta_i$ ( i = 1, 2, 3 . . . 6) is the regression coefficients.

ANOVA of dependant variable is shown below-

**ANOVA: Priority Sector Lending by Commercial Banks**

| | df | SS | MS | F | Significance F |
|---|---|---|---|---|---|
| Regression | 5 | 96857018 | 19371404 | | |
| Residual | 4 | 992599.6 | 248149.9 | 78.06332 | 0.000446 |
| Total | 9 | 97849618 | | | |

**Note**: SS = Sum of Squares, MS= Mean sum Square

The other results obtained from the regression analysis are summarized in Table 12.10.

The aforesaid analysis relating to determinants of priority sector lending by banks shows a high degree of explanatory power ($R^2$ =0.989). This indicates 98 per cent variation in the bank financing of priority sector in the district is explained by independent variables. It is further confirmed by 'F' ratio which turned to be statistically significant. This implies that the independent variables like mounting over dues, interest rate, credit-deposit ratio, branch expansion and volume of business are the perfect determinants of dependent variable viz., priority sector advances. The â (beta) value of C/D ratio, volume of business and branch expansion are positive and statistically significant. However, the â coefficient of interest rate is positive and of mounting overdues of bank is negative, but both are not statistically significant. The aforesaid analysis indicates that three factors viz., volume of business, C/D ratio and branch expansion out of five identified factors are the most affecting factors of deployment of bank credit to priority sector.

**Table 12.10**
**Regression Summary of Independent Variables**

| Independent variables | 'β' value | t stat | Sig. | S E | Adjusted $R^2$ | $R^2$ | SE |
|---|---|---|---|---|---|---|---|
| Intercept ($\beta_1$) | - | | | | | | |
| Percentage of overdues ($\beta_2$ ) | -75.6425 | -1.1076 | 0.3301 | 68.288 | | | |
| Interest rate on credit($\beta_3$) | 229.019 | 0.418 | 0.6974 | 547.881 | 0.977176 | 0.989856 | 498.146 |
| Credit/Deposit ratio($\beta_4$) | 119.747 | 2.5568 | 0.06284 | 46.833 | | | |
| Branch expansion of banks($\beta_5$) | 1027.795 | 8.9536 | 0.00086 | 114.79 | | | |
| Volume of business ($\beta_6$) | 4.7405 | 3.5671 | 0.02343 | 1.3289 | | | |

The stumpy performance intensity of credit delivery institutions, ie, unhealthy C/D ratio, does present an impression that flow of credit to priority sector has come down substantially despite various measures undertaken. The adequacy of credit delivery centers i.e., branch expansion of banks, is also a credit supporting variable to activities relating to small business entrepreneurs and agriculture. The volume of business per branch ensures to achieve higher degree of productivity and hence improves the heath of the banks so that it gets strength to support the required sector of the economy. Higher recovery ensures bank to endorse higher quantum of credit to priority sector. It may be suggested that there should be proper recovery of loan amount from loanee in order to restore the performance of commercial banks in the area under study, other wise banks would face liquidity crisis for recycling the fund.

## NOTES AND REFERENCES


1. Narasimham, M. 1994. *Financial Sector Reform: The Unfinished Agenda*, Platinum Jubilee Conference Volume, Indian Economic Association, Indira Gandhi Institute of Development Research, Bombay
2. http://www.articlesbase.com/business-articles/priority-sector-lending-by-commercial-banks1106151.html#ixzz19 Pmxg wvk (visited on 10th Sept,2010)
3. Niranjana, S and Anbumani, V. 2002. *Social Objectives and Priority Sector Lending*, Banking and Financial Sector Reforms in India, Deep and Deep publications, P- 231
4. Government of India (1991a) *Report of the Committee on Financial System, Ministry of Finance,* (Narasimham Committee), December.
5. Govt of India (1998) *Report of the Committee on Financial System, Ministry of Finance*, (Narasimham Committee-II), April.
6. Majumder, N.A. 2001. *The New Architecture of Rural Credit System*, Prof. M. L. Dantwala Monograph Series, Department of Economics, University of Mumbai, August 2001.
7. Reddy, Y. V. 2001. *Address at the Conference of Indian Society of Agricultural Marketing* at Vizag (A.P.) February

8. Reserve Bank of India. 2009. *Master Circular on Priority Sector Lending*, 30th June 2009.

9. Shete, N. B. 2002. *Priority Sector Advances By Public Sector Banks during the Post Reform Period (1992-93 to 2000-01).* Working Paper, NIBM, Pune, March, 2002.

10. Radelet, S and Sachs, J. 1998. *The Onset of the East Asian Financial Crisis*, NBER Working Paper 6680.

11. Hardy, D.C and Pazarbasioglu.1999. *Determinants and Leading Indicators of Banking Crisis: Further Evidence*, Washington D.C, IMF Staff Papers, 46(3).

12. Kaminsky, G.L and Reinhert, E.S. 1999. *The Twin Crisis: The Causes of Banking and Balance of Payment Problems*, American Economic Review, 89, http://home.gwu.edu/graciela.

13. Salas and Saurina, J. 2002. *Credit Risk in two Institutional Regime: Spanish Commercial and Saving Banks*, Journal of Financial Services Research, 22(3): 203-224.

14. Meyer, A. P and Yeager, T. J. 2001. *Are Small Rural Banks Vulnerable to Local Economic Downturns* Federal Reserve Bank of St Louis Working Paper, pp. 1-28.

15. Gambera, M. 2000. Simple *Forecasts of Bank Loan Quality in the Business Cycles: Emerging Issues Series*, Federal Reserve Bank of Chicago, pp,1-31.

16. Marcucci, J and Quagliariello, M. 2005. *Is Bank Portfolio Riski-ness Pro-cyclical? Evidence from Italy Using A Vector Auto-regression*, University of York, Discussion Papers in Economics, http://www.york.ac.uk/depts/econ (Retrieved on 5th January 2009).

17. Hoggarth, G, Sorensen, S and Zicchino, L. 2005. *Stress Tests of UK Banks Using a VAR Approach*, Bank of England Working Paper, No. 282, pp.1-44.

18. Baboucek, I and Jancer, M. 2005. A VAR *Analysis of the Effects of Macroeconomic Shocks to the Quality of the Aggregate Loan Portfolio of the Czech Banking Sector*, Czexh National Bank Working Paper Series, pp- 1-68

19. Rikta, N. N. 2006, *Institutional Lending and Financing Policy for SMEs in Bangladesh*, Policy Note, Federation of Bangladesh Chamber of Commerce and Industry, Dhaka

20. Report (2009) *Egypt; Country Strategy Paper Mid-Term Review 2007-2011*, Country Regional Department North I (Orna), April 2009, Progress report

21. Joshi, P,N. 1972. *Financing of Priority Sectors by Commercial Banks*, The Journal of Indian Institute of Bankers, XLIII(1):27-34

22. Chawala, A.S. 1979. *Nationalization and Growth of Indian Banking*, Deep and Deep Publication, New Delhi

23. Angadi, V.B. 1983. *Bank's Advances to Priority Sectors: An Enquiry in to the Causes of Concentration*, Economic & Political Weekly, XVIII (13):503-510 (March 26)

24. Joshi P.N. 1986. *Profitability and Profit Planning in Banks*, The Journal of Indian Institute of Bankers (April-June) 57 (2)

25. Singh, S. 1987. *Profitability of Commercial Banks in India*, Punjab National Bank Monthly Review, (October) II (II)

26. Muhammad Yunus. 1988. *The Poor as the Engine of Development*, Economic Impact, 63:27-31

27. Rangarajan, C. 1991. *Banking Development Since 1947; Achievement and Challenges*, Financial System in India, II

28. Government of India (1991a) *Report of the Committee on Financial System*, Ministry of Finance, (Narasimham Committee), December

29. Krishnoswamy, K.S. 1992. *More a Lawyer's Belief than Report*, Economic & Political Weekly, XXVII (8):391-393, (February, 22)

30. Rajagopal, S. 1994. *The Priority Sector*, IBA Bulletin, XVI (1): 52-54 (January)

31. Patel, S.G. 1996. *Role of Commercial Banks' Lending to Priority Sector in Gujarat - An Evaluation*, Finance India, X(2): 389-393

32. Government of India (1998) *Report of the Committee on Financial System, Ministry of Finance*, (Narasimham Committee-II), April

33. Kohli, R. 1997. *Directed Credit and Financial Reforms*. Economic and Political weekly, XXXII(42):2267-2276 October 18

34. Ajit, D. 1997. *Para Banking in India, Some Issue*. Economic and Political weekly, (October 18) XXXII (42)

35. RBI, Department of Banking Supervision (1999) *Some Aspects and Issues Relating to NPAs in Commercial Banks*, RBI Bulletin, LIII(7): 913-930

36. Report of the *Expert Committee on Rural Credit* (V S Vyas Committee), 2001, NABARD, Mumbai, November 12.

37. Niranjana, S and Anbumani, V. 2002. *Social Objectives and Priority Sector Lending*, Banking and Financial Sector Reforms in India, Deep and Deep publications, P- 231

38. Shete, N.B 2002 *Priority Sector Advances By Public Sector Banks During the Post Reform Period (1992-93 to 2000-01).* Working Paper, NIBM, Pune, (March 2002)

39. World Bank (2004) *Indian Bank Profits Hit by Priority Sector Lending,* 15th June 2004, weblink:http://www.domain-b .com/finance/banks/world_bank/20040615_profits.html, (accessed on 13/05/09)

40. RBI Internal Working Group (2005) *Priority Sector Lending,* Rural Planning and Credit Department Central Office, RBI, Mumbai (September)

41. Ahmed, J.U. 2005. *Bank Financing of Small Scale Industries: A Diagnostic Evaluation*, Ahmed, J.U (ed.) Industrialization in North Eastern Region, Mittal Publications, New Delhi

42. Bhati, S. 2006, *Trust between Branch Managers and Loan Officers of Indian Banks,* International Review of Business Research Papers, 2(4):51-58, December

43. Rajesham, Ch and Rajender, K. 2007. *Management of NPAs in Indian Scheduled Commercial Banks,* The Chartered Accountant of India, June

44. Narasaiah, M and Naik, N.T.K., 2007. *Venture Capital for Small and Medium Business: A Proposal for South- South Co-operation.* Indian Economic Panorama, October 2007, 17(3): 24- 25

45. Sooden, M and Kumar, S. 2007. *Priority Sector Lending in Post Reform Period*, Finance India, (December), XXI(4): 1389-1404

46. Paramjit, N and Priyanka, M. 2007. *Analysis of Non-Performing Assets in Priority Sector: A Comparative Study of Public and Private Sector Banks,* Indian Journal of Agricultural Economics, (July)

47. RBI (2007) *Report of the Technical Group to Review Efficacy of Existing Legislative Framework Governing Money Lending and its Enforcement Machinery,* Mumbai

48. Roy, Anup. 2008. *NABARD Asks Banks to Speed up Farm Lending to Meet Yearly Disbursal Target*, The Week in Review, visited on 15th Sept, 2010, http://www.livemint.com/2008/11/19230033/Nabard-asks-banks-to-speed-up.html

49. Reserve Bank of India (2010) RBI *Comes Up with Stricter Norms for Priority Sector Lending*, http://www.accommod ationtimes.com /real-estate-news/rbi-comes-up-with-stricter-norms-for-priority-sector-lending/ visited on 12th August 2010

50. Verma, S and Antony, A. 2010. *RBI May Reject Trade-Ability for Priority Sector Lending Papers, The Financial Express,* 28th December 2010

51. Government of Assam (2007) *Statistical Hand book,* Directorate of Economics and Statistics, Guwahati, Assam.
52. Office of the *Joint Director of Agriculture*, South Assam Zone, Silchar
53. Calculated on the basis of data obtained from *Directorate Economics and Statistics & District Industries Centres* of the area under study
54. UBI (2009) Lead Bank Office, United Bank of India, Silchar, Assam.

# 13

# Screen-based Trading: A Boon for Small Investor

**A. Rajmani Singh**

Capital market of the world has been changing very fast over the last few decades. A series of stock market structure reforms has been implemented in different stock markets around the world. These reforms have been aimed at improving market efficiency, including modernization of trading and information systems, expanding membership globally and revamping the regulatory framework. Stoll (2006) emphasizes the main benefits to be expected from the introduction of modern sophisticated trading technology. There have been numerous studies on the causes and effectiveness of microstructure reforms in the more established stock markets, focusing in particular on trading and information systems; and most of the studies suggest that such structure reforms have had a positive impact, creating efficiency gains in the price discovery process, increased liquidity, investor friendly and lower volatility unlike past. Examples include studies of Milan (Amihud *et al.*, 1990; Tokyo (Amihud and Mendelson, 1991), New Zealand (Blennerhassett and Bowman, 1998) Tel Aviv (Amihud *et al.*, 1997; Kalay *et al.*, 2002), Paris (Pagano and Schwartz, 2003), London (Chelley-Steeley, 2008), and Dublin (Chelley-Steeley and Lucey, 2008)

Screen Based Trading System (SBTS) or On line trading or e-trading or scrip less trading has been found to be more cost-effective, less time consuming, more transparent, and user-friendly in comparison with scrip based trading. In recent past, many developed markets of the world have been putting their effort to automate and introduce screen based trading systems.

The last decade has witnessed a dramatic change in both the number and the market share of screen-based trading systems. The adoption of screen based trading systems has transformed the economic landscape of trading venues and is proving a force for change in market architecture and consequential trading possibilities. It has been removing geographical constraints and allowing much higher trade volumes to be handled, and in customized ways that until recently would have been technically impossible or prohibitively expensive.

Within the fixed income market sector, screen based trading has made most inroads into many government bond markets. As per a survey by the Bond Markets Association of USA, there were 97 electronic, fixed-income trading systems operating in the U.S. and Europe in late 2008 versus 11 in 1997. Of these 97 electronic trading systems, 56 were based mainly in the USA and 41 in Europe. Information provided by trading platform vendors suggests that fixed income trading executed electronically has increased in volume steadily over the past several years. The Survey concluded that online bond trading grew significantly with average growth of 78 per cent on 2008.

The National Stock Exchange (NSE) has been the most proactive in bringing about most of these technological innovations, including online trading. It started way back in February 2000 with the Kochi-based Geojith Securities conducting the first Net transaction when 100 shares of Reliance was traded by SEBI chairman D R Mehta for Geojith chairman A P Kurian. Much water has flown under the bridge since then.

From a base of about Rs 3 crores in April 2000, volumes for online trading have risen to nearly Rs 1,500 crores per month in January 2001. A Nasscom-BCG study estimates the market will grow to Rs12,000 crores per month by 2005. In spite of these optimistic numbers, online trading in India is at a very nascent stage (about 2 percent of total traded volumes) compared to countries like South Korea (60 percent), US (40 percent) and UK (20 percent). Online trading in the year 2000-2001 accounted for only Rs 50,170 crores out of total traded volume of Rs 25,08,445 crores.

## What is Screen Based Trading?

The trading on stock exchanges in India used to take place through open outcry without use of information technology for immediate matching or recording of trades. This was time consuming and inefficient. This system has imposed limits on trading volumes and its level of efficiency. In order to provide efficiency, liquidity and transparency, NSE introduced a nationwide, on-line, fully automated screen based trading system (SBTS) where a member investor can punch into the computer for the quantities of a security and the price at which he would like to transact, and the transaction is executed as soon as a matching sale or buy order from a counter party is found. We can trade while working in the office or at home and if we do not have computer/internet at home, we can go to Cyber café. Now, investors can also use their mobile for track and invest in the online trading market. Thus, it is truly a powerful medium to place our orders without any manual intervention and trades are executed in a matter of a few seconds.

SBTS (Screen-Based Trading System) gives us the ability to click in instantly execute trades when connected to trade execution infrastructure through partner clearing firms and execution providers. SBTS, when used alongside helps empower to analyze options, quote markets, and execute orders - all at the same time. With SBTS, we can create defaults for a number of contracts, order durations, and order types, and track the status of orders in the SBTS message Log.

Screen based trading uses modern tele-communications and computer technology to combine information transmission with trading in financial assets. Trading members are connected to the exchange from their workstations to the central computer located at the exchange via satellite. Buy and sell orders from the brokers reach the central computer located at stock exchange and are matched by the computer. They are registered with one or more Stock Exchanges. Mostly Online Trading Websites in India trade in BSE and NSE.

## Screen Based Trading System in India

Since the beginning of economic liberalization process in 1991, the size of Indian capital market had expanded manifold. The traditional system of trading through physical transfer of securities failed to cope up with the requirements of growing capital market and hindered further growth of the market.. Physical settlement mechanisms give rise to inefficiencies and risks of bad deliveries, delays in transfer and registration, fake certificate and forgeries.

The old scrip based trading system of securities transactions involves enormous paper work involving certificates and transfer deeds. Every securities transactions in the physical scrip based system are required to be accomplished by physical movement of securities certificates along with transfer deeds to and registration with the company. In the process of purchasing of securities and till getting the certificates duly transferred and endorsed in the name of the buyer, there are wide varieties of problems encountered by the buyer/ seller such as:

- Bad deliveries of share due to signature difference

- Mistakes in completion of transfer deeds/ incomplete transfer deeds
- Tearing and mutilation of certificates
- Fake certificates
- Fraudulent interception of certificate in transit
- Cost of transfer stamps duty
- Processing time taken by the company
- Postal delays in disbursement and higher charges etc
- Exploitation of investors by the middlemen/intermediaries
- Greater paper work and procedure and
- Theft or share lost before transfer

In order to overcome the above problems/difficulties in one side and enable to provide efficiency, liquidity, investor friendly and transparency, for the first time, National Stock exchange introduced a nationwide, on line, fully automated SBTS started from November 4th 1994 in India.

Minimization of settlement risks and shortening of settlement cycle are the basic requirements for greater depth and expansion of markets by upgrading the existing trading system into a modern internationally competitive one. A need was felt for the introduction of scrip less trading system or screen based trading system movements, culminating in the promulgation of Depositories Ordinance 1995 (later re-promulgated in 1996). Thus, Depositories Act has paved the way for institutions an infrastructure for eliminating various risks associated with capital market transactions and increasing the efficiency of clearance and settlement systems. It allows for de-materialization and re-materialization of securities in depositories through electronic book entry thus reducing settlement risks and removing some of the infrastructural bottleneck.

## Status of SBTS in India

NSE was the first stock exchange in the country to provide nation wide order driven screen based trading system on November $4^{th}$ 1994. Today, all stock exchanges in India follow screen based trading system. The NSE model was gradually emulated by all other stock exchange in the country. Till date NSE has rendered a yeoman's services and covering 1,200 trading members, 1,500 cities, 1,80,000 terminals, 1,400 equity shares, and 2,000 debt instruments.

After a gap of one year, BSE had replaced its open outcry system with the BSE On-line Trading (BOLT) facility in 1995. This totally automated, screen-based trading in securities was put into practice nation-wide within a record time of just 50 days. BOLT has been certified by DNV for conforming to ISO 27001:2005 security standards. The capacity of the BOLT platform stands presently enhanced to 80 lakh orders per day.

Today, BSE is the world's number 1 exchange in the world in terms of the number of listed companies (over 4900). It is the world's 5th most active in terms of number of transactions handled through its electronic trading system. And it is in the top ten of global exchanges in terms of the market capitalization of its listed companies (as of December 31, 2009). The companies listed on BSE command a total market capitalization of USD Trillion 1.28 as of Feb, 2010. BSE is the first exchange in India and the second in the world to obtain an ISO 9001:2000 certification. It is also the first Exchange in the country and second in the world to receive Information Security Management System Standard BS 7799-2-2002 certification for its BSE On-Line trading System (BOLT). Presently, BSE got ISO 27001:2005 certified, which is a ISO version of BS 7799 for Information Security.

The main stock exchanges in which screen based trading is being followed from initial stages are:

1. National Stock Exchange (NSE)
2. Over the Counter Exchange of India (OTCEI)
3. Inter-connected Stock Exchange of India (ICSE)

Procedure for Screen Based Trading

There are some steps which an online trader has to follow in order to online stock trading. They are as follow:-

- **Step-1:** Those investors interested in doing the trading over internet system, that is, NEAT- ISX, should approach the brokers and register with the Stock Broker.
- **Step-2:** After registration, the broker will provide a login ID and password for both Demat and trading account to the member.
- **Step-3:** Actual placement of an order will be executed. An order can be placed by using the place order window as under:
  - (a) First by entering the symbol and series of stock and other parameters such as quantity and price of the scrip on the place order window.
  - (b) Second, fill in the symbol, series and the default quantity.
- **Step-4:** It is the process of review. Thus, the investor has to review the order placed by clicking the review option. He may also re-set to clear the values.
- **Step-5:** After the review has been satisfactorily done, the order has to be sent by clicking on the send option.

- **Step-6:** The investor will receive an "Order Confirmation" message along with the order number and the value of the order.
- **Step-7:** In case the order is rejected by the Broker or the Stock Exchange for certain reasons such as invalid price limit, an appropriate message will appear at the bottom of the screen. At present, a time lag of about ten seconds is there in executing the trade.
- **Step-8:** It is regarding charging payment, for which there are different modes. Some brokers will take some advance payment from the investors and will fix their trading limits. When the trade is executed, the broker will ask the investor for transfer of funds by the investor to his account.

## Advantages of Screen Based Trading

The following are the advantages of trading securities through screen based trading:

- No risk of loss/ theft/fraud of shares
- No risk of receiving fake/forged/stolen certificates
- No stamp duty while transferring share from one investor to another
- Fast, secure and speedy transactions with minimum cost
- Reduction in paper of stockbrokers and stock exchanges.
- No delay in transfers
- Executes trades instantly with greater Transparency
- Allows traders on and off the floor to send orders and receive trade confirmations.

- Helps empower traders to simultaneously analyze options, quote markets and execute orders.
- Investment in IPOs, equities, Mutual Funds and Bonds are possible through online trading.
- Check the trading history; demat account balance and bank account balance at any time.
- No geographical and time limitations
- Orders directly sent to stock exchanges rather than stock broker. This makes order execution very fast.
- It provides almost each and every information which is required for a trader on a single screen including stock market charts, live data, alerts, stock market news etc through E-mail or SMS..
- Real time stock trading without calling or visiting broker's office.
- Display real time market watch, historical data, graphs etc.

## Disadvantages of Screen Based Trading

The following are the disadvantages of screen based trading:

- Depend on the Website performance - sometime the website is too slow or not enough for user friendly response.
- Infant stage - difficult for those investor especially who doesn't know much about computer and internet.
- Brokerage charges are little high.
- Location constraints - You cannot trade if you are not on the computer where you have installed trading terminal software.

- It requires high speed internet connection.
- These trading terminals are not easily available for low volume share traders.
- There is lack of personal touch while doing stock trading through screen.

## SBT Mechanism with special reference to NSE

NSE stresses on innovation and sustained investment in technology to remain ahead of competition. NSE is the first exchange in the world to use satellite communication technology for trading. It uses satellite communication technology to energize participation from about 2648 VSATs from nearly 201 cities spread all over the country covering 1,200 trading members, 1,500 cities, 1,80,000 terminals, 1,400 equity shares, and 2,000 debt instruments. Its trading system, called National Exchange for Automated Trading (NEAT), is a state of-the-art client server based application. At the server end all trading information is stored in an in-memory database to achieve minimum response time and maximum system availability for users. It has uptime record of 99.999%. For orders entered by the user, the response time within trading system is around 10ms. NSE has been continuously undertaking capacity enhancement measures so as to effectively meet the requirements of increased users and associated trading loads. NSE has also put in place NIBIS (NSEs Internet Based Information System) for on-line real-time dissemination of trading information over the Internet. Fig given below depicts how NSE operating its online trading connecting mainframe computer and PCs of member via VSAT and other computer peripherals.

NSE has the main computer which is connected through Very Small Aperture Terminal (VSAT) installed at its office. The main computer runs on a fault tolerant mainframe computer at the Exchange. Brokers have terminals installed at their

**Fig. 13.1: Network system of NSE NEAT**

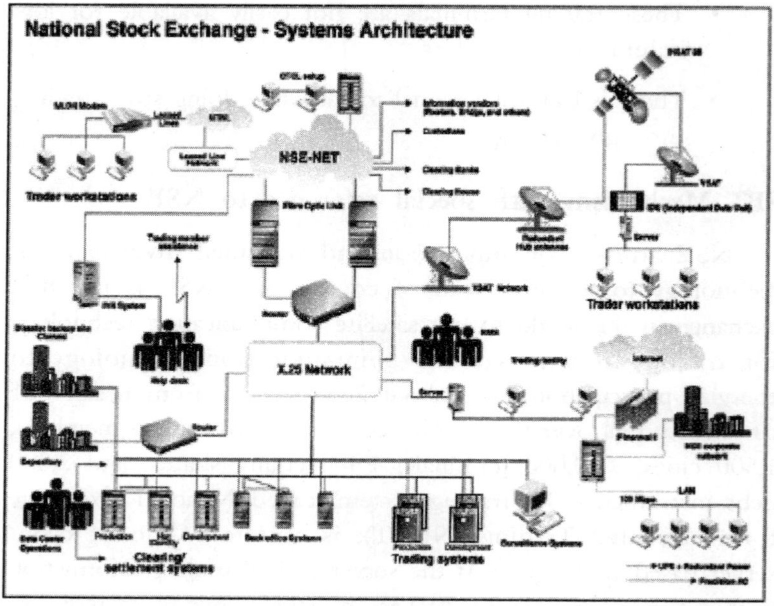


premises which are connected through VSATs/leased lines/ modems.

An investor informs a broker to place an order on his behalf. The broker enters the order through his PC, which runs under Windows NT and sends signal to the Satellite via VSAT/leased line/modem. The signal is directed to mainframe computer at NSE via VSAT at NSE's office. A message relating to the order activity is broadcast to the respective member. The order confirmation message is immediately displayed on the PC of the broker. This order matches with the existing passive order(s), otherwise it waits for the active orders to enter the system. On order matching, a message is broadcast to the respective member.

The trading system operates on a strict price time priority.

All orders received on the system are sorted, with the best priced order getting the first priority for matching i.e., the best buy orders match with the best sell order. Similar priced orders are sorted on time priority basis, i.e. the one that came in earlier gets priority over the later order. Orders are matched automatically by the computer keeping the system, transparent and fair. Where an order does not find a match, it remains in the system for the day till a fresh order comes in or the earlier order is cancelled or modified.

## Facilities of the Online Trading in India

The investor has to register with an online trading portal and get into an agreement with the firm to trade in different securities following the terms and conditions listed down in the agreement. The order processing is done in correct timings as the servers of the online trading portal are connected to the stock exchanges and designated banks all round the clock. They can also get updates on the trading and check the current status of their orders either through e-mail or through the interface.

- **Products and services of the online trading in India:** The major financial products and services of the Online trading in India are like equities, mutual funds, life insurance, general insurance, loans, share trading, commodities trading, portfolio management and financial planning.
- **How to place order:** An investor informs broker to place an order on his behalf. The broker enters the order through his PC, which runs under windows NT and sends signal to the satellite via VSAT. The signal is directed to mainframe computer at NSE via VSAT at NSE office. A message relating to the order activity is broadcasted to respective member.

- **Online Trading in NSE and BSE, Buying/Selling Shares and Brokers**: Investing in share market can bring very good returns compared to other kind of investments like bank fixed deposits, bonds, PPF, NSC etc. Selecting the right stock in the right sector at the right time is important for success in equities. Price of the stocks increases according to the growth of the company plus companies will give bonus and dividend at periodic intervals.
- **Buying/Selling a Share:** Once the account is active you can buy shares from BSE or NSE. For every buy or sell transaction you will have to pay a brokerage to the broker which normally ranges between 0.4% to 0.8%. Suppose you buy 100 shares with price 100. So total amount is Rs 10000. For a .5% brokerage firm you will have to pay 0.5% of 10,000 ie Rs50. Same amount you have to pay when you sell it. So totally Rs 100 will be reduced from your total profit.Apart from this brokerage you will have to pay many other charges like Service tax on the brokerage ie 12.25% for above transaction it is 12.25% of Rs 50 ie 6.125 for buy and another 6.125 for sell. Then there are other charges like Securities Turnover Tax (.125%), Stamp duty, Education cess, minimum buy/sell commission etc. These amount varies from broker to broker.
- **Online Brokers:** There are currently close to 50 online brokerage firms in India like Sharekhan, Geojith Securities, ICICIDirect, HDFCSecurities, IndiaBulls, Investsmart Online, Kotak Street, Motilal Oswal, 5 Paisa etc are the prominent online brokers.
- **Electronic Contract Notes**: In screen based trading, electronic contract notes are issued. The electronic contract notes should be as per the prescribed standard format in

the bye-laws, rules and regulations of stock exchange. The electronic contract notes become valid legal document when digital signatures are inscribed on it.

- **Electronic Fund Collection**: In screen based trading, the funds are settled through settling bank. Brokers get their funds directly credited to their accounts and the clients can in turn get their accounts credited or debited for the net funds through settling bank. Settling bank is the bank which has connection between stock exchange, broker and client.

## Online Trading: Boon or Bane for Small Investor

Different online trading studies across the globe has proved that there has been improving the securities market manifold and expanded its market operation to masses including small investor. Side by side it has also created confusion among the small investor for taking right investment decision at right time. Online trading has provided ample scope and opportunities to small investor which was never happened in the past. It has charges lower fees and commissions in comparison with traditional ways of trading; it enables to make an opportunity to act on price movement immediately; direct access to information on real time prices and charts; absence of broker gives any trader an opportunity to take his/her own decisions without hurry; completing or denying a trade can be performed within a few seconds so it's easier to manage investments and shorten losses. However, the major drawback of online trading is the absence of a middleman (broker) and as a result the absence of an investment plan, which full service broker will definitely help you to create. So if you are not yet advanced investor, you should better search for broker before you begin to trade and consult him. The middleman is also very important assistant, because in case you have not access to computer and Internet, you should know that you can call your broker and manage your trades. Having such a broker is very profitable, of course you'll have to pay money for broker service but at the same time you'll have an opportunity for direct control. Choosing a broker is an important and serious step which should be well considered as far as your success in online trading will partially depend on your broker. Don't ever forget to learn more about online trading, if you want to succeed. Considering the pros and cons of online trading, the benefits getting through online trading by the small investor has been on the upper side. Now small investor can easily access to securities market which they never dream before. Awareness and knowledge on online trading through internet must be learned by the investor if he / she wanted to trade. If proper knowledge, investment analysis and selection of portfolio have been considered along with right timing of investment, it will certainly be a BOON for small investor to earn money otherwise it will be a BANE for the small investor.

## Way Forward

In spite of the problems and issues, the future looks bright. Explains Shukla:

> "All hope is not lost as players like Reliance and Bharti have started laying optic fibre across the length and breadth of the country, and in a matter of say two years, the last mile connectivity issue will be solved."

Adds Gada:

> "The solution lies in balancing a technology-centric approach to transactions with the human touch factor which will be a key factor in making the transition from the traditional method of broking to e-broking."

Organizations like ICICI-Direct have a very rosy view of the future too. Says Bagchi:

"We are pleasantly surprised by the acceptance of online trading by our customers over the last 18 months. At ICICIDirect, we are routinely processing about 12,000 trades per day even in these market conditions. The risk appetite of the investors has come down but the participation levels have stabilized as shown by our growing customer base of over 135,000 customers."

Gada adds, "Online trading is a certainty and this is endorsed by its rapid acceptance in developed and structured capital markets. We do not believe anything has gone wrong with trading online in particular." While the numbers may not match up to growth figures of online trading made last year, viewed from the overall context of the depressed market sentiment the world over, the increase in both, brokers providing online services and investors who are trading online is indeed a reinforcement of the increasing acceptance of online trading.

Increasing smart phone penetration and the availability of Internet browsers as a basic feature in entry-level phones is increasing the base of subscribers with access to the Internet. In the second quarter of FY10, a total of 127 million subscribers were capable of accessing data services through mobile handsets. The non-voice revenue mix of Indian wireless operators remains low at 10-11 per cent, compared with 25-30 per cent for mature markets due to non-availability of 3G services.

Thus, as these services become operational, we expect data mix to increase to 20-25 per cent by 2015. Apart from mobile applications, 3G services will also allow GSM operators to offer mobile broadband services—a fast-growing market with a significant potential, given the negligible fixed broadband penetration in India. 3G spectrum will provide telecom companies the opportunity to offer real-time trading, as well as interactive and real-time equity research-based services, thus leading to increased revenues through subscription-based research services and increased data usage. Mobile trading is an extension of traditional online trading and works either through a browser or an application provided by the broker. The low Internet speeds on mobiles also limits features, compared to a web version of online trading.

## CONCLUSION

With the launching of online trading in Indian capital market, now more and more penetration of small investor in securities market emerged. Earlier offline trading was considered as the main source of stock trading in India. Now online stock trading system has been increasing its popularity. The main advantage of online trading is that it is more consistent and more transparent. There is need for revolution of information technology for successful online trading for the masses. Online trading can be successful only where infrastructural facilities for internet are available for the investors at cheaper price with dedicated line without interruptions.

Today online trading is the most popular way to trade and earn money due to computers. Each investor aims at successful online trading but before you try your hand at online trading do remember that it's not a gambling. Make sure that you are aware of ***online trading concepts, online trading tips and safe online trading*** before you start trading. There is no doubt that online trading is a perfect opportunity to earn money but it doesn't mean that this occupation is for everyone. Online trading has not only benefits but also drawbacks, that's why before you begin to trade, you should consider all online trading pros and cons.

Knowledge and awareness on online trading must be imparted to each and every investor before you start to take investment decision. Taking right decision in right time with online trading knowledge will make you to get boon if not you have to accept for the bane.

## REFERENCES

Christopher J. Green at el (2010) Share Liquidity and Market Microstructure Reform: The Case of Screen-based Trading in Mumbai, Korean Securities Association

Indian Securities Market: A Review 2009

Camilleri, S. J., and C. J. Green, 2009, The impact of the suspension of opening and closing call auctions: Evidence from the National Stock Exchange of India, *International Journal of Banking, Accounting and Finance* **1**, pp. 257–284.

Indian Economy (2008) Pratiyogita Darpan. Upkar Prakashan, Agra-2

Bhat Sudhindra (2008) Security Analysis and Portfolio Management, Excel Books, New Delhi-28

Walia and Kumar (2007) "Online Stock Trading in India" Indian Journal of Marketing volume XXXVII • Number 4 • April

Interpal Singh at el (2007) Security Analysis and Portfolio Management, Kalyani Publishers Ludhiyana.

Lau, Chau and yen (2001) "adoption of online trading in Hong Kong financial market" journal of electronic commerce Research, vol 2, no.2, 2001

Li, Lee and Cude (2001) "Intention To Adopt Online Trading: Identifying the Future Online Traders" Association for Financial Counseling and Planning Education.

Barber and Odean (1999) "online investors: Do the Slow Die First"

www.gsm.ucdavis

www.theonlinetradingguide.com

www.onlinetrading.co.in

# 14

# Security Trading; Pricing of IPOs: A Scrutiny of Procedure

**Nayan Barua & Sujit Sikidar**

Security constitutes an important avenue for investment for a segment of the members in the society. Security trading by nature may be somewhat riskier but its return is comparatively higher at some interval of time. Some investors can directly participate in security trading through equity stock in share market. While those who are risk averse can go for a slightly softer instrument like debt instrument i.e. mutual fund. Before going into the trading proper we proceed to examine the definition and nature of securities as given in the concerned legislation as discussed hereunder.

## Objectives

The objectives of the paper are as follows:

1. To examine the nature of securities and the pricing mechanism in IPO; and
2. To make a critical review of the IPO pricing policy.

The paper is descriptive in nature. It encompasses the recent guidelines issued by SEBI with regard to securities trading and other related matters.

## Meaning of Securities as per Securities Contract and Regulation (SCR) Act 1956

Section 2(1)(b) dealing in securities means an act of buying, selling or otherwise dealing in any security by any person either as principal or as agent. Securities include

(i) Shares, scripts, stocks, bonds, debentures, debenture stock or other marketable securities of a like nature in or of any incorporated company or other body corporate;

(ii) Government securities;

(iii) Such other instruments as may be declared by the Central Government to be securities; and

(iv) Rights or interests in securities [sec 2(h)]. Government security means a security created and issued by the Central Government or a State Government for the purpose of raising a public loan [sec 2 (b)].

Any stock exchange, which is desirous of being recognized may make an application to the Central Government in specified form Form A under Rule 3 of the Securities Contract (Regulations) Rules 1957 (SCRR).

(1) Securities Contracts (Regulation) Rules 1957; Securities contracts (Manner of Increasing and Maintaining Public Shareholding in Recognised Stock Exchanges) Rules 2006 (MIMPS) are regulating securities market.

(2) MINPS maintains dispersal of shareholding in stock exchanges as follows. Traders on a stock exchange must always be in a minority amongst shareholders; they can not together own more than 49 pc. Within this limit, a single foreign institution can own 26 pc at most but none has been allowed to do so.

## Mechanism of Allotment

There is a Brokers Pool Account; Registrar and Transfer Agent facilitating securities trading. The company going for IPO again through NSDL passes the shares to depositories (DP). NSDL operates through NSDL central system. NSDL has 286 DPs as in March 2010. DPs levy a charge and securities are deposited as pledge; it results in transposition in a D-mat account. Delivery instruction slip (DIS) is issued to the DPs. Generally banks and other limited companies duly registered with SEBI can act as DPs. ISIN in shares of companies.

## ASBA

- Allotment must be completed within seven days of the closure of IPO. SEBI has introduced Application Supported by Blocked Amount (ASBA). Money from ASBA must be released within 15 days from the date of allotment. This SEBI order comes into force from July 2010. IPO investor will use ASBA – A form with their name, address and bank account number. The amount applied for will be blocked in your bank account and on this the investor will not lose any interest income. The investor applicant would earn interest income even on the amount blocked from the concerned bank. So there is no loss of interest income for the IPO applicant from his blocked amount with his bank.
- There are 12,000 D-mat accounts in Guwahati as in March 2010. Further Standard Chartered Bank has also introduced D-mat account facilities from January 2011 for security traders in equity stock.
- On allotment, amount will be unblocked and account will be debited only to the extent required to pay for allotment of shares. Hence, there will be no need for

refunds etc. ASBA form can be obtained from the designated branches of the Self Certified Syndicate Bank (SCSB), the list of such banks is given in the ASBA form. The details of ASBA form is also found in the Red Herring Prospectus. The name of the Escrow Collection Banks are also found in ASBA form.

Now we proceed to discuss about fresh issue of shares and its pricing mechanism as discussed hereunder.

## Pricing of Fresh Issue of Shares

There are two ways of fresh issue of shares by a company or a government company registered under the Companies Act, 1956. One is (a) IPO and the other is (b) follow-on offer (FPO) for the shares already listed in the market. While an FPO may be issued in two ways namely: (a) Auction method, auction route; and (b) Book-building route.

**(a) Auction method, auction route:** Auction method followed in the case of NTPC FPO in February 2010, was perhaps responsible for subdued response in terms of the pricing. Auction method has been permitted by SEBI.

In case of French auction, allotments are made at the bid price while in the case of Dutch auction, allotments are made at single price to all bidders.

**(b) Book Building Method:** Book building process must indicate justification for proposed issue price of security, basis of price fixation, whether book-building process is followed. Due Diligence Certificate from SEBI-approved merchant bankers is necessary to be procured by the company. The merchant bankers are appointed in order to advise the management.

## Pricing of Securities

The merchant bankers hold joint consultation with qualified institutional buyers (QIBs), foreign institutional investors (FIIs), mutual funds (MFs) and other intermediaries in order to feel the pulse of the prevailing market price and also at the same time to estimate the net worth of the company for which a bid for the price be offered. (Bathwal S.K., Pricing of Public Issue (IPO) - How Far Fair?, Chartered Secretary, (A-21) January 2011, p. 37). Bids are invited from QIBs, MFs and retail investors within specified price band. Price band is then circulated through newspaper and other media for public information. However, there is a scope for lowering the price band if the response of the QIBs is not encouraging; and the date of closing of subscription may be extended.

## Open Bidding

This open bidding method is often abused in favour of MFs and merchant bankers (MB). About 70 pc of public issue is reserved for QIBs and MFs, as per SEBI guidelines. They take a upper hand in terms of tax provision and dominant share in purchase of securities. Sometimes FIIs participate in IPOs under the double taxation avoidance agreement (DTAA) from Mauritius and other places. It comes in the form of re-entry of Indian money parked in a foreign country in the name of FII in portfolio.

The two depositories in India are National Securities Depository Ltd. (NSDL) and Central Depository Services Ltd. (CDSL) in November 2009. There is a proposal from the govt. to introduce an electronic voting platform to be unveiled in November 2009 by one of the two depositories in the country, replacing the practice of seeking shareholder consent through the postal ballot.

## SEBI revised investment cap in IPO in October 2010

1. Maximum application size for retail investors raised to Rs. 2 lakh.
2. Norms tightened for preferential issue of shares to promoters. Promoters not exercising warrants after subscribing will be ineligible for issue of shares or convertible warrants for one year.
3. Companies to have a pre-announced fixed pay date for payment of dividends and for credit of bonous shares.
4. SEBI to soon notify norms for rights issue of Indian depository receipts (IDR).

## SEBI QIP FIAT TO BRING DOWN BANK FLOAT

1. QIBs currently bring in only 10 pc of the bid amount.
2. Anchor investors have to bring in 25 pc of the bid amount and follow it up with the remaining 75 pc within two days of the closure of the public issue.
3. An anchor investor (who cannot be a promoter of the company) can subscribe upto 30 pc of the 60 pc portion reserved for qualified institutional buyers (QIBs) in an IPO. Such an investment is subject to a lock-in period of one month.
4. Currently, HNI and retail bring in 100 pc of the bid amount.
5. The float money remains with the bank for about ten days.
6. Banks invest the money in overnight markets like CBLO and repo.
7. The merchant banker (MB) has to issue Due Diligence Certificate (DDC) and also to accord justification to

the price of IPO. The MB is offered remunerative fees for the job.

An International Organization of Securities Commission (IOSCO) in a Discussion Paper on Stock Exchange Demutualization 2010, revealed that a stock exchange has two main identities:

(a) It is a commercial entity carrying on the business of running a stock exchange and seeking to protect and promote its business.

(b) On the other hand, it also supports the integrity and efficiency of capital markets by setting and enforcing appropriate rules to regulate its market.

(c) The commercial role of a stock exchange is to provide services to generate revenues from listing, trading services, settlement fees, fees for membership and charges for the sale of market information.

This often conflicts with its other role when members are asked to set rules in the public interest that may negatively affect their own commercial interests and monitor and enforce rules against each other. (Ref Mythili Bhusnurmath, Pro bono Publico, *The Economic Times* dated 1 January, 2011).

Self regulation and self-governance could be an answer, Demutualisation, which is characterized by a separation of ownership of an exchange from its members could be an answer; as the interest of the owners act as a constraint on actions that would benefit the interests of member firms.

NSE, BSE to start Pre-market call auction from October 18, 2010

The NSE and BSE have decided to implement pre-market call auctions which is a special 15-minute trading window starting at 9 am from October 18, 2010. It implies that all other segments; including derivatives and non-index stocks will trade only at 9-15 am. The aim of pre-market call auction exercise is to enable better price-discovery in the market. The call auction is the solution to take care of the uncertainty that is prevailing in people's mind about where a stock should be priced at the open.

## Its Working

At 9 am investors will be able to place their buy and sell order for the Nifty or the Sensex stocks for a period of 7 minutes. During these 7 minutes, no trade will be executed. However, the exchanges will discover an indicative price for these stocks and the indicative index levels. While these indicative levels will continue to change through the course of the 7 minutes, they will be reflective of the general direction of the market and investors can then accordingly place their bids.

If based on these indicative prices investors wish to change or cancel their orders they will be allowed to do so. The exchanges will suddenly halt this order taking randomly between 9.07 am and 9.08 am in order to check any market manipulation.

After this stoppage, till 9.12 am is when orders will be matched and opening prices of the stocks and the opening levels for the indices will be discovered. It is during this time that the trade will be executed at the single discovered price for every stock. The opening price for a stock will be the price at which the maximum amount of shares can be traded.

## New Index for IPOs

The Bombay Stock Exchange (BSE) on August 24, 2009 launched on IPO index to help investors track the value of companies for two years after listing on the bourse.

Base date of the index is May 3, 2004, while the base value is 1000 points. The index on 24 August, 2009 closed at 1947.54, an annual compounded return of 12.88 pc. The broader 30 share Sensex and BSE 500 yielded much higher returns of 20.57 pc and 18.90 pc respectively.

According to a BSE statement, a robust 6.7 pc growth rate for 2008 -09 and hopes of further improvement will boost the primary market. It is an appropriate time to introduce an indicator that will track primary market conditions in the Indian Capital Market.

The IPO index, which comprises 48 companies, will include only new listings and no follow-on public issues. For being listed on the index, a scrip must have a minimum free float (non-promoter holding) market capitalization of Rs. 100 crores on its first day of listing. The market capitalization weightings of the index constituents will be limited to 20 pc. After two years of listing, the scrip will be excluded from the index on the second Monday of the month. (Ref News information collected from *Economic Times*, several issues.)

# 15

# A Review of the Operational Performance of Assam State Transport Corporation

**Abhigyan Bhattacharjee & Nayan Barua**

**Abstract**: The present paper tries to appraise the operational performance of the Assam State Transport Corporation for a period of five years from 2004-05 to 2008-09. The review on operational performance of the Corporation was taken as the focal point for the study. The main thrust of the paper is focused towards- firstly, to understand the extent to which the ASTC was able to keep pace with the growing demand for public transport, secondly, to know the extent to which the Corporation was running its operations efficiently and finally to know the extent to which economy was ensured in cost of operations. The methodology adopted is a case study approach of the ASTC and audit report of the five years ending 2009 of the Comptroller and Auditor General of India for Government of Assam being the prime source of information.

## Brief Overview of ASTC

Assam State Transport Corporation was incorporated on March 1, 1970 under the Section 3 of the Road Transport Corporation

Act, 1950 as a wholly owned Corporation of the State Government of Assam. The Corporation is under the administrative control of the Transport Department of the Government of Assam. The management of the Corporation is vested with the Board of Directors comprising Chairman, Managing Director and seven other Directors appointed by the Government of Assam. The day-to-day operations are carried out by the Managing Director, who is the Chief Executive of the Corporation, with the assistance of Deputy General Manager, one Regional Manager and nine Divisional Managers. The Corporation has Regional office, 10 Divisional offices, one central workshop, five Divisional workshops and 109 bus stations.

The bus body building is carried out through external agencies. The Corporation has a fleet strength of 325 buses as on 31 March 2009(data available). The Corporation's share in the passenger transport operations in the State was 2.32 per cent and the remaining 97.68 per cent was accounted for by private operators. The turnover of the Corporation was Rs 37.86 crore in 2008-09, which was equal to 0.05 percent of the State Gross Domestic Product. The Corporation employed 2,667 employees as on 31 March 2009.

## Scope of the Present Study

The data gathered for the study was based on the audit review conducted during February 2009 to June 2009 which covers the performance of the Corporation during the period from 2004-05 to 2008-09. The review on operational performance of the Corporation was taken as the focal point for the study.

## Objectives

i) To understand the extent to which the ASTC was able to keep pace with the growing demand for public transport.

ii) To know the extent to which the Corporation was running its operations efficiently.

iii) To know the extent to which economy was ensured in cost of operations.

The criteria adopted for assessing the achievement of objectives were:

i) All India averages for performance parameters

ii) Performance Standards and operational norms fixed by the Association of State Road Transport Undertakings (ASRTU).

## Methodology

The methodology adopted for the study is a case study approach of Assam State Transport Corporation. The Audit Report of Comptroller & Auditor General of India for a period of five years from 2004-2009 was the basis of the study. Review of the same was made focusing the *operational performance* of the Corporation during the same period. Secondary data was sourced from the Report of the Comptroller and Auditor General of India (CAG), (Commercial), for the year ended 31 March 2009 for the Government of Assam. Other related literature for the study was availed from the official website of ASTC.

## Research Questions

1. Whether the growth of ASTC as public transport is faster in comparison to All India Average?
2. Whether the Corporation is running its operations efficiently?
3. Whether the Corporation is successful in ensuring economy in its cost of operations?

## Operational Performance

The operational performance of the Corporation for the five years ending 2008-09 was taken for the study. The operational performance of the Corporation was evaluated on various operational parameters.

Parameters of Operational Performance

i) Percentage share of corporation in passenger transport

ii) Fleet strength and its Age profile

iii) Route Planning

iv) Cost of operations

## Discussion

In order to understand the operational performance on parameters, the following discussion is underway:

Table 15.1 depicts that the ASTC has not been able to keep pace with the growing demand for public transport. Although, total vehicle density per one lakh population increased from 39.15 in 2004-05 to 46.04 in 2008-09, the Corporation's vehicle density per one lakh population reduced marginally from 1.12 in 2004-05 to 1.07 in 2008-09.

The main reasons for the low fleet holding was found as per audit were:

- Absence of any perspective planning
- Inability of the Corporation to generate resource for adequate replacement of condemned vehicles and addition of new buses to the fleet.
- Absence of any transport policy of the State Government.

**Table 15.1**
**Growth of Public Transport in India**

| Sl No | Particulars | 2004-05 | 2005-06 | 2006-07 | 2007-08 | 2008-09 |
|---|---|---|---|---|---|---|
| 1. | Corporation's buses* | 316 | 328 | 404 | 331 | 325 |
| 2. | Private stage carriages (3-1)* | 10,724 | 11,222 | 12,151 | 13,666 | 13,672 |
| 3. | Total buses for public transport* | 11,040 | 11,550 | 12,455 | 13,997 | 13,997** |
| 4. | Percentage share of Corporation | 2.86 | 2.84 | 2.44 | 2.36 | 2.32 |
| 5. | Percentage share of private operators | 97.14 | 97.16 | 97.56 | 97.64 | 97.68 |
| 6. | Estimated population (crore) | 2.82 | 2.87 | 2.93 | 2.98 | 3.04 |
| 7. | Vehicle density per one lakh population (Total) | 39.15 | 40.24 | 42.51 | 46.97 | 46.04 |
| 8. | Corporation's bus density per one lakh population | 1.12 | 1.14 | 1.04 | 1.11 | 1.07 |

**Source:** Compiled From CAG Audit Report (Commercial), 2009

* Figures at the end of the respective years

** In the absence of availability of total buses in 2008-09, figures of 2007-08 have been adopted for comparison purpose

- Increased competition from private operators arising from unbridled issuance of permits to private operators by Government.

## Fleet Strength and Utilisation

The corporation has its own fleet of buses. In September 2001, it allowed privately owned buses (POBs) to operate under its banner and on its routes under 'Self Employment Scheme'. Accordingly, the Corporation entered into an agreement with the private bus owners to operate their buses on approved routes in the state.

The Association of State Road Transport Undertaking (ASRTU) had prescribed (September 1997) the desirable age of a bus as eight years or five lakh kms, whichever was earlier.

Table 15.2 shows the age profile of the buses held by the Corporation for the period of five years ending 2008-09.

The table shows that the Corporation was not able to achieve the norm of right age buses. It is seen that during 2004-09, the Corporation added 188 new buses at a cost of Rs 32.54 crore. The expenditure was incurred out of fund (plan as well as non plan) provided by the State Government for the purpose. To achieve the norm of right age buses, the Corporation was required to buy 77 new buses additionally, which would have cost Rs 13.33 crore approximately. However, the Corporation did not generate adequate internal resources through its operations to finance the replacement of buses.

The average fleet requires high maintenance and results in extra cost and less availability of vehicles compared to underage fleet, other things being equal. This went on to increase operational inefficiencies and cause losses which in turn, affects the ability of the Corporation to replace its fleet on a timely basis.

**Table 15.2**
**Age Profile of the Buses Held By ASTC**

| Sl No | Particulars | 2004-05 | 2005-06 | 2006-07 | 2007-08 | 2008-09 |
|---|---|---|---|---|---|---|
| 1. | Total number of buses at the beginning of the year | 367 | 316 | 328 | 304 | 331 |
| 2. | Additions during the year | 25 | 32 | 50 | 43 | 38 |
| 3. | Buses scrapped during the year | 76 | 20 | 74 | 16 | 44 |
| 4. | Buses held at the end of the year (1+2-3) | 316 | 328 | 304 | 331 | 325 |
| 5. | Of (4), No. of buses more than 8 years old | 90 | 135 | 108 | 123 | 77 |
| 6. | Percentage of over-age buses to total buses | 28.48 | 41.16 | 35.53 | 37.16 | 23.69 |

**Source:** Compiled From CAG Audit Report (Commercial), 2009

## Survival Strategy

- The Corporation's ability to survive and grow will depend on its efforts to remove operational inefficiencies.
- Cut costs
- Tap non-conventional revenue avenues so that it can fund its capital expenditures and be self-reliant.

## Fleet Utilization

Fleet utilization represents the ratio of buses on road to those held by the Corporation. The Corporation fleet utilization did not set any target of fleet utilization and the fleet utilization of the Corporation decreased sharply in 2005-06 and although gradually it increased thereafter. In 2008-09 it stood at 79.38 per cent as compared to All India average of 92 per cent.

It is seen that the Corporation was not able to achieve an optimum utilization of its fleet strength, which in turn impacted its operational performance adversely. It is also found that the Corporation has neither monitored fleet utilization on a regular basis nor analyzed the reasons for poor fleet utilization for taking corrective measures.

## Reasons for Poor Fleet Utilization

The main reasons for poor fleet utilization as found in Audit report in respect of eight divisions for the five year 2004-09 were:

- Vehicles remaining off the road for want of repair and maintenance
- Suspension of uneconomic services and
- Strikes, bandhs and natural calamities

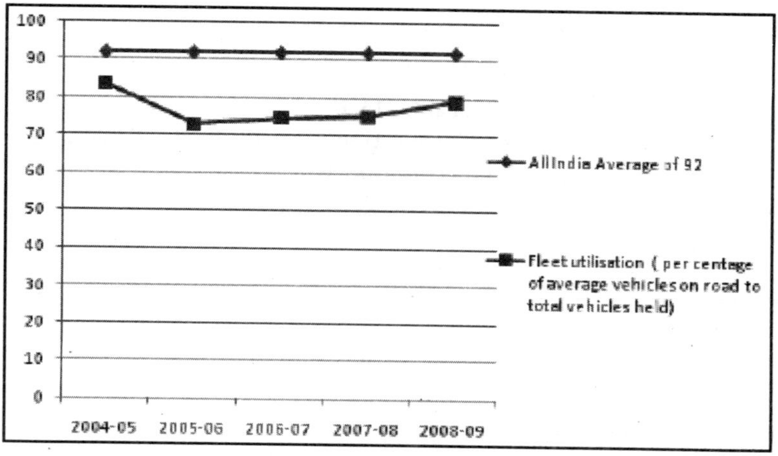


**Source:** Compiled From CAG Audit Report (Commercial), 2009

**Fig. 15.1**

## Route Planning

Appropriate route planning to tap demand leads to higher load factor. The Corporation does not have a system of route planning on a regular basis. As against 560 routes available for operation as on September 2009 (data available), the Corporation and the privately operated buses (POBs) under ASTC banner are operating 522 routes (Table 15.3).

### Observations Made as per Audit Analysis

- Board decided (Februray 2006) that the Corporation should operate only on economic routes and allot uneconomic routes to POBs.
- It was observed that no route rationalization has been undertaken by the Corporation so far (as on September 2009).
- On 56 long distance (i.e. 300 km and above) and inter-state routes, only POBs were exclusively operating at high load factor.

- The Corporation has not explored the possibility of operating its own buses on these routes, which may bring in more revenue.

**Table 15.3**

**No. of Services by the Corporation and POBs in Economic and Uneconomic Routes**

| Routes | | No. of Routes Operated | No. of Services plying |
|---|---|---|---|
| Economic | ASTC | 34 | 120 |
| | POB | 20 | 98 |
| Uneconomic | ASTC | 113 | 150 |
| | POB | 355 | 1194 |
| Total | | 522 | 1562 |

**Source:** Compiled From CAG Audit Report (Commercial), 2009.
**Note**: Load factor represents the per centage of passengers carried to seating capacity.

**Table 15.4**

**Total Number of Routes and Routes Making Profit**

| Year | Total No. of routes | No. of routes making profit | No. of routes not meeting total cost* | No. of routes not meeting variable cost |
|---|---|---|---|---|
| 2004-05 | 139 | 108 (77.70) | 139(100) | 31(22.30) |
| 2005-06 | 139 | 111 (79.86) | 139(100) | 28 (20.14) |
| 2006-07 | 127 | 101 (79.53) | 127 (100) | 26 (20.47) |
| 2007-08 | 133 | 102 (76.69) | 133 (100) | 31 (23.31) |
| 2008-09 | 134 | 105 (78.36) | 134 (100) | 29 (21.64) |

*Calculations made by Audit
**Note**: Figures in parentheses indicate percentage to total routes.
**Source:** Compiled From CAG Audit Report (Commercial), 2009.

## Observations

- In 2008-09, 78.36 per cent routes were profit making.
- For the purpose of determining the profitability of routes here, the Corporation had considered recovery of variable cost only.
- Poor traffic earnings coupled with increasing maintenance costs of over aged buses and poor vehicle productivity incapacitated these services to cover the cost.
- Given the scenario of mixed routes and obligation to serve uneconomical routes, the Corporation should have decided an optimum quantum of services on different routes so as to optimize its revenue while serving the cause.

## COST OF OPERATIONS

The following discussion is underway to meet the third and final objective of the present study. To study the cost of operations, mainly three factors were considered

i) Repairs and Maintenance

ii) Manpower cost

iii) Fuel cost

## Repairs and Maintenance

On review of the Audit Report, it was found that the Corporation does not maintain date of repair and maintenance expenditure.

Table 15.5 shows a summarized picture of fleet holding, over-aged buses, total repairs and maintenance (R&M) expenditure for the last five years up to 2008-09:

**Table 15.5**
**Summarized Picture of Fleet Holding, over-aged Buses, Total Repairs and Maintenance (R&M) Expenditure**

| Sl No. | Particulars | 2004-05 | 2005-06 | 2006-07 | 2007-08 | 2008-09 |
|---|---|---|---|---|---|---|
| 1. | Total buses (Number) | 316 | 328 | 304 | 331 | 325 |
| 2. | Over-age buses (more than 8 years old) | 90 | 135 | 108 | 123 | 77 |
| 3. | *Percentage* of over age buses | 28.48 | 41.16 | 35.53 | 37.16 | 23.69 |
| 4. | R&M Expenses (In crore) | 1.46 | 1.61 | 2.68 | 2.54 | 2.87 |
| 5. | R&M Expenses per bus (in Rs.) (4/1) | 46,203 | 49,085 | 88,158 | 76,737 | 88,308 |

**Source:** Compiled From CAG Audit Report (Commercial), 2009

i) **Repairs & Maintenance**: From Table 15.5, it can be inferred that the expenditure on R & M has increased substantially from Rs 46, 203 per bus in 2004-05 to Rs 88,308 per bus in 2008-09. Further, the R&M expenditure as mentioned did not include the labour cost since the Corporation does not have a system of allocation of labour cost.

ii) **Manpower Cost**: Manpower is an important element of cost which constituted 48.18 per cent of total expenditure of the Corporation in 2008-09. Therefore, it is imperative that cost is kept under control and the manpower is utilized optimally to achieve high productivity.

Table 15.6 provides the details of manpower, its cost and productivity.

The analysis shows that manpower cost per effective kilometer was continuously on the increase over the period except 2007-08, when it marginally decreased but remained above the AIA at Rs 7.50.

It can be noticed from the table that the number of crew per bus was almost within the norms fixed by the Corporation (i,e three per bus). However, in the overall manpower position, the Corporation holds surplus staff of 1.7 per bus in 2008-09 as compared to AIA, which could have been off-loaded by implementing Voluntary Retirement Scheme etc. Although the Committee on Public Undertakings (COPU) in its 30$^{th}$ Report (Dec 1997) recommended that staff bus ratio of the Corporation, be fixed at 6:1, however, no action on the COPU's recommendation was taken by the management (up to September 2009).

## Fuel Cost

Fuel is a major cost element, which constituted 22.58 per cent of total expenditure in 2008-09. Control of fuel costs by

**TABLE 15.6**
**Details of Manpower of the Corporation**

| Sl No | Particulars | 2004-05 | 2005-06 | 2006-07 | 2007-08 | 2008-09 |
|---|---|---|---|---|---|---|
| 1. | Total buses at the end of the year | 316 | 328 | 304 | 331 | 325 |
| 2. | No. of drivers | 376 | 373 | 376 | 369 | 364 |
| 3. | No. of drivers per bus | 1.19 | 1.83 | 1.93 | 1.51 | 1.51 |
| 4. | No. of conductors | 605 | 600 | 588 | 499 | 492 |
| 5. | No. of conductors per bus | 1.91 | 1.83 | 1.93 | 1.51 | 1.51 |
| 6. | Other staff | 1847 | 1837 | 1799 | 1832 | 1811 |
| 7. | No. of other staff per bus | 5.84 | 5.60 | 5.92 | 5.53 | 5.57 |

**Source:** Compiled From CAG Audit Report (Commercial), 2009

**Table 15.7**

**Actual Fuel Consumption, Mileage Obtained Per Litre (Kilometre Per Litre, AA and The Extra Expenditure**

| Sl No | Particulars | 2004-05 | 2005-06 | 2006-07 | 2007-08 | 2008-09 |
|---|---|---|---|---|---|---|
| 1. | Gross Kilometres (in lakh) | 130.14 | 136.28 | 139.00 | 145.88 | 144.22 |
| 2. | Kilometre obtained per litre (KMPL) (1/4) | 3.54 | 3.65 | 3.62 | 3.67 | 3.70 |
| 3. | AIA in the category | 4.94 | 4.94 | 4.94 | 4.94 | 4.94 |
| 4. | Actual consumption (in lakh litres) | 36.74 | 37.32 | 38,36 | 39.78 | 39.02 |
| 5. | Consumption as per AIA (in lakh litres) (1/3) | 26.34 | 27.59 | 28.[illegible]4 | 29.53 | 29.19 |
| 6. | Excess Consumption (in lakh litres) (4-5) | 10.40 | 9.73 | 10.22 | 10.25 | 9.83 |
| 7. | Average cost per litre (in Rs) | 25.66 | 30.86 | 32.09 | 32.21 | 34.50 |
| 8. | Extra expenditure (Rs in crore) (6x7) | 2.67 | 3.00 | 3.28 | 3.30 | 3.39 |

**Source:** Compiled From CAG Audit Report (Commercial), 2009

a road transport undertaking has a direct bearing in its productivity.

Table 15.7 shows Actual Fuel Consumption, Mileage obtained per litre (Kilometre per litre, AA and the extra expenditure.

## Conclusion

From the analysis drawn so far, the paper comes up with the following conclusions and recommendations:

- The Corporation could not keep pace with the growing demand for public transport as its share declined from 2.86 per cent in 2004-05 to 2.32 per cent in 2008-09.
- The Corporation was not running its operations efficiently as its performance on important operational parameters was below A.A.
- The Corporation did not ensure economy in operations as its manpower and fuel costs were higher than the A.A.
- The Corporation could not recover the cost of operations in any operational inefficiencies, weak financial management and inadequate monitoring by top management.

## Recommendations

- In order to increase its share in public transport, increase productivity of its fleet and minimize R & M expenditure, the Corporation should phase out over age buses by inducting new buses.
- Proper route planning would help to achieve optimum quantum of services to optimize its revenue.

- Proper monitoring by the top management is required in order to ensure accountability at all levels. The management is required to maintain a proper data base and evolve Management Information System (MIS) covering all operational parameters for record, monitoring and control.

## REFERENCES

*Report of the Comptroller and Auditor General of India* for the year ended 31 March 2009(Commercial), Government of Assam.

http://www.assamtransport.com/

# 16

# Budgetary Support of the Government for Protection against Climate Change

**Sujit Sikidar & Prashanta Sharma**

The Corporate houses compete for maximum utilization of resources at their control. The competition among corporations in industrial field makes terrible threat to environmental degradation and climatic change. There ought to have adequate measure for protecting environment and preventing climatic change. As, the Government is entrepreneur, planner, and controller for all round development, how public resources are allocated for preventing climatic change is to be interpreted. In this article the budgetary allocation of the Union Government and Government of Assam for climate change has been discussed.

## Methodology

The study is mainly based on secondary source of data. The researcher has collected information from the Appropriation Accounts and Finance Accounts of the Government of India and the Government of Assam. The investigation covers the period 2005-06 to 2008-09.

## Limitation of the study

To examine the public resource allocation for climatic change only two activities of Government of Assam (viz Soil & Water Conservation and Forestry & Wildlife) and three activities of Government of India (viz Soil & Water Conservation, Forestry and Wild life and Plantation) have been chosen.

## Budgetary Grant for Soil and Water Conservation

The budgetary grant shows the government preference in allocating public resources in different activities. It has been observed that the budgetary allocation of Union Government and Government of Assam for Soil and Water Conservation has not been enhanced progressively. The percentage of the budgetary allocation for Soil and Water Conservation out. of the total Budgetary Grant of Union Government was 0.00056%.It became 0.00101% in 2006-07.It was reduced to 0.00049% in 2008-09. Graph 16.1 exhibits the downward trend of the P.C of Budgetary Grant for Soil and Water Conservation.

In case of the budgetary allocation of the Government of Assam for Soil and Water Conservation, it has been observed that the percentage of the budgetary allocation out of total budgeted grant was 0.133% in 2005-06. It became 0.136%in 2006-07, after that it reduced to 0.103% and 0.098% respectively in 2007-08 and in 2008-09. Table 16.2 and Graph 16.2 indicate the downward trend of the budgetary allocation of Government of Assam for Soil and water conservation.

## Budgetary Grant for Forestry and WildLife

The budgetary grant of the Government of India for Forestry and Wildlife was not significantly changed in 2005-06 to 2008-09. Table 16.3 exhibits that it was 0.02% in 2005-06.It increased to 0.03% of total budgetary Grant in 2006-07.In 2007-08 and

**Table 16.1**
**Budgetary Allocation for Soil and Water Conservation**

**(Rs.in crores)**

| Years | Total Budgetary Grant | Budgetary Grant for Soil and Water Conservation | P.C of Budgetary Grant for Soil and WaterConservation on total Budgetary Grant |
|---|---|---|---|
| 2005-06 | 1717120.02 | 9.7 | 0.00056 |
| 2006-07 | 1752017.59 | 17.68 | 0.00101 |
| 2007-08 | 2391461.75 | 17.45 | 0.00073 |
| 2008-09 | 2625417.67 | 12.81 | 0.00049 |

**Sources**: Annual Financial Statements of Union Government

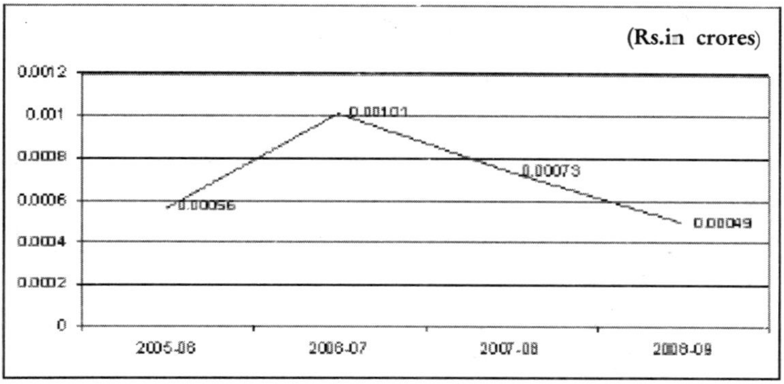


**Sources**: Annual Financial Statements of Union Government

**Graph 16.1: P.C of Budgetary Grant for Soil and Water Conservation on total Budgetary Grant of Union Government**

2008-09,again it reduced to 0.02%.

**Table 16.2**
**Budgetary Grant of Government of Assam for Soil and Water Conservation**

(Rs. in crores)

| Years | Total Budgetary Grant | Budgetary Grant for Soil and Water Conservation | P.C of Budgetary Grant for Soil and Water Conservation out of total Budgetary Grant |
|---|---|---|---|
| 2005-06 | 21451.09 | 28.45 | 0.133 |
| 2006-07 | 21864.36 | 29.64 | 0.136 |
| 2007-08 | 23567.1 | 24.31 | 0.103 |
| 2008-09 | 27204.1 | 26.72 | 0.098 |

**Source**: The Appropriation Accounts of the Government of Assam

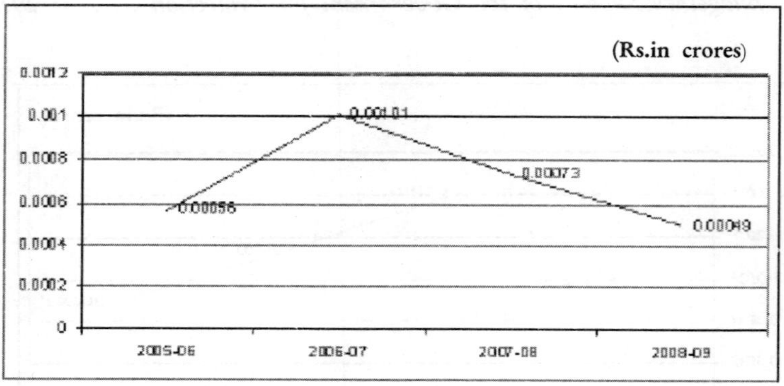


**Source**: The Appropriation Accounts of the Government of Assam

**Graph 16.2: P.C. of Budgetary Grant for Soil and Water Conservation out of Total Budgetary Grant**

**Table 16.3**
**Budgetary Allocation of Union Government for Forestry and Wildlife**

(Rs. in crores)

| Years | Total Budgetary Grant | Budgetary Grant for Forestry & Wildlife | Percentage of Budgetary Grant for Forestry and Wildlife on total budgetary Grant |
|---|---|---|---|
| 2005-06 | 1717120.02 | 420.68 | 0.02 |
| 2006-07 | 1752017.59 | 466.36 | 0.03 |
| 2007-08 | 2391461.75 | 488.84 | 0.02 |
| 2008-09 | 2625417.67 | 547.82 | 0.02 |

**Sources**: Annual Financial Statements of Union Government.

In case of Government of Assam, the percentage budgetary grant for Forestry and Wildlife out of total budgetary grant was 0.92% in 2005-06.It increased to 1.03% in 2006-07.In 2007-08 and in 2008-09 it reduced to 0.87% and 0.81% respectively. The down ward trend of the budgetary grant as stated in Table

16.4 shows that the Forestry and Wildlife is not given due preference in allocating public resource.

**Table 16.4**
**Budgetary Grant of Government of Assam for Forestry and Wildlife**

(Rs. in crores)

| Years | Total Budgetary Grant | Budgetary Grant for Forestry & Wildlife | Percentage of Budgetary Grant for Forestry and Wildlife on total budgetary Grant |
|---|---|---|---|
| 2005-06 | 21451.09 | 198.19 | 0.92 |
| 2006-07 | 21864.36 | 225.56 | 1.03 |
| 2007-08 | 23567.1 | 203.99 | 0.87 |
| 2008-09 | 27204.1 | 219.24 | 0.81 |

**Source**: The Appropriation Accounts of the Government of Assam

## BUDGETARY GRANT FOR PLANTATION

As in case of Soil and Water Conservation and Forestry and Wildlife, the percentage of budgetary allocation for Plantation out of total budgetary allocation shows the downward trend. As exhibited in Table 16.5, it was 0.02% in 2005-06 and in 2006-07. It reduced to 0.01% in 2007-08 and in 2008-09. The Government of Assam has no separate activity for Plantation in Appropriation Accounts (Table 16.5).

The aforesaid observations do not indicate the preference of both the State and Union Government in distributing public resource for the activities preventing climate change.

### Budgetary Grant under Capital Head of Account

The Government Expenditures are divided into two groups i.e. Revenue Expenditures and Capital Expenditures. The

Revenue Expenditures are for maintaining fixed facilities and services and Capital Expenditures are incurred mainly for creation of assets and facilities. The proper implementation of the Government policy needs both the Revenue Expenditures and Capital Expenditures. The budgetary allocations of Union Government in Capital Head of Accounts for the activity-' Soil and Water Conservation' exhibited upward trend in2005-06 to 2008-09.It was Rs.0.35 crores in 2005-06 and it increased to Rs.2 crores in 2008-09.But, the budgetary allocations of Union Government in Capital Head of Accounts for the activity-'Forestry and Wild Life' was not increased progressively. As shown in Graph 16.4, it was Rs.2.4 crores in 2005-06.The budgetary allocations of Forestry and Wildlife in 2006-07 and 2007-08 were Rs.1.99 crores and Rs.2.03 crores, which were lesser than the amount of 2005-06. In 2008-09, it became Rs.3.05 crores.

**Table 16.5**

**Budgetary Allocation of Union Government for Plantation**

(Rs. in crores)

| Years | Total Budgetary Grant | Budgetary allocation for plantation | Percentage of Budgetary Allocation for plantation on total budgetary Allocation |
|---|---|---|---|
| 2005-06 | 1717120.02 | 386.69 | 0.02 |
| 2006-07 | 1752017.59 | 346.05 | 0.02 |
| 2007-08 | 2391461.75 | 316.26 | 0.01 |
| 2008-09 | 2625417.67 | 357.01 | 0.01 |

**Sources**: Annual Financial Statements of Union Government

In case of Plantation, the Government of India had no budgetary allocation in 2005-06 to 2007-08 under the capital head

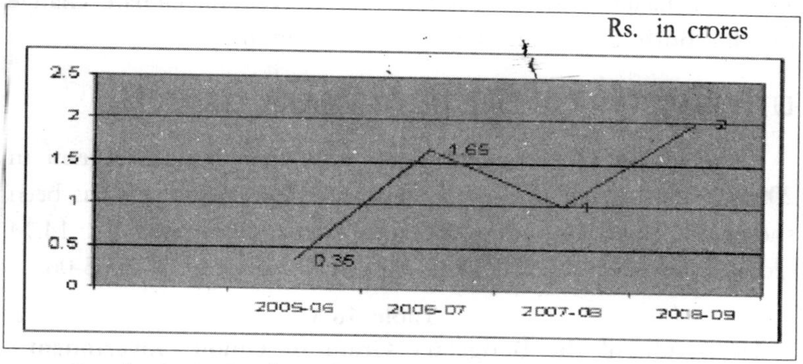


**Graph 16.3: Budgeted Capital Expenditures of Union Government for Soil and Water Conservation**

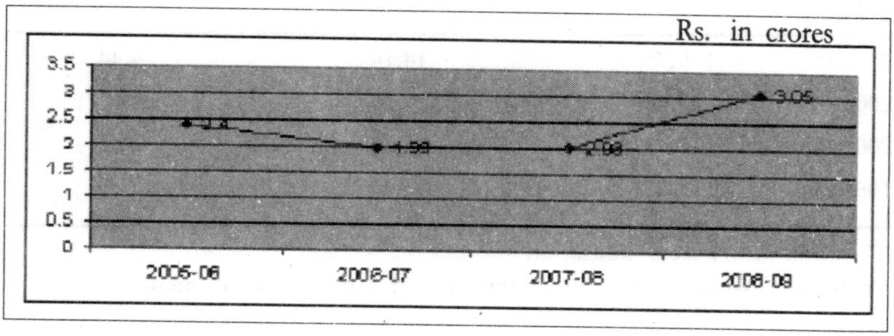


**Graph 16.4: Budgeted Capital Expenditures of Union Government for Forestry and Wildlife**

of accounts. The union Government allocated Rs. 15 crores as budgeted capital expenditures for Plantation only in 2008-09.

In case of Government of Assam, no amount had been estimated as Capital Expenditures for Soil and Water Conservation and for Forestry and Wildlife during the period 2005-06 to 2008-09.

The aforesaid observations indicate that capital expenditures had not been given due weightage for enhancing the basic facilities in the activities for preventing climate change by the both State and Union Government.

## UTILISATION OF THE BUDGETARY GRANTS

The Union Government spent more than budgeted grant in 2005-06 and in 2008-09 for soil and water conservation. It has been shown in Table 16.6 that the actual expenditure was Rs. 14.14 crores whereas budgeted grant was Rs.9.7 crores in 2005-06.

**Table 16.6**
**Utilisation of the Budgetary Grant of Union Government for Soil and Water Conservation**

(Rs.in crores)

| Years | Budgetary Grant | Utilised amount | Unutilised amount |
|---|---|---|---|
| 2005-06 | 9.7 | 14.14 | -4.44 |
| 2006-07 | 17.68 | 14.25 | 3.43 |
| 2007-08 | 17.45 | 11.32 | 6.13 |
| 2008-09 | 12.81 | 15.06 | -2.25 |

*(-) indicates excess utilisation
**Sources:** Annual Financial Statements of Union Government.

Similarly, the utilized amount was Rs.15.06 crores against the budgeted grant Rs.12.81 crores in 2008-09.The unutilized amount for Soil and Water Conservation was Rs.3.43 Crores and 6.13 crores in 2006-07 and in 2007-08 (i.e 19.40% and 35.13% of the budgetary Grant.). In 2007-08 the utilization of the budgetary grant was significantly inadequate.

The union Government also spent more than budgetary allocation for the activities-'Forestry and Wild Life' in 2005-06 to 2008-09. Table 16.7 shows that in every year the actual expenditures of 'Forestry and Wildlife' were more than the budgetary allocation.

**Table 16.7**
**Utilisation of Budgetary Grant for Forestry and Wildlife**

(Rs. in crores)

| Years | Budgetary Allocation | Utilisation | Unutilisation |
|---|---|---|---|
| 2005-06 | 420.68 | 432.14 | -11.46 |
| 2006-07 | 466.36 | 499.55 | -33.19 |
| 2007-08 | 488.84 | 605.13 | -116.29 |
| 2008-09 | 547.82 | 611.08 | -63.26 |

*(-) indicates excess utilisation
**Sources**: Annual Financial Statements of Union Government

In case of Plantation, as exhibited in Table 16.8, the Government of India spent more than budgetary allocation in 2005-06, 2007-08 and in 2008-09. The actual expenditure was less than budgeted expenditures only in 2006-07.

**Table 16.8**
**Utilisation of the Budgetary Allocation for Plantation**

(Rs. in crores)

| Years | Budgetary Grant | Utilised amount | Unutilised amount |
|---|---|---|---|
| 2005-06 | 386.69 | 430.08 | -43.39 |
| 2006-07 | 346.05 | 340.03 | 6.02 |
| 2007-08 | 316.26 | 320.7 | -4.44 |
| 2008-09 | 357.01 | 441.67 | -84.66 |

*(-) indicates excess utilisation
Sources: Annual Financial Statements of Union Government.

Though the Union Government spent more than the budgeted estimates of the aforesaid activities in majority years of the period - 2005-06 to 2008-09 as shown in Table 16.6, Table 16.7 and in Table 16.8, the utilization of the State Government budgetary grant in Assam is completely reverse one. The unutilized amount of the budgetary grant of the Government of Assam was more than 18% in 2005-06 to 2008-09. In 2008-09, it was 28.93%.

Similarly, it has been observed in Table 16.10 that the unutilized amount of Forestry and Wildlife was 18% to 36% in 2005-06 to 2008-09.

Without adequate implementation of the budgetary plan in the state level the activities will not ensure the achieving of the goal for prevention of the climatic change.

**Table 16.9**

**Utilisation of Budgetary Grant of the Government of Assam for Soil and Water Conservation**

(Rs. in crores)

| Year | Budgetary allocation | Actual Utilisation | Unutilised amount |
|---|---|---|---|
| 2005-06 | 28.45 | 23.23 | 5.22 |
| | (100%) | (81.65%) | (18.35%) |
| 2006(07 | 29.64 | 24.18 | 5.46 |
| | (100%) | (81.58%) | (18.42%) |
| 2007(08 | 24.31 | 19.79 | 4.52 |
| | (100%) | (81.41%) | (18.59%) |
| 2008(09 | 26.72 | 18.99 | 7.73 |
| | (100%) | (71.07%) | (28.93%) |

**Source**: The Appropriation Accounts of the Government of Assam

**Table 16.10**
**Utilisation of the Budgetary Grant of the Government of Assam for Forestry and Wildlife**

(Rs. in crores)

| Year | Budgetary allocation | Utilised amount | Unutilised amount |
|---|---|---|---|
| 2005-06 | 198.19 | 136.42 | 61.77 |
| | (100%) | (68.83%) | (31.17%) |
| 2006-07 | 225.56 | 161.69 | 63.87 |
| | (100%) | (71.68%) | (28.32%) |
| 2007-08 | 203.99 | 198.19 | 75.16 |
| | (100%) | (100%) | (36.84%) |
| 2008-09 | 219.24 | 179.16 | 40.08 |
| | (100%) | (81.72%) | (18.28%) |

**Source:** The Appropriation Accounts of the Government of Assam.

## CONCLUSION

The budgetary allocations of the Union and the State Government need to be enhanced for the activities related to prevention of climate change. The Government should pay attention for creation of assets and expansion of fixed facilities for the function related to climate change. At the state level proper and adequate utilization of fund are to be ensured.

# 17

# Short-Run Managerial Decision Analysis

**A.R. Mujibur Rehman**

**Abstract:** The objective of this paper is : (i) to present the theoretical framework of analysis for short-term managerial decision, and (ii) to demonstrate its application for such decision-making in different situations. Hence, this paper sets out the analytical framework in terms of the differential or incremental costs and revenues and also deals with the application of the analytical framework in various decision situations.

## SHORT-RUN DECISIONS AND DECISION-MAKING

Short-run decisions are those operating decisions which basically relate to the period during which the operating capacity of a business is supposed to be fixed. Examples of short-run operating decisions are make or buy, accepting special orders, increase or decrease in the volume of production, optimal product-mix decision, reduction in selling price to boost up sales volume, add or drop a product.

Short-term decisions are peculiar in nature. The information needed for such decisions is termed as 'relevant data'. The relevant data refers to decision-making components of a given situation. The first component of the relevant data is that, it relates to a future period. Therefore, these decisions imply some future activity. Since the conventional accounting data are inadequate to serve the purpose these data have to be modified in the form of addition/deletion to tailor the historical costs to the requirement of decision-making.

The second component of the relevant data is that, it is mainly tangible. Therefore it is amenable to precise and direct measurement and hence quantitative-which can be expressed in numerical terms.

Decision-making is essentially a process of evaluating two or more alternatives leading to a final choice of the best alternative. This is also called Alternative Choice Decisions.

## Decision Situations

This paper demonstrates the application of incremental/ differential costs and revenue data for managerial decision-making in the following decision situations:

1. Make or buy decisions
2. Increase in volume of output and acceptance of export order
3. Reduction in selling price of products
4. Profitability of product mix/sales mix
5. Dropping a product
6. Replacement of machinery
7. Operate or shut down decisions
8. Loss leaders
9. Comparing machines with hand labour

10. Estimation of cost savings and their conversion into present value

## Make or Buy Decisions

Sometimes, under certain circumstances firms have to choose between manufacturing certain parts or components themselves or buying those from outside suppliers. Incremental analysis is useful in getting solutions to this kind of decision-situations. In case the firm has adequate idle (unutilized) capacity to make the components, the relevant input data is the committed or avoidable costs. Interestingly, this is because the firm would not be required to incur fixed costs to manufacture the components. But if it is necessary to enhance the existing plant capacity or the existing capacity of the plant is diverted for the manufacture of the components, opportunity cost in terms of lost contribution will be relevant to the decision analysis.

*Example-1* (Make or buy decision)

The XYZ Company manufactures most of its own parts and components. The per unit cost data are as follows:

| | |
|---|---:|
| Raw material | Rs. 8 |
| Direct wages | 3 |
| Variable overheads | 2 |

The company will require a new part for its current year's output. This part can be manufactured in the company without any expansion of existing facilities. However, it would be necessary to incur additional cost of product testing by Rs. 5,000 per month.

The alternative choice before the company is to purchase the part from an outside supplier at Rs. 13.40 per unit. The company has estimated that it will need 2,00,000 new parts during the current year.

Advise the company whether it should buy or manufacture the new parts. What would be your answer if the requirement of new parts was only 1,00,000 parts?

## *Solution*

The decision analysis is shown in Table 17.1

**Table 17.1**
**Decision Analysis**

| Volume of parts (2,00,000 units) | Make costs | | Buy costs | |
|---|---|---|---|---|
| | Total Rs. | Per unit Rs. | Total Rs. | Per unit Rs. |
| Raw material | 16,00,000 | 8.00 | | |
| Direct wages | 6,00,000 | 3.00 | | |
| Variable overheads | 4,00,000 | 2.00 | | |
| Additional fixed costs: | | | | |
| Product Testing | | | | |
| (Rs. 5,000x 12) | 60,000 | 0.30 | | |
| Purchase costs | - | - | 26,80,000 | 13.40 |
| Total costs | 26,60,000 | 13.3 | 26,80,000 | 13.40 |
| Differential costs favour the decision of making the component | Rs. 20,000 (Total) Re. 0.10 per componnet | | | |

**Advice:** The company should make the new part.

| Volume of parts (1,00,000 units) | Make costs | | Buy costs | |
|---|---|---|---|---|
| | Total Rs. | Per unit Rs. | Total Rs. | Per unit Rs. |
| Raw material | 8,00,000 | 8.00 | – | – |

(*contd.*)

| Volume of parts (1,00,000 units) | Make costs | | Buy costs | |
|---|---|---|---|---|
| | Total Rs. | Per unit Rs. | Total Rs. | Per unit Rs. |
| Direct wages | 3,00,000 | 3.00 | – | – |
| Variable overheads | 2,00,000 | 2.00 | – | – |
| Additional fixed costs | 60,000 | 0.60 | – | – |
| Purchase costs | – | – | 13,40,000 | 13.40 |
| Total costs | 13,60,000 | 13,60 | 13,40,000 | 13.40 |

**Advice:** In case, the requirement of the new part is 1,00,000 units, the company should buy the new part from the outside supplier.

## Increase in the volume of output and acceptance of export order

Sometimes the business enterprise may propose to achieve expansion in terms of increase in the volume of production. In such a case, the increase in the production is advisable if the increased production leads to additional profit. Therefore it becomes necessary to compare the profitability of the existing production volume with that of the profitability after increased production. A statement of comparative profitability comprising sales revenue, marginal cost, contribution and profit under the present level of production as well as after expansion would clearly indicate whether the proposed increase in production would generate additional profit or not.

The same principle will also apply in case of special orders or export orders received by the firm.

*Example-2 (Increase in production)*

A factory produces 24,000 units of a product. The cost sheet provides the following data:

| | Rs. |
|---|---|
| Direct materials | 1,20,000 |
| Direct wages | 84,000 |
| Variable overheads | 48,000 |
| Fixed overheads | 80,000 |
| Total Cost | 3,32,000 |

## *Solution*

**Table 17.2**
**Statement of Comparative profitability**

| Particulars | Present | | After expansion | |
|---|---|---|---|---|
| Production and sales-units | 24,000 | | 36,000 | |
| | Per unit Rs. | Amount Rs. | Per unit Rs. | Amount Rs. |
| Sales | 20.00 | 48,000 | 20.00 | 7,20,000 |
| Direct materials | 5.00 | 1,20,000 | | |
| Direct wages | 3.50 | 84,000 | | |
| Variable overheads | 2.00 | 48,000 | | |
| Variable costs | 10.50 | 2,52,000 | 9.50 | 3,42,000 |
| Contribution | 9.50 | 2,28,000 | 10.50 | 3,78,000 |
| Fixed cost | | 80,000 | | 90,000 |
| Profit | | 1,48,000 | | 2,88,000 |
| BEP(units) | $\frac{80,000}{9.50}$ = 8,421 units | | $\frac{90,000}{10.50}$ =8,571 units | |
| $= \frac{\text{Fixedcosts}}{\text{Contributionperunit}}$ | (before expansion) | | (after expansion) | |
| P/V Ratio= $\frac{\text{Contribution}}{\text{Sales}}$ | 47.5% | | 52.5% | |

The product is sold at Rs. 20 per unit.

The management is considering increase in production. Fixed costs are expected to increase by Rs. 10,000 when plant expansion is completed. The present plant capacity is 24,000 units a year. After the expansion, the capacity will increase by 50%. Variable costs are expected to go down by Re. 1 per unit with the expansion. The current selling price of Rs. 20 per unit is expected to remain same under either alternative.

Ascertain the Break Even Points under both the situations. Which alternative is better and why?

The profitability after expansion is improved and therefore it is worthwhile to expand.

## Reduction in the selling price of products

When the volume of sales remains stagnant or starts to decline, management may propose to reduce the selling price of the product in anticipation of achieving a greater volume of sales. Consequently, this step may also lead to an increase in the net profit over the present level.

In such a situation, it will be necessary to determine the level of desired profit as well as the minimum volume of sales to be maintained to achieve the desired profit. For this purpose, the likely future contribution per unit, changes in the per unit variable cost as well as change in the fixed cost must also be taken into consideration. Finally, the minimum units to be sold to ensure maintaining the desired profit can be determined.

*Example-3 (Reduction in selling price)*

The Modern Electronics decides to effect a 10% reduction in the selling price of its product because they feel that such a step may lead to a greater volume of sales.

It is anticipated that there is no prospect of a change in total fixed costs and variable cost per unit. The directors wish to maintain net profits at the present level.

The following information have been obtained from its books:

| | Rs. |
|---|---|
| Sales : 10,000 units | 2,50,000 |
| Variable costs per unit | 20 |
| Fixed costs | 40,000 |

How should management proceed to implement this decision?

## *Solution*

**Table 17.3**
**Statement of sales, contribution and profit**

| Present profit: | Rs. |
|---|---|
| Sales | 2,50,000 |
| Less: Variable costs | 2,00,000 |
| Contribution | 50,000 |
| Less: Fixed costs | 40,000 |
| Profit | 10,000 |
| **Future contribution per unit:** | |
| Selling price (Rs. 25-2.50) | 22.50 |
| Less: Variable cost | 20.00 |
| Contribution per unit | 2.50 |

Volume of sales required for the desired profit

$$= \frac{\text{Fixed cost} + \text{Desired Profit}}{\text{Contribution per unit}} \times \text{Selling price per unit}$$

$$= \frac{\text{Rs.}40,000 + 10,000}{\text{Rs.}2.50} \times 22.50$$

Rs. = 4,50,000

Minimum units that must be sold $= 20,000 \text{ units} \left(\frac{\text{Rs.}4,50,000}{\text{Rs.}22.50}\right)$

**Comment**: The management should reduce the selling price only when it is sure of increasing the sales by additional 10,000 units.

## Profitability of Product/Sales Mix

The decision whether a firm should continue, modify or eliminate a particular product mix or sales mix rests on the contribution made or the loss incurred by the product/product mix. The marginal costing approach will assist in taking an appropriate decision in this regard. This approach is also useful to management when the profitability of a new product/sales mix is examined in a situation where the firm decides to replace the existing mix with a new mix.

*Example-4*

The following product/sales mix is capable of being achieved in a factory:

(i) 2,000 units of product 'A' and 2,000 units of product 'B'.

(ii) 2,000 units of product 'B' and 2,000 units of product 'C'.

(iii) 2,000 units of product 'A' and 2,000 units of product 'C'.

**Cost per unit is as follows:**

| | A' | 'B' | 'C' |
|---|---|---|---|
| | Rs. | Rs. | Rs. |
| Direct materials | 24 | 28 | 24 |
| Direct wages | 16 | 12 | 12 |
| Variable overhead | 4 | 6 | 8 |
| Selling Price | 60 | 64 | 62 |

Fixed cost is Rs. 20,000.

Determine the marginal cost and contribution per unit of 'A', 'B', 'C' and the profits resulting from sales mix (i), (ii) and ?(iii).

***Solution***

**Table 17.4(a)**
**Statement of Marginal Cost and Contribution (per unit)**

| | A<br>Rs | B<br>Rs | C<br>Rs |
|---|---|---|---|
| Selling Price | 60 | 64 | 62 |
| Direct material | 24 | 28 | 24 |
| Direct wages | 16 | 12 | 12 |
| Variable overhead | 4 | 6 | 8 |
| Marginal Cost | 44 | 46 | 44 |
| Contribution | 16 | 18 | 18 |

## Dropping a Product

When a firm produces a number of products, it may sometimes so happen that a particular product may generate a low profit or may even incur loss. In such a situation, management contemplates dropping of the loss incurring or low profit product so as to strengthen the manufacturing activity of the other profitable products. But before arriving at a final decision, management should carefully study the following vital factors:

(i) The quantum of 'contribution' of the product. Although the product is not profitable, yet it is contributing towards recovery of the fixed cost. This would not be available if the product is dropped.

(ii) The loss incurring product should be dropped only if the released capacity could be profitably utilised towards other alternative channel where the expected 'contribution' and the 'P/V ratio' must be higher than those of the dropped product.

**Table 17.4(b)**
**Statement of Comparative Profitability of Sales Mix**

| Sales Mix (units) | Contribution Rs. | Total contribution Rs. | Fixed cost Rs. | Profit Rs. | P/V Ratio | Rank |
|---|---|---|---|---|---|---|
| (i) A – 2,000<br>B – 2,000 | 32,000<br>36,000 | 68,000 | 20,000 | 48,000 | 27.40% | III |
| (ii) B – 2,000<br>C – 2,000 | 36,000<br>36,000 | 72,000 | 20,000 | 52,000 | 28,5% | I |
| (iii) A – 2,000<br>C – 2,000 | 32,000<br>36,000 | 68,000 | 20,000 | 48,000 | 27.80% | II |

*Example-5 (Sales Mix Decision)*

Calculate the effect of existing sales-mix and new sales-mix from the following data by comparing the P/V ratio and Break-Even Point.

| Products | A Rs. | B Rs. | C Rs. | D Rs. |
|---|---|---|---|---|
| Sales | 50,000 | 40,000 | 30,000 | 20,000 |
| Variable Cost | 25,000 | 30,000 | 24,000 | 15,000 |
| New Sales Mix | 40,000 | 50,000 | 20,000 | 30,000 |
| Fixed cost Rs. 25,000 | | | | |

## *Solution To Example 5*

**Table 17.5 (a)**
**Statement on the effect of Sales Mix Existing Sales Mix**

| Products | A<br>Rs. | B<br>Rs. | C<br>Rs. | D<br>Rs. | Total<br>Rs. |
|---|---|---|---|---|---|
| Sales | 50,000 | 40,000 | 30,000 | 20,000 | 1,40,000 |
| Variable Cost | 25,000 | 30,000 | 24,000 | 15,000 | 94,000 |
| Contribution | 25,000 | 10,000 | 6,000 | 5,000 | 46,000 |
| P/V Ratio | 0.5 | 0.25 | 0.2 | 0.25 | 0.328 |

Break-Even Point $= \frac{\text{Fixed Cost}}{\text{P/V ratio}} = \frac{\text{Rs.}25,000}{0.328} = \text{Rs.}76,220$

*Solution To Example 5*

**Table 17.5(b)**
**Statement on the effect of Sales Mix**
**New Sales Mix**

| Products | A<br>Rs. | B<br>Rs. | C<br>Rs. | D<br>Rs. | Total<br>Rs. |
|---|---|---|---|---|---|
| Sales | 40,000 | 50,000 | 20,000 | 30,000 | 1,40,000 |
| Variable Cost (assessed) | 28,000 | 35,000 | 14,000 | 22,000 | 99,000 |
| Contribution | 12,000 | 15,000 | 6,000 | 8,000 | 41,000 |
| P/V Ratio | 0.3 | 0.3 | 0.3 | 0.26 | 0.292 |

Break-Even Point $= \frac{\text{Fixed Cost}}{\text{P/V ratio}} = \frac{\text{Rs.}25{,}000}{0.292} = \text{Rs.}85{,}616$

**Comment**: The above analysis shows that the new sales mix is not favourable because this reduces the P/V ratio from 0.32 to 0.292 and increases the Break-Even Point from Rs. 76,220 to Rs. 85,616 of sales.

Nevertheless, an Income Statement comparing between 'Keeping the product' and 'dropping the product' must show that the impact of dropping the concerned product would be positive on operating income.

### *Example-6 (Dropping a product)*

The Eastern Ltd. has three product lines, all produced in one factory. The past records show that product C has continuously incurred net loss. The estimated income statement of the three products is given below:

| Particulars | A<br>Rs. | B<br>Rs. | C<br>Rs. | Total<br>Rs. |
|---|---|---|---|---|
| Sales | 5,00,000 | 4,00,000 | 1,00,000 | 10,00,000 |
| Variable expenses | 2,50,000 | 2,40,000 | 70,000 | 5,60,000 |
| Contribution Margin | 2,50,000 | 1,60,000 | 30,000 | 4,40,000 |
| P/V Ratio | 50% | 40% | 30% | 44% |
| Fixed Expenses<br>(Salary, insurance and depreciation) | 1,70,000 | 90,000 | 45,000* | 3,05,000 |
| Operating Income | 80,000 | 70,000 | (-)15,000 | 1,35,000 |

* Includes product-line supervisor's salary of Rs. 20,000.

The management is considering dropping of the product C. Advise the management.

### *Solution*

**Table 17.6**
**Income Statement**

| Particulars | Keeping Product-C<br>Rs. | Dropping Product-C<br>Rs. | Difference<br>Rs. |
|---|---|---|---|
| Sales | 10,00,000 | 9,00,000 | 1,00,000 |
| Variable Expenses | 5,60,000 | 4,90,000 | 70,000 |

*(contd.)*

| Particulars | Keeping Product-C Rs. | Dropping Product-C Rs. | Difference Rs. |
|---|---|---|---|
| Fixed Expenses | 3,05,000 | 2,60,000 | 45,000 |
| Total Expenses | 8,65,000 | 7,50,000 | 1,15,000 |
| Operating Income | 1,35,000 | 1,50,000 | 15,000 |

**Comment**: The above Income Statement reveals that it would not be appropriate to discontinue the unprofitable product C. Because all the fixed expenses except supervisor's salary of Rs. 20,000 would continue (Rs. 25,000). Thus, the net effect of dropping product C would be to forego the contribution of Rs. 30,000 in order to save Rs. 20,000 salary.

## Operate or shut down decision

When the firm faces difficulties due to recessionary trend and the sales revenue is on continuous decline, the management considers whether the plant should be shut down temporarily or not till the recessionary trend is over.

The decision criterion in such a situation will be based on the comparison between the shut-down losses and the losses associated with continuing operations.

*Example-7 (Operate or shut down decision)*

The B. Ltd. Manufactures 2,00,000 units of product per year when it operates at normal capacity. The unit cost of manufacturing at normal capacity is as follows:

| | Rs. |
|---|---|
| Direct materials | 8 |
| Direct labour | 2 |

*(contd.)*

| | |
|---|---|
| Variable overheads | 3 |
| Fixed overheads | 4 |
| Product cost per unit | 17 |
| Selling price | 20 |

During the next 3 months, only 10,000 units can be produced and sold. Management plans to shut down the plant for 3 months, estimating that the fixed manufacturing overhead can be reduced to Rs. 75,000 when the plant will not operate; the fixed overhead costs are incurred at a uniform rate throughout the year. Additional costs of plant shut down for the 3 months are estimated to be Rs. 15,000.

You are required to answer:

(a) Should the plant be shut down for 3 months? Show computations.

(b) What is the shut down point for the three months in units of product?

***Solution (a)***

**Table 17.7**
**Decision Analysis (Shut Down Plant)**

| Particulars | | Operating Plant Rs. | Shut Down Plant Rs. |
|---|---|---|---|
| (i) Estimated Revenue | | 2,00,000 | – |
| (10,000 units × Rs. 20) | | | |
| (ii) Estimated cost: | Rs. | | – |
| Direct Materials | 8 | | |
| Direct labour | 2 | | |
| Variable overheads | 3 | | |
| | 13 | | |
| Total Variable Costs | ... | (1,30,000) | – |

*(contd.)*

| Particulars | Operating Plant Rs. | Shut Down Plant Rs. |
|---|---|---|
| (iii) Estimated contribution (i-ii) ... | 70,000 | – |
| Less: Fixed costs $\left(\frac{2,00,000 \text{ unit}}{4 \text{ quarters}} \times \text{Rs.}4\right)$ | (2,00,000) | -75,000 |
| Shut down costs | – | -15,000 |
| Net Loss | (60,000 ) | (90,000) |

**Comment:** The plant should not be shut down for 3 months as the loss while operating the plant is Rs. 60,000 only, whereas shut down of the plant would entail a higher loss i.e. Rs. 90,000.

**(b)** The shut down point is the point at which losses from continued operation are equal to the shut down costs. That is,

$$\frac{\left(\text{Fixed cost when plant is operating}\right) - \left(\text{Shut down cost when plant is not operating}\right)}{\text{Contribution Margin per unit}}$$

$$= \frac{\text{Rs. } 2,00,000 - \text{Rs. } 90,000}{\text{Rs.}7}$$

$= 15,714$ units.

## Loss Leaders

In some situations of extremely competitive market and other related factors, an item may be deliberately offered at a price which is so low that the firm has to incur loss in the expectation that additional sales will be generated which, in turn, will eventually offset the loss. Such sales are called loss leaders. In such a case, it is necessary to determine the level of increase in sales revenue in order to justify the promotional effort.

*Example-8 (Loss Leaders)*

The regular monthly gross sales average of a firm is Rs. 5,00,000. Monthly fixed costs are Rs. 1,25,000. The contribution margin ratio of the firm is 50%. To increase the sales, the firm decides to sell a special product at Rs. 8 each. If 10,000 units of this product can be purchased for Rs. 12 per unit, determine the increase in the sales revenue of the normally priced products to make the promotion viable.

***Solution***

**Table 17.8**
**Decision Analysis (Loss Leaders)**

| Particulars | | Rs. |
|---|---|---|
| Incremental revenue | | 80,000 |
| Less: Incremental cost | | 1,25,000 |
| (Incremental Loss) | | – 45,000 |
| Desired increase in sales revenue | $= \frac{\text{Loss(Rs.45,000)}}{\text{P/V ratio (0.5)}}$ | 90,000 |

**Comment:** In order to justify the promotional campaign, the increase in the sales revenue must exceed Rs. 90,000.

## Replacement of Machinery

When the present machine is working and can still operate for the rest of its working life for some years, replacement of the existing machine with a new machine appears to be unprofitable. This is not the correct approach. The management knows that a new equipment can be purchased to do the same job and having an expected economic life without any salvage value. But the utility of the new machine lies in its greater operating efficiency, which will eventually reduce the operating expenses from the present level. This is why management often replaces the existing machine with a new machine.

*Example-9 (Replacement of Machinery)*

A company purchased a machine two years ago at a cost of Rs. 1,20,000. The machine has no salvage value at the end of its effective life of six years and the company is writing off deprecation as per the straight line method. The company feels that a new machine can be purchased at a cost of Rs. 1,60,000 to perform the same job and having an expected working life of 4 years without any salvage value. The new machine will reduce the variable operating expenses from the present level of Rs. 3,30,000 to Rs. 2,60,000 per annum. The sales volume is expected to continue at Rs. 4,00,000 per annum for the next four years.

Your are required to appraise the usefulness of the proposal.

***Solution***

**Table 17.9**
**Statement showing profitability of the Present and the New Machine**

| Particulars | Present machine<br>Rs | New machine<br>Rs | Increase/ (decrease) in costs<br>Rs |
|---|---|---|---|
| 1 | 2 | 3 | 4 |
| 1. Sales<br>(Rs. 4,00,000× 4 years) | 16,00,000 | 16,00,000 | – |
| 2. Variable costs (4 years) | 13,20,000 | 10,40,000 | (2,80,000) |

(*contd.*)

| 1 | 2 | 3 | 4 |
|---|---|---|---|
| 3. Loss on account of writing off old machine | 80,000 | 80,000 | – |
| 4. Depreciation of new machine | – | 1,60,000 | 1,60,000 |
| Total costs | 14,00,000 | 12,80,000 | (1,20,000) |
| Net profit | | 2,00,000 | 3,20,000 |
| Average Annual Incremental Income (Rs. 1,20,000/4 years) | | | 30,000 |
| Incremental Investment ... | | 1,60,000 | |
| Return on incremental Investment $\left(\frac{\text{Rs. } 30,000}{\text{Rs. } 1,60,000} \times 100\right)$ | ...18.75% | | |

**Comment:** The above analysis shows that there will be 18.75% return on additional investment of Rs. 1,60,000. The return appears to be quite satisfactory. Therefore, it will be advisable for the company to replace the present machine by a new machine.

## Comparing Machines with Hand Labour

The management may also contemplate substituting machines for hand labour. However, in such a case it is normally presumed that the selling prices of the products, whether produced by hand labour or machines, will be the same and that the required fund will be available without any difficulty for purchasing the machine.

For this purpose, the management will need financial data and other non-financial information before arriving at a final decision. With regard to the method to be employed, the following costing approaches can be adopted:

1. **Total cost approach:** The method which will have the lowest total cost, deserves to be selected.
2. **Marginal costing approach:** The method which will generate highest contribution, is to be selected.
3. **Cost savings** converted into present value.

*Example 10 (Comparing machines with Hand Labour)*

A Co. Ltd. has developed a new product. It has taken decision to produce 1,000 units per annum. The required data are as under:

| Particulars | Machine Rs. | Hand Labour Rs. |
|---|---|---|
| Purchase price | 20,000 | – |
| Direct material | 5,000 p.a. | 5,000 p.a. |
| Direct labour | 500 p.a. | 3,000 p.a. |
| Variable overhead cost | 2,000 p.a. | 1,000 p.a. |
| Fixed costs excluding depn | 1,500 p.a. | 1,000 p.a. |

The selling price of the product is fixed at Rs. 30 each. If the machine is purchased, it will have an estimated life of 10 years with no scrap value.

Show the marginal costs, contribution and total cost including interest at 5%.

***Solution***

**Table 17.10(a)**
**Statement of Marginal Costs and Contribution**

| Particulars | Machine Rs. | Hand Labour Rs. |
|---|---|---|
| Sales (1,000 units @ Rs. 30 each) | 30,000 | 30,000 |
| Direct material | 5000 | 5,000 |
| Direct labour | 500 | 3,000 |
| Variable overhead | 2,000 | 1,000 |
| Marginal costs | 7,500 | 9,000 |
| Contribution (Sales- Marginal costs) | 22,500 | 21,000 |

Table 17.10(a) clearly shows that the machine is preferable as it yields a higher contribution.

**Table 17.10(b)**
**Statement of Total Costs**

| Particulars | | Machine Rs. | Hand Labour Rs. |
|---|---|---|---|
| Direct material | | 5,000 | 5,000 |
| Direct labour | ... | 500 | 3,000 |
| Variable overhead | ... | 2,000 | 1,000 |
| Fixed overhead | ... | 1,500 | 1,000 |
| Depreciation: 1/10th of Rs. 20,000 | | 2,000 | – |
| Total cost | ... | 11,000 | 10,000 |
| Interest @ 5% | ... | 550 | 500 |
| | | 11,550 | 10,500 |

From the point of view of the total cost approach, hand labour is preferable.

## Estimation of Cost Savings and their Conversion to Present Values

After making a comparison of the cost data and revenue data of the alternatives, the amount of cost savings of the best alternative is estimated and then the present value of the amount of cost savings is determined. The present value of cost savings is calculated for the expected life (in years) of the profitable alternative at a given interest rate per annum.

*Example-11 (Estimation of Cost Savings and their Conversion to Present Values)*

A manufacturing enterprise undertakes certain job with the help of 10 labourers and incurs a total cost of Rs. 1,00,000 per year. The enterprise is planning to use a machine in place of labourers. The cost of the machine would be Rs. 80,000 with an expected life of 10 years. There will be no residual value of the machine after the expiry of its life. The operating costs in case of machine employment would be Rs. 60,000 excluding depreciation. Discount any savings in cost at the rate of 6% per annum.

Advise whether the change is justified.

## Solution

**Table 17.11**

| Operating costs | Rs. |
|---|---|
| In the case of Hand Labour | 1,00,000 |
| In the case of machine | 60,000 |
| Cost Savings | 40,000 |

The present value of cost savings for 10 years at 6% interest per annum (as per table) will be

| | Rs. |
|---|---|
| Rs. 40,000 × 7.36 | 2,94,400 |
| Less: Total depreciation | 80,000 |
| Net cost savings | 2,14,400 |

## Advice

The decision should be to employ machine since it will ensure net cost savings of Rs. 2,14,400.

# Our Contributors

**Ahmed, Dr. Jaynal Ud-din**, Associate Professor, Department of Management, North Eastern Hill University, Tura Campus, Chandmari, Tura -794002, West Garo Hills, Meghalaya, India. E-mail: jaynaluahmed@yahoo.co.in/ juahmednehu@gmail.com

**Bal, Dr. Ranjan Kumar**, Professor of Commerce, P. G. Department of Commerce, Utkal University Bhubaneswar, Orissa.

**Barua, Nayan**, Professor, Deptt. of Commerce, Gauhati University, Guwahati.

**Bhattacharjee, Abhigyan**, Assistant Professor, Department of Commerce, Assam University, Diphu Campus, Karbi Anglong. E-mail: abhigayn09@rediffmail.com

**Bhowal, Amalesh**, Professor, Dept. of Commerce, Assam University, Diphu Campus, Karbi Anglong.

**Bora, Dr. Bhaskarjyoti**, Reader, Department of Commerce, Gauhati University, Guwahati -781 014, Assam, India. Email: bhaskarjb2001@yahoo.com

**Das, Purnashree**, Research Scholar, Deptt. of Commerce, Gauhati University, E-mail : daspurnashree@yahoo.com.

**Dey, Nikhil Bhusan**, Professor, Department of Commerce, Assam University, Silchar. e-mail: nikhil.b.dey@gmail.com

**Gautam, H C**, Professor, Department of Commerce, Gauhati University.

**Ghosh, Suparna**, Research Scholar, Deptt. Of Commerce, Gauhati University, E-mail:suparna 1181@gmail.com

**Meetei, Dr. Kh. Dhiren**, Associate Professor, Department of Commerce, Manipur University, Imphal

**Panda, N.**, Professor, Department of Commerce, North-Eastern Hill University, Shillong-793022.

**Paul, Dr. Pinku**, Senior Lecturer, Centre for Management Studies, Bhubaneswar, Orissa.

**Prasain, Dr. G.P.**, Professor & Head, Department of Commerce, Manipur University, Imphal.

**Rehman, Dr. A.R.M.**, Professor, Department of Commerce, Nagaland University, Kohima Campus, Kohima-797001

**Saleem, Dr. Shaikh**, Director, Millennium Institute of Management, Dr. Rafiq Zakaria Campus, Aurangabad, Maharashtra, India. Email:- director_mim@yahoo.com. Phone No.:- +91-0240-2390371 / 72, Mobile No.:- +0091-09325211184

**Shankar, A.N.**, Lecturer, Department of Commerce, Mizoram University, Aizawl-796009.

**Sharmacharjee, Rajat**, Assistant Professor, Department of Commerce, Assam University, Silchar. email: rajatau@rediffmail.com

**Prashanta Sharma**, Assistant Professor (Sr. Grade), Deptt. of Commerce, Gauhati University, Guwahati. E-mail: Prashanta_Sharma@rediffmail.com

**Sikidar, Sujit**, Professor, Deptt. of Commerce, Gauhati University, Guwahati-781014.

**Singh, Dr. A. Rajmani**, Associate Professor of Finance, Department of Commerce, Manipur University. Email:-rajaheibam2@gmail.com

**Singh, Dr. Elangbam Nixon**, Associate Professor, Department of Management, Mizoram University, Aizawl.

**Thappa, Sankar**, Assistant Professor, Department of Business Administration, North Eastern Regional Institute of Management, Guwahati

**Upadhyaya, Jiban**, Assistant Professor Dept. of Commerce, Sikkim Government College, Tadong, Gangtok- 737 102, Sikkim, India , Email: jugangtok@yahoo.co.in

# Index

❑❑❑